Dedicated to all those who served Queen and Country
in Cyprus during the troubled years of 1955 to 1961.

To those whose pleasure it had been to serve at
'Hell on the Hill',
and most especially to those who failed to return
from the conflict.

Copyright © Ian Tillotson 2018

First edition 2018.

The moral right of the author has been asserted.

This book is copyright. All rights reserved. Without limiting the rights under copyright reserved above, no part of this publication may be reproduced, stored or introduced into a retrieval system, or transmitted, in any form or by any means (electronic, mechanical, photocopying, recording or otherwise), without the prior written permission of the copyright owner.

ISBN: 9781731438102

PARADISE MISLAID

A VOYAGE INTO UNKNOWN TERRITORY,
DISCOVERY AND ENLIGHTENMENT.

A CONVOLUTING RITE OF PASSAGE
FROM ONE WORLD TO THE DOORSTEP OF THE NEXT.

280 SIGNALS UNIT
CAPE GATA.

IAN TILLOTSON.

Paradise Mislaid

Prologue. i

Chapter 1. The Call to Arms - The Kitchenerian Finger Beckons. 1

Chapter 2. The Bumpy Road to Gata. 11

Chapter 3. Those early apprehensive days. 35

Chapter 4. The Quest for Elysian Domesticity. 46

Chapter 5. In Defence of the Nation - the selfless daily toil. 72

Chapter 6. Skiving - The noble art of being unobtrusively obvious. 88

Chapter 7. A more honest approach? - but skiving none the less. 101

Chapter 8. Those well-earned moments of rest and repose. 122

Chapter 9. The best laid plans... gang aft a-gley. 164

Chapter 10. Nothing if not valiant on the sporting field of valour. 184

Chapter 11. That sweet illicit nibble on the other side of the fence. 198

Chapter 12. The winds of change were blowing,… 227

Chapter 13. Time gentlemen please! 236

Epilogue. 242

Appendix. 247

Acknowledgements. 257

The Author. 258

PARADISE MISLAID

Prologue.

Much has been penned, over the years, about military conscription and National Service, and many the expressed views about its value to the nation's defences and the benefits to those conscripted. It is not the intention that this narrative should make repeat of earlier chronicles, but suffice to chart the chronology of my personal initiation and passage through this formative period in my life in service to Queen and country. The greater proportion of my service period was spent at 280 Signals Unit, Cape Gata, Cyprus.

At the termination of the Second World War, and with little threat of any imminent requirement to defend Britain's shores and dependencies, the military fighting force had become temporarily in excess of necessity. However, military policing remained an urgent requirement, in reoccupied territories in the Far East, in Palestine, in India, in parts of Europe and notably in occupied Germany. A substantial proportion of the occupying troops had been wartime conscripts, and the requirements of the day dictated that demobilisation for these deployments would necessarily be delayed. It had been decreed that the objective would be the demobilisation of those who had served during the wartime period by 1948, and their replacement by a newly conscripted force as considered necessary.

Conscription recommenced in 1949, provisionally for a period of five years, and thereafter to continue on a year-on-year basis. Initially, conscripts were to serve for eighteen months to be followed by four years in a reserve capacity, later adjusted to twelve months with five years in reserve. The ensuing emergencies in Berlin, the USSR, Malaya and Hong Kong set political nerves jangling, and the prompt readjustment to the eighteen plus four. The Korean War rang more warning bells, and conscription was increased once more, and for the final time, to two years, with a reserve period of three and a half. This is the way that it remained until late in the 1950's and the very early 1960's when the reduction of annual intake began, and finally concluded in January 1963, when the last National Serviceman finally hung up his boots.

***

For most of recorded time, the bejewelled island of Cyprus has occupied a geographical position of strategic importance. Though popular mythology informs us that Cyprus is the home of Aphrodite, the Goddess of Love, she seems to have failed somewhat in her task and calling, as a succession of empires have seen fit to rape, pillage, violate, and appropriate this lovely lady and her domain, as they sought to derive military and pecuniary benefit from occupancy.

Long ago, the Assyrians had a pop at Aphrodite, until the superior authority of the empirical Egyptians gave them the boot. For a considerable time the Ottoman Empire and the Persians ruled supreme, but Greece later harvested the benefit of greater proximal advantage, and established a social governance that was to enjoy a measure of permanence. In turn, the English, the Venetians and the Turks made their individual contributions to the confusion of social, corporate and cultural identity. In 1878 the British Empire finally assumed the administration, though nominal sovereignty remained initially with the Turks. At that time, the Turks were the losing side in a war against Russia, and as it was not in the British interest to permit the island to fall into Russian hands, the British intervened to help to kick the Russian bear into touch. The quid pro quo was the establishment of British administration.

Though the indigenous population was to derive considerable social and domestic benefits from this arrangement, it did nothing to resolve the increasing differences and conflict between Greek and Turk, the former being dominant numerically, while the latter deriving advantage from the pact between the British government and the Turkish Sultan.

During the first two decades of the twentieth century, the investment of British infrastructure and expertise afforded enormous social and structural benefit to the island population. However, during this period Greek continued to agitate for Enosis, permanent union with Greece, while the Turk vociferated equally in support of the Turkish equivalent. A significant adjustment to international relations and to the governance of the island became imposed when Turkey elected to take up arms in support of Germany during the First World War. This action later precipitated the annexation of Cyprus by the British government, and its declaration as a British Crown Colony.

Cyprus remained strategically important to Britain during the second global conflict, as a centre for some military operations in Palestine, the Middle East, and in North Africa, and as a staging post onward to India and the Far East. However, it was not until 1956, that growing tension between Britain and Egypt elevated the importance of the island to a far greater and critical level.

Throughout the twentieth century, a significant proportion of import and export to and from Britain had passed through Ferdinand de Lesseps' splendid waterway, the Suez Canal. In 1956, President Gamal Abdel Nasser, assumed Egyptian ownership of the Anglo-French Suez Canal Company, founded the Suez Canal Authority, and imposed heavy charges on any nation aspiring to make use of it. Conflict in the region resulted and quickly escalated, precipitated the Suez Crisis, and became the touch paper of a combined Israeli / Anglo / French invasion of Egypt.

This action did not find universal approval or support, and the United Nations instructed early termination and withdrawal. A cease-fire was declared within a month of invasion, and withdrawal was completed before the end of the year. Cyprus had become of increasing strategic importance during this period, and by the conclusion of this conflict, it had become clear that the island was destined to become the base for the only British military presence in the Middle East. On withdrawal from Egypt, it was to Cyprus that the majority of personnel, equipment, arms, vehicles and machinery were transferred.

With no tangible indication of reduction of tension in the region, and with the continuing requirement for global surveillance, it had become clear that the strategic importance of

Cyprus was unlikely to be reduced in the foreseeable future. To accommodate these requirements, the base at RAF Akrotiri became subject to considerable expansion, bases for military personnel were established at a number of locations, and signals and communications units were located at strategic points around the coastline, and at elevation in the Troodos Mountains.

During this period, the peace and tranquillity of Cyprus had been further and grossly disrupted by an internal terrorist uprising. 1954 had witnessed the arrival, from Greece of General Georgios Grivas Dhigenis. He became the founder and leader of 'EOKA' (ETHNIKI ORGANOSIS KYPRION AGONISTON), a pseudo military and militant organisation, the singular purpose of which was to cast off the authority and the burden of British colonial rule. Together with the Greek Archbishop Makarios, Grivas and EOKA embarked upon a campaign of terror and killing which was to endure for a period of six years before the signing of a truce in 1960, and later, the declaration of the Republic of Cyprus in 1962.

The violence of this offensive took the form of concealed explosive devices as means to ambush, and equally to kill and maim through concealment in domestic buildings, in military installations and in aircraft. It involved the murder of military personnel, members of the Cyprus police, and civilians, and it involved the placement of small explosive devices designed to explode at a touch or a switch, and to cause maximum injury to the victim. It was an offensive that combined guerrilla tactics and murder most foul as its principal strategies, it was indiscriminate in its approach, and thus it imposed its havoc upon service personnel and families alike.

In 1956, Archbishop Makarios was deported from Cyprus to exile in the Seychelles, a period that coincided with an escalation in EOKA activity as the British military presence became reduced to accommodate the requirement of the Suez crisis. The exile was short-lived, and Makarios returned in early 1957, no doubt refreshed and reinvigorated from his 'holiday'. The continued EOKA offensive escalated through late 1958 and early 1959, more sporadically during the latter half of that year, and finally coming to a close in early 1960.

During the negotiations to establish a final settlement, EOKA capitulated and relinquished its demand for ENOSIS in return for sovereignty and independence from British governance. The British government retained sovereignty over a number of military bases, and though these have been reduced in number and area, this arrangement continues to the present day.

Alas, peace and tranquillity among the meadows and mountains of Aphrodite's island did not prevail. Greek and Turk continued to hurl abuse, each in the direction of the other, Greek seeking union with Greece, Turk demanding a Turkish homeland. The outcome, in 1974, became civil war in the wake of the invasion of Northern Cyprus by forces from mainland Turkey, and an ultimate death toll of monstrous proportions.

Today, Aphrodite looks down upon an island unhappily divided. To the north, Turk. To the south, Greek. Between the two, the imposed tragedy of a physical, ethnical, and psychological barrier. The lamentable division between Cypriot and Cypriot, the separation of family from family, the tormenting schism that insists upon the supremacy of theistic and cultural intolerance, and the denial of the benevolence of humanity. Cyprus remains a sparkly, but somewhat tarnished little jewel in the Eastern Mediterranean, but one that now requires the begrudged stamp of visa authority to allow its countrymen to venture from coast to coast.

Perhaps Aphrodite, and the many who lie in the huge cemeteries in Nicosia and in the demilitarised zones, dream that one day Cyprus may once again become - simply Cypriot.

Chapter 1. The Call to Arms - The Kitchenerian Finger Beckons.

*

*"My boy, here is a word of sincere advice
from an old soldier.
Never, never, ever, volunteer for anything!"*

*

The 1950s. The last decade in black and white. At its genesis, Europe had taken purposeful strides towards post-war recovery. Much of the rubble of destruction had been cleared, urban centres had been demolished, repaired or replaced, industry had chuffed its way into positive and purposeful production, and agriculture was cultivating cabbages, cows and chickens for our consumption. Although rationing continued to dictate the quality, the quantity, and the limited multiformity of our daily diet, and the ingredients of Sunday lunch were made to last until Wednesday, many of the ravages and deprivations of the previous decade were becoming relegated to memory, still painful, but slowly being replaced by hope.

The first half of the twentieth century had been dominated by global warfare. None but the most remote had escaped its influence. It had left the human race bludgeoned, bloodied and bewildered, and perhaps just a little bit chastened. That was it! There would be no more! The human race would take stock, repair the damage of its own stupidity, and endeavour to adopt a more harmonious approach to its tenancy of the planet. Who was it who first coined the phrase 'Nation shall speak peace unto Nation?' Churchill? Hitler? FDR? Truman? Stalin? A biblical musing? Or perhaps simply a contrived phrase designed to promulgate a fanciful aspiration. It doesn't matter! It didn't work anyway. The Fifties proceeded, and by the end of the decade, the conflict roster read like a gazetteer of global attrition. Korea, Algeria, Malaya, Puerto Rico, India, Cuba, Indochina, Kenya, Laos, Sudan, Spain, Tibet, Lebanon, China, Morocco, Indonesia, Hungary, Iraq, Poland, Egypt, Thailand, United States of America, Taiwan, Netherlands, USSR, Cameroon, Spain, Vietnam, Iran, Greece, Paraguay, Pakistan, Madagascar, Palestine, Costa Rica, Israel, Burma, Guatemala, Ethiopia, Congo, the burgeoning cold war... Oh, and I almost forgot... Cyprus.

On the home front a youthful generation, mere babies during the turmoil, was beginning to flex its self-assertive muscles. Most would harbour some memory of the carnage, the pointless brutality, and the most abominable facet of human character. In protest, some would adopt a pacifist stance, while others would mutter continued belligerence from behind a flag of victory. While a pragmatic adult population attempted to view the reality that lay beyond euphoria, many of the next generation continued to suffer a considerable degree of emotional turmoil and social confusion. They had been nudged into sub-adulthood by a senior generation that they now held responsible for the deprivations of childhood. They harboured resentment, and as the character of post-war youth evolved, some became increasingly rebellious.

They were a generation that had been raised on conkers in the playground; fed on Bisto gravy, spam fritters and polony; suffered and spat the horrors of Eucryl tooth powder; twirled among hula hoops; and for those more fortunate, mingled with the Redcoats and knobbly knee competitions at Butlins. The pubs closed at ten, remained so all through Sunday, and potato crisps contained small blue packets of salt. Then, as now, football was pursued with religious fanaticism. However, those were the days when the national sport was played at local level. The heroes were local lads playing for local teams, each enjoying the utterly dedicated support of a local populace. No less enthusiastic were the grubby kids who played in streets where the perils of traffic were merely brief and occasional interruptions, and which were permitted passage by the simple removal of one of the jacket-goalposts. In the decade that witnessed the birth of the mini, motoring became an everyman pursuit, and football became permanently expunged from the streets of residential Britain.

They were a generation that required the inspiration of success or celebration. They had a coronation and with it the promise of change. By chance, and on the same day, they rejoiced and applauded the first successful ascent of Mount Everest. They helped to clear the all-pervading sense of post-war doom as the nation proudly exhibited its technological progress at the Festival Of Britain. Here, on London's South Bank the public echoed its perplexity at the impossible spectacle of the Skylon, towering above its needle point balance and apparently held in place by no more than a few steel strings. They marvelled at the abundant revelations of the Dome of Discovery, delighted in the many diversions and attractions of the Pleasure Gardens, and gasped at the stereophonic and stereoscopic advances in cinematography. In a purpose-built theatre on the South Bank, and wearing cardboard spectacles, each with one red and one green lens, audiences started and twitched as figures from fantasy and mythology bore down upon them from the distorted screen.

"Marvellous innit? Bloody marvellous."

During the nineteen fifties, the public availability of television was in early embryo, and even by the end of the decade, it had become a facility limited to a tiny, indistinct screen, and graced the sitting rooms of only the relatively wealthy. Who can forget the viewing of their very first television programme? Mine had been, 'Billy Bunter, the Grey Owl of the Remove', on a screen that may have measured nine inches in each direction. Later innovation placed large convex magnifying screens in front of the woefully small cathode ray tube, thus imposing a distorting dome upon an image already dominated by central corpulence and peripheral diminution.

The cinema continued to provide entertainment for the masses, and everyone went to the pictures. Towards the end of the decade, Disney and the emerging dominance of Hollywood were producing imagery and extravagant musicals in 'Glorious Technicolor'. It would take time for this to usurp the still dominant and ubiquitous black and white, which continued to provide the flickering images on our screens through most of the decade. However, and as Dylan insisted, 'The times they were a-changin', and the straight-laced censorship that had hitherto imposed strict limits upon public viewing, were beginning to relax.

Richard Attenborough's 'Brighton Rock' exploded the violence of tormented youth upon the silver screen, while James Dean continued to be rebellious, with or without a cause, until he secured his own immortality in the wreckage of his Porsche. The ludicrous Bill Haley proceeded to rock around the clock, mainly in the direction of the exit, as Elvis oscillated through the auditorium, capturing the minds, the passion, and a significant proportion of the bodily functions of a hundred million dribbling teenyboppers. The more homespun Tommy Steele had a handful of songs, he flashed, banged and walloped, and while he led a small white bovine on a string, Lonnie Donegan seemed to lose his way in a confusion of boots and daisy roots somewhere deep in the Cumberland Gap. Dean Martin and Perry Como pursued their aspiration to convince the world of the aphrodisiac qualities of Italian cuisine, Fats Domino collected blueberries, and Bing Crosby made a seasonal, and mercifully brief, visit to the world's Yuletide radio waves.

Among the lady warblers, Alma Cogan afforded solemn warning against dancing on the streets of Buenos Aires with an Inuit, while Doris Day's bed had apparently sustained a modicum of anonymous overcrowding. Kay Starr struggled to afford guidance to parental misdirection on the adaptation of ballroom elegance to rocking and rolling, while Connie Francis made serious threats of bodily mutilation to a little guy with a bow and arrow.

To the open-mouthed and dribbling delight of a youthful male population, the censor had also lifted the skirts of female presentation. While the lid on the box labelled 'Sexual Revolution' remained firmly closed during the fifties, the female form was being presented in ever more revealing and beguiling manner. In 'La Dolce Vita' the statuesque Anita Eckberg cantilevered into view a considerable proportion of the magnificent pinnacles of her framework. But then came apoplexy for the active and vociferous group of moral crusaders, with the release of 'And God Created Woman', and with it a phrase unknown to Samuel Johnson became added to the common vocabulary. 'Full-frontal' was the word on the street that was describing a fleetingly brief sequence of Brigitte Bardot's performance.

The film was screened on two consecutive nights in my local cinema. At the first screening, The Coliseum cinema was filled to capacity and beyond by a significant proportion of the heavily breathing male adolescent and early adult local population. Their panting anticipatory passion was obliged to wait impatiently, apprehensively, and somewhat noisily, as the mandatory programme sequence of the day preceded the main feature. It was always the same. News bulletin, current affairs or topical documentary, a cartoon, the main feature presentation, and the National Anthem, which required the audience to stand respectfully to some measure of attention. A feverishly expectant hush accompanied the credits as this main feature commenced. Apart from the occasional outpouring of expletive exuberance, this pregnant quietude was maintained throughout the entire performance. Abruptly, the much-anticipated spectacle was gone. In less than the blink of an eye, the lithesome Brigitte had briefly crossed several hundred fields of vision, and had pertly disappeared from view.

At the end of the film, the National Anthem was ignored and abandoned in the rush to seek the exit and the opportunity to exchange and compare the visual experience. Out in the street the expletives were flowing in abundance, as were the expressions of intent that indicated clear purpose for a number of Bardot anatomical parts.

"Did you see it? Yeah! Bloody Hell, never seen anything like that on the screen. Fantastic! Fabulous tits… and did you see the bush?"

However, in spite of the abundant claims of cinematic voyeurism, many, perhaps the majority, had seen nothing. The brief naked Bardot passage had not appeared from the obvious and expected quarter, and had then been further confused because the brief frontal view had been limited to an image reflected in a wall mirror. Thus, many had become aware only as the pert Bardot rear was exiting the door through which she had been widely expected to arrive. The Coliseum was no less crowded on the following evening.

Later in the decade, and beyond, as television became a more widespread living room phenomenon, our very own Sabrina, still in black and white, laid down her own challenge to the current mammary supremacy. However, television censorship took a much more severe view of unclad frolicking, and though Sabrina's generous monticules were always contained within a swaddling garment, they stood proud and prominent however small the screen. These cautious steps by the broadcasters injected a little welcome glamour among the familiar line-up of 'This is your Life', 'Dr, Kildare', 'The Saint', 'What's my Line', and 'The Man from U.N.C.L.E'. Thus, the fifties witnessed the genesis of the 'couch potato' age.

Supermac was telling them all that they had never had it so good. And it was! The dolly tub and mangle were being replaced by washing machines that resembled paddle steamers. The refrigerator was usurping the use of the outside meat safe. Huge cast iron radiators heralded the onset of the central heating age and the demise of the kitchen range and the paraffin stove. The freezing outside privy, bucket or flush, became converted to a coal house as the comfort of the comprehensive bathroom relegated the dunny forever into redundancy.

This was the maelstrom of mixed messages and confused emotions into which the class of '51 had been thrust. Here was an entire generation, male, female, or indifferent, that longed to dip an anatomical extremity into a permissive realm, visible but not yet quite revealed, available but just slightly out of reach. They remained shackled and hamstrung by the unspeakable retribution of vindictive convention, by the unwavering condemnation of pious denunciation, and by the horrors of the emotional ducking stool.

Whatever the confusion, real or imagined, in the minds of the almost-adult population of the fifties, it evolved, as ever before and since, and up to the present day, into every one of the seven deadly sins. Shiny young men in smart suits, straight cut ties and waistcoats, and riding the popular Vespas or Lambrettas, converged in two-stroke battalions on the resort towns of south east England. Here they engaged in noisy and often bloodstained confrontation with black-clad, grease stained hell riders on their roaring AJS, Triumph, Matchless, Royal Enfield machines, or even the occasional mighty Ariel Square Four, or Vincent Black Prince. Thus and there, and to the annoyance of the resident and visitor alike, the Mods clashed with the Rockers. Nothing was achieved, save unnecessary mayhem, and sunset bore witness to retreat to respective high-rise apartment or underground garrison.

For the girls of the early decade, fashion assured attractiveness. Girls had not yet abandoned the mantle of young ladies, and were alluringly appealing in dresses, and blouses, and even stockings with seams. Alas for young woman-kind, the urge had evolved to emulate the appearance and the attitudes of their confused brothers. This perhaps in the belief that beating each other senseless on a regular basis bestowed a more enjoyable way of life on their male counterparts. The fashion industry responded in kind. The late fifties witnessed suits, ties, short haircuts, and side-by-side differences that were hardly detectable. Those alluring young ladies had become shapeless, lumpy and androgynous; sharing stance, street corner, public bar, and drooping cigarette with their more flamboyant boyfriends.

For the males, a slightly divergent path. They had clearly lost the plot. With excess testosterone oozing from every pore and orifice, and not the faintest idea what to do with or about it, they urgently required a safety valve that would relieve the pressure in their boilers. Continued and constant street warfare did not reduce numbers, failed to satisfy any imagined purpose, and fuelled the testosterone levels to the point of scrotal cataclysm. They required a uniform that conveyed a clear message. "Don't mess with me! I'm hard, and I mean really hard! This is my territory. Here you play to my rules!"

Thus, posturing became the new warfare, and a mercifully short-lived fashion statement became the ammunition. Not since the eighteenth century had society witnessed a young male population that disported its-self in quite such a ludicrous manner. Apparently, modelled on a long extinct Edwardian fashion, the future leaders of men now became Teddy Boys. Drapes, zoot suits, coffin-cut jackets of knee length, topped with a velvet collar. Flashy silk waistcoats adorned with a bootlace or Slim Jim tie. Drainpipe or stovepipe trousers cut sufficiently short to flaunt garish socks, and crepe-soled, blue suede brothel-creepers that increased stature by at least a tottering and unsteady couple of inches. These soft-soled bumpers imposed and infused every step on a smooth surface with a sound like a crushed mouse. So great was the apparent population of pulverised rodents at the Saturday night dance, that the music became merely an incidental beat to direct the flailing rock 'n' roll lower limbs.

Then someone introduced 'Slipperene', the dead mice disappeared, the flailing limbs lost contact with the substratum, and jostling quickly degenerated into the weekly skirmish as unsteady bodies adopted their own misdirected trajectories. As the accumulated testosterone became nuclear, fists, bottles, furnishings and an ill-defined opposition flew, and the blood began to flow. Among the young ladies, those who continued to favour the more feminine skirt and blouse simpered into a neutral corner, while the more butch among them occupied the battle periphery and cheered - or simply joined in, contributing in no small measure to the affray.

For the strutting young male, the crowning glory was the carefully sculpted tonsure. Making abundant use of heavy-duty Brilliantine, the coiffure, fore and aft, became a thing of artistic splendour not to be disturbed, let alone touched. To the fore a resplendent quiff was raised in an extravagant pompadour style, or fashioned in the form of the popular elephant's trunk, while the rear had been formed, lovingly and carefully into the celebrated duck's arse. While orifice of duck may have afforded a slightly unfortunate reference to this aspect of tonsorial art, the DA, as it was known and loved, took its reference from the elegantly folded wings of a male Mallard. Thus attired, adorned, embellished, bewigged and bejewelled, the future of the nation lounged menacingly on street corners, gathered in sheepish groups in dance halls, postured and primped in public places, or contorted, gyrated and flailed to the strains of Rock Around the Jailhouse.

Talk within the male company centred heavily on conquest. Not that of the mod versus rocker conflict, more of the quiet corner behind the dance hall kind.

The answer to the question "Have you ever er... you know?" was always in the affirmative. Truth or otherwise, male pride would never, ever permit a negative, if honest, response. Truthfully of course, the converse was frequently the case. The era of sexual freedom had not yet arrived, and a furtive fumble, often accompanied by a slap across the ear, was often as far as conquest would proceed.

"Go on then, tell us who with." "Can't tell you that." "Don't believe you then." "Well don't spread it around." … "Go on! I didn't know she did."

For the male, conquest and boast often enhanced a personal reputation, for the female, the same boast and empty talk frequently imposed the opposite effect. "What her!!! Who hasn't? Station bicycle!"

As the angst and bombast of male adolescence proceeded, an entire generation became acutely aware that its freedom of expression, its carefree way of life, those idyllic years between education and the burdensome responsibilities of profession and family, could become abruptly terminated. Striking terror into the hearts of every youth, callow, intellectual, or bumptious, was the threat of the dreaded call-up. In the fifties, military National Service was approaching the end of its purpose, and by the early sixties it had been phased out. Just why it imposed such mortal dread upon the minds and hearts of those approaching its teenage deadline, remained unclear to me, but many and diverse were the contrived fabrications that were put forward as supplications for exemption. Clear evidence of acceptance to full-time further education was one of the few valid and acceptable justifications for immunity. Professional training, apprenticeship, or working in agriculture could allow deferment, and for some, was offered in the hope that the service would simply terminate, or that they would be overlooked. Conscientious objection was treated with contempt, as was religious intolerance. Bogus and spurious medical conditions were very rapidly rumbled. Identity denial could be readily out manoeuvred by the local office of public records. Burning the summons papers merely attracted a posse of military policemen at the door. Regular changes of location and address served no other purpose than delay. Claims of family dependants were no match for a brief interrogation. The sudden development and attempted demonstration of a limp, impaired vision, defective hearing, insanity, illiteracy, incontinence, flat feet, kneebophobia (morbid fear of the knees bending in the wrong direction), terminal flatulence, or a chronic intolerance to uniforms were rewarded only with summary indifference.

My papers duly arrived. Maybe I could have worked a flanker, though it didn't occur to me to try. I was just half way through a four-year course of study in forestry that required practical training and home study to occupy two of the four years. In view of the call to arms, and Kitchener's unwavering finger, my college placement would tolerate a deferment, to permit my response to the call, and my service to queen and country.

Though five years at boarding school may have induced a small measure of independent spirit, it was a slightly brutal, cloistered existence and was totally removed from the reality of an outside world. Thus, it was a very timorous bus journey that whisked me from the safe and peaceful embrace of my rural village existence and brought me to the rude and noisily alarming centre of Middlesbrough and the place appointed for my initiation into a world that could hardly be more alien to my earlier life. At the simple stroke of a pen, I was about to relinquish the last few tattered remnants of childhood.

As it turned out, the interview was friendly enough. Not the harrowing interrogation overseen by burly, heavily armed military policemen that my worst fears had foolishly envisaged. A simple registration that was without inquisition had required no more than a few questions and a signature. Personal details were logged, ethnic origin, religious adherence, sexual orientation, any permanent physical characteristics, all were quietly noted.

"In which of the services would you prefer to serve?"
"The Royal Air Force please." So polite!
"What would you like to do in the Royal Air Force." Was this bloke taking the mickey?
"Flying duties."
"Ah! I am afraid that flying duties are not allocated to National Servicemen. Anything else?"

Stumped! I muttered something about aircraft.
"Home base or overseas preferred?"

Though I hadn't anticipated this one. Never having ventured beyond the home shores, and not even very far from Yorkshire, my response was staccato.

"Oh! Overseas please sir." The added "sir" was reactive rather than calculated.

So the interview concluded, a veritable ocean of peace before the tempest of embarrassment and discomfiture that was to follow. As each innocent was ushered away from his personal details, it quickly became clear that he was being slotted into his place on a production line, the nature of the end product of which was not yet apparent, nor anywhere in view. The next room was furnished with long trestle tables and benches, and just a few people, some in uniform, some not so, whose purpose was to introduce each incomer to his next interrogation. Still kindly presented at this stage, the intelligence test demanded answers to a list of somewhat elementary questions. A glance at the content quickly revealed that this was not so much a test to reveal the level of literacy, numeracy, and general knowledge, but more to expose its presence or absence. New to most of us, the system provided a choice of multiple answers, and the requirement to indicate choice by placing a tick in a box. The resulting assessment would dictate preferred or directed choice of service. Though there were a few who were left chewing the pencil, most passed through this vestibule fairly quickly, and then on into the next chamber of increasing horror.

Another room, but this time a clear distinction between the uniformed disciplinarians and the white coated examiners. This was the province of the weight, height, heart, reflexes, ear, nose, throat, and dental examination. A wooden spatula became the tool of gentle persuasion after the weigh in, stethoscope and rubber hammer. Aided further by use of a torch, mouth, throat, teeth, ears and nostrils were afforded critical scrutiny. The doctor, a title indicated by the white coat, and assumed by the victim, muttered a few words as he pursued the procedure, and these were entered upon a sheet of paper by an aide.

Entry into the next hall quickly revealed that the milk of human kindness had become seriously eroded and drained. The town hall had been commandeered for these purposes, and this was our timorous entry into its main chamber, a veritable Tower of Babel, and a confusing and somewhat clamorous profusion of many people. Authority was being wielded by those in uniform, some of whom wore the terrifying stripes and badges of authority. Others were sitting anonymously at tables, while the majority, in white gowns seemed to be in pursuit of unspeakable practices upon a long line of naked men.

A sergeant at the door directed the incomers to a row of benches and hooks.

"Right! Over there! Strip naked, join that line and stand to attention."
"Naked! But all those people."
"Naked laddie! Naked! Just like what you was on the day when you was born."

Slowly, timorously, defensively, and embarrassed in the extreme, each innocent debutant did as instructed, and took his place at the end of the line.

My own emotions at this time were clearly not so extreme as some. Perhaps the rigours and shared facilities of boarding school had afforded familiarity with some of the diversities of the male human form. However, a glance down the line revealed the entire plethora of human emotion. Fear and bravado. Embarrassment and exhibitionism. Terror and supplication. Patience, tolerance, and fast failing resistance. For most simple resignation to whatever was about to befall, and the simple desire to comply, to complete, and to escape.

As revealing as the array of exposed emotions was the diversity of the equally exposed physical attributes. This was a twitching, fidgeting, shuffling column of debagged, denuded, and collectively mortified manhood. Some were big lads in every respect, content to stand proudly and be viewed by all present, while others attempted vainly to hide behind hands, crossed legs and deep blushes. Bravado or bashfulness, one feature of this intimate encounter, exacerbated every exhibited sentiment. Together with the doctors, administrators, people wielding clipboards and pens, recorders, and those wearing ominous surgical gloves, were a number of young female nurses. For each and every one of these young conscripts, stalwart or stunted, to be thus and publicly unclad was humiliation beyond endurance, and especially so in the presence of young and pretty beings so frequently spoken of in bold and boastful terms of conquest.

As inspection proceeded, a uniformed disciplinarian patrolled the rear of the line to ensure rigid upright posture. Extreme distress in one individual was painfully apparent, and he became subject to a few tortured moments before he was allowed to leave the ranks.

The disciplinarian approached from the rear. The boy had adopted a semi-crouched posture. Knees and back were bent, hands clasped, elbows thrust defensively into his groin, he had become overwhelmed by terror.

"Attention lad. Stand to attention."

There was no reactive movement.

"Do you know what attention means laddie? Attention is what you do when you has just sat on a broken bottle. STAND TO ATTENTION!"

The unhappy boy slowly uncurled. Whatever his years, his physical development had failed to keep pace. He was under-developed, puny in size, lacking significant body hair, and possessed of a body that suggested very early teenage at most. At this point, one of the medics approached, and gently removed him from the line.

For those remaining, the first instruction was to step forward and on to a low bench. It quickly became apparent that this required manoeuvre raised each individual and his genitals to an elevation more appropriate for inspection. Another white coated medical man, wielding another wooden spatula, proceeded along the line, his steely and critical gaze intent upon the detection of any suspicious blemish or pimple. Those anatomical parts, formerly deeply private, and possibly not having been seen by another living soul since the last nappy change, had abruptly become public property. The deftly wielded spatula lifted, moved left, moved right, and made the scrotal adjustments necessary for superficial inspection, before two surgically clad fingers peeled back the foreskin of those for whom parental choice or theological doctrine had not deprived them of this appendage. While we remained thus elevated, the instruction to touch our toes was delivered by the uniformed disciplinarian, an action that permitted another white coat, visual access to the remaining bodily orifice. The later knowledge that this had been our 'Freedom from Infection' or FFI inspection, did little to restore dignity.

"Step down!" "Legs apart!"

Now the head scrotologist, accompanied by a medical orderly, passed along the rear of the line, pausing at each individual. Two fingers gently raised two testicles. Each individual breathed a momentary word of silent gratitude and relief that it was a white coat and not one of the pert nurses that was tickling his goolies.

"Cough."
"Aurgh."
"No lad! When I say cough, I mean cough. Try again."
"Aurghargh."

"That's better."

"OK!"

And that was it! Unless of course, the abused testicles had failed to twitch in the approved and expected manner, in which case, the operation was repeated. The unhappy fate of those whose testicles failed to twitch at all was not something that we cared to speculate upon at that moment. A twitch was all that had been required to obtain relief from our unwitting exhibitionism.

The following orderly made the appropriate notes, and added his own instruction.

"Please read the test card from top to bottom."

"Now provide a specimen please."

A small bottle was proffered to accommodate this requirement. As the first in line adjusted in an attempt to satisfy this impossible request and equally impossible task in quite such a public arena.

"Not here lad, over the bucket!", the following instruction directed sternly.

The unhappy victim of this tirade, now clutching his turgid member, followed the pointing finger to the intended vessel in a corner of the room.

Though the entire grisly and embarrassing procedure had been mercifully brief, gazing nonchalantly at the ceiling or the unadorned upper wall had become a painfully prolonged experience for all concerned. However, for two even more unhappy individuals somewhere in the middle of the long line of nakedness, the occasion had transported their emotions to a point in excess of bodily tolerance. Whatever the strength of clearly failing willpower, they both began to rise to the occasion. Along a line of totally naked men, two proud, if somewhat embarrassed, testimonies to youthful manhood, proclaimed their defiance in bold upward and forward display, and in so doing, rapidly became the subject of cruel but unrestrained sniggering. In a gesture that added insolence to defiance, one of those for whom standing to attention had abruptly adopted an additional meaning, stood proudly and rigidly to attention. Clearly officer material. It was one of the nurses who found sympathy for their plight. As she navigated the few short paces toward the protruding appendages, she removed a pencil from the breast pocket of her tunic. One deft, but sharp flick, with practised hand and eye, applied smartly to the end of each of the offending organs, and deflation was rapid.

Part of the old cockney rhyme came to mind.

Big ones, small ones
Some as big as your head
Give 'en a twist, a flick of the wrist
That's what the showman said.

Proceedings completed, I left the metropolis, caught the bus home to my sleepy rural backwater, and pondered the while. Perhaps I had just joined the Royal Air Force.

Chapter 2. The Bumpy Road to Gata.

... "There's another one for ladies, further down." ...

*

"Your country needs you."
It will provide a luxury cruise to take you to the chosen resort,
and the last and latest word in air travel to bring you back.

Innocents and tenderfeet, they were plucked from the fortresses
of their cities, and the fastness of their rural retreats,
and in the blink of an eye and without ceremony or preparation,
they became thrust into the military maelstrom.

In that moment, and in the interests of survival,
the final vestiges of innocence were abandoned
and were replaced by cunning, expanding worldly wisdom
and the developing art of deviousness.

For some, those whose lives had better prepared them
for this step into the unknown, the transition was brief and relatively painless.

These individuals would become the first survivors,
and would achieve early dominance in the ensuing skirmish for survival.

For others, the metamorphosis was to be slow and painful,
and would persist through the months that lay ahead.

Many of these individuals would fall by the wayside,
and would endure only a persistent longing to obtain release.

With benefits of street wisdom, and in spite of
the impoverishment and deprivation that would dominate the months ahead
it soon became clear that there was little at Cape Gata
that could not be obtained, located, discovered, or simply misappropriated.

Scruples and moral ethics were destined to endure a severe beating.

*

Six weeks or so later, my instructions arrived, complete with a travel warrant to Bedford railway station. I was to report to RAF Cardington on 2nd. June 1958. Prised, mentally kicking and screaming, from the bosom of family and from sleepy rural living, like a latter-day Dick Whittington, I headed to the unknown south. The long train journey, splendidly steam hauled of course, was a new venture for me. In my youth I had spent very little time in the distant southern parts, a solitary motor cycle visit to London a year or so earlier, when a field near Enfield had provided camping accommodation, and daily train access to the city.

Now, heading south once more, but to a camp site of a very different nature. RAF Cardington, just five miles from Bedford, occupied the former home location of the huge British airships, R100 and R101. Central to the station were the immense hangars in which these largest of all flying machines had been constructed in 1929, and had been based during their flying trials. These immense metal cathedrals, measuring more than 800 feet in length, almost 200 feet wide, and 160 feet in height, bore hollow testimony to a brand of warfare that had failed to materialize.

For we shy, nervous, apprehensive, incoming conscripts, Cardington was to prove a mere moment of transience. Residence of no more than a few days permitted the RAF to process the steady stream of fresh faced, and relatively innocent young men, and to pass them through its portals in both directions as quickly as possible. Each trepidatious rookie hoped to identify a potential friend among the blur of unfamiliar faces, or for the more timorous, a larger figure behind which to remain anonymous. We were kitted, administrated, medicated, and ever so slightly indoctrinated, and with our new, free suit of clothes, we took our first faltering steps toward the acceptance of a military way of life. The relative freedom from the anticipated harsh treatment, cruelty and verbal abuse that was allegedly an integral part of introductory National Service, induced a modicum of false security. Perhaps a couple of in-service years would not be so bad after all.

A confusing miscellany of forms and documents passed before each of us, all to be completed and signed. They were borne away to an unknown depository, taking with them every known detail of life to date. The outcome of all this administration was the issue of our identity cards, document number 1250. This document carried the indelible number by which each of us would be identified throughout our respective RAF careers, and which none of us would ever forget. Punishment for the loss of a twelve-fifty would be mediaeval in quality. It was to prove a saviour to me later in my service when tight moments threatened life, limb and integrity.

Another day, and another long line of shuffling bodies heading slowly to the service counter of the soup kitchen of kit issue. One size fits all, is not a maxim that can apply to the issue of uniforms. The requirement to ensure that each individual is neither strangled by his shirt collar, castrated by his underpants, nor enshrouded in trousers of Brobdingnagian proportions, imposes a process of measurement, guesswork and tentative fitting that is inevitably ponderous. Thus kitted, each proud recruit returns to his billet to remove his civilian vestments for the last time, and to become familiar with the 'blue' that will dominate his daily apparel for the next two or three years.

The medical moments of our visit to Cardington were approached with considerable apprehension. Lurid tales of inoculations, intimate personal inspections, blood tests of Frankensteinian character and dimension, and physical demands more appropriate to an Olympian athlete, had begun to circulate from the day of our arrival. To collective relief, the reality was much less dramatic. The medics examined eyes, ears and throat, they studied medical histories, they tested blood pressure, they unleashed a barrage of questions to which most of the answers were 'yes', and they peered into places where peering is considered less than desirable by both parties. It was an event that was spared discomfort and which imposed only a little embarrassment. The converse would follow in due course.

While this modest rite of passage and induction had been far less humiliating and discomfiting than most had feared, for some, what was to follow was torment beyond endurance. Cardington welcomed them all. The long and the short and the tall, and the indescribably indifferent. It rapidly cloned them into identical facsimiles of each other and projected them, startled and confused, into the bright sunlight of their brave new world.

Early wardrobe victims to this transition had been the drapes, the brothel creepers and the technicolour socks. For most, modesty had come of age at an earlier indoctrination, and had become replaced by a shrugged and nonchalant 'who cares'. However, for those whose extravagantly styled locks might have rivalled those of the French seventeenth century nobility, the ultimate indignity was about to unfold. They had arrived with their luxuriant waves, curls, cowlicks, quiffs and pompadours petrified into immobility by the extravagant use of Brilliantine, or concreted into permanence by liberal quantities of Brylcreem. It was even alleged that some made use of hairnets to ensure minimum disturbance as they slept, or perhaps that they might crack if rapped with large spoon. Damocles was about to lose his grip.

The barber's shop was a busy line of seats and scissors. Each seated individual was afforded a brief but identical few moments of concentrated attention, though some did take a little longer than others. A few swift sweeps of the electric clipper, a few skilfully directed clipped incisions with oversized scissors, and each unwilling sheep became instantly shorn of its finery. Carefully sculpted tonsorial masterpiece followed lovingly crafted coiffure with a barely audible swish, to the floor. Here, the crowning glories of a lost civilian life gathered in an ever increasing pile around the chair until a break in proceedings initiated unceremonious despatch with an anonymous broom.

Outside, among a similarly denuded throng, the discomfiture and outrage of the earlier hirsute was matched only by the mirth and ribaldry of those whose short back and sides, had remained relatively unscathed.

Cardington provided the venue for our first pay parade. The entire station complement had been ordered into one of the vast airship hangar buildings, and had been instructed to fall into ranks. It seemed as if hundreds of smartly attired individuals had materialised from unseen corners of the station. They had coalesced into a huge parade of well-disciplined penguins, filling only a fraction of the colossal internal void once occupied by the R101. At one end of the hangar, three or four tables, each with three chairs awaited their respective masters of ceremonies. Each became occupied by an officer, a sergeant and an orderly. One of the sergeants brought the parade smartly to 'Attention' and then 'At Ease'.

Each and every pay parade procedure followed an identical pattern. In alphabetical order, each payee was identified by his called out name. He responded by calling out 'Yes Sir', and his last three numbers at the top of his voice, as he stamped to ramrod rigid attention. He marched from the ranks, stamping at each turn, and to his ordained table where he stamped to attention once more and saluted the officer. He then received his paltry pay from the sergeant, and this was recorded by the orderly. "Thank you sir." The payee saluted once more, stamped, and then stamped again through three turns of ninety degrees as he marched back to the ranks whence he had come.

Much worse for those languishing at the rear of the cavernous building was the noise, and the grave risk of failing to hear your own name when it was called. The din seemed to hang in the air, to be trapped in the void, and to echo from the walls and the distant roof.

'Baker', 'Yes Sir, 123 Sir.' Stamp. 'Jones', 'Yes Sir, 456 Sir.' Stamp. 'Jackson', 'Yes Sir, 789 Sir.' Stamp. Stamp. Stamp. Stamp. Stamp. 'Smith', 'Yes Sir, 567 Sir.' Stamp.

The entire massive void was filled to capacity with panic- stricken raised voices and the sound of boots being venomously struck against the concrete. The duration was interminable and while Aaronson wilted in the heat, Zacharia was unable to risk so much as a blink of lost attention.

This was early June, and as luck had it, a particularly warm early June. The temperature inside the hangar steadily increased to the point when frying an egg on the toe of a burnished boot might not have been considered impossible. The area worst affected was the totally unventilated rear of the building, and those unfortunates who were destined to endure the longest wait. Those bearing the names Aaronson, or Absalom stood a reasonable chance of early relief and the opportunity to spend some the awarded cash in the NAAFI. However, poor old Zacharia stood little chance of survival let alone a beer. With a surname beginning with 'T', I was well down the pecking order, but long before I was to receive my paltry stipend, one by one the more susceptible crashed to the floor, and remained there until an attendant medical orderly was directed to administer relief.

The weekly pay for a National Service conscript was one guinea per week. For reasons that were beyond comprehension, it was not the practice to pay one pound and one shilling each week. Instead, and on alternate weeks, each individual was paid one pound, and one pound and one florin (two shillings). The Youngs and Zacharias must have wondered if it had been worth it.

Cardington also provided the venue for lectures of the informative kind, though from very different areas of information. There were talks about the Royal Air force in general, how if functioned, what it did, how rank and file made the best contribution to its purpose. We were introduced to an array of trades and professions to which we could afford consideration, pending the moment in a few weeks when we would be invited to make a choice. From a much more basic aspect of the information equation came the stern warning of the horrors of sexually transmitted disease. This wisdom was supported by grossly graphic projected images and film, produced and edited to afford maximum shock. The somewhat lurid images of discharges, sores, and horrid discolorations, left few in any doubt that perhaps it would have been better to have left the testosterone at home in a bottle.

Departure from Cardington was without rancour or particular memory. Association had been brief and introductory, and now we innocents were moving on to the next stage in our military interlude. We had each arrived at this place, alone, apprehensive, fearful even, of the unknown that lay ahead of us. We made our departure in small associations of growing friendships. For some, my own included, those friendships would persist, station by station, posting by posting, through the entire experience to demobilisation two years hence, and for a smaller number, these days marked the start of lifelong association. As if to demonstrate that comradeships formed in adversity or grossly out of context, do not fade, reunion some fifty years later, and after the total preoccupation of profession, family life, interests and pursuits, rekindles, without hesitation or interruption, the shared participation of those distant years.

Now, we were back on board the train, and heading for the distant township of Bridgnorth and the next step on the road to Gata. We were destined for our weeks of basic training. In the popular vernacular this was 'square bashing', though pounding the square was only a small part of the discipline and sufferance to which our tender bodies would be exposed. We were to be brutally divested of the last token traces of civilian life, thrust through the mincing machine of military indoctrination and moulded into small portions of the function of the Royal Air Force.

The steep township of Bridgnorth nestles in an upper middle portion of the valley of the River Severn. Local topography, or perhaps Isambard Kingdom Brunel had been enduring a bad day at the office, had dictated that its railway station had been located in a deep ravine. It was here that we were to encounter our first indication of the tenor of life that would dominate the next six weeks.

From the alighting platform a long and steep flight of steps led to the highway, and to a modest fleet of three-ton trucks. Celebratory bunting was entirely lacking, as were signs bearing any slogan that might have indicated a welcome to Bridgnorth. Substituting these were a group of gleaming, hard faced, grim booted, strategically located drill instructor corporals. Their apparent sole function and purpose was to dedicate the entire period of disembarkation in competition to identify the individual who could instil the greatest degree of terror into the stumbling arrivals.

"PICK YOUR FEET UP."

"MOVE. MOVE. MOVE."

"AT THE DOUBLE! WHAT DID I SAY LAD? I SAID AT THE BLOODY DOUBLE."

It was the middle of June. It was hot. After a long train journey, we were trapped in the narrow and stifling confines of a deep cutting. We faced the ascent of a steep and single file stairway. We were dressed in our heavy 'best blue' uniforms, and we were carrying all of our worldly possessions in heavy kitbags.

"MOVE YOUR BLOODY ARSES!"

The breathless summit brought scant and brief relief. The waiting trucks were of the high tailgate variety, and though these were hinged and could readily be lowered to floor level, this, of course, had not been done. The scene was one of shipwrecked mariners all scrabbling to grasp the security of the rescuing rope ladder, or of startled rabbits all desperately seeking the comfortable anonymity of the dark interior as the oppressors approached. The ascent of the tailgate was akin to a similar exercise on the north face of the Eiger, and we fell in an untidy scrummage into the truck, each seeking the relative anonymity of the forward portion.

Though the entrance to RAF Bridgnorth was not particularly forbidding, it quickly became clear that those portals afforded access to a new and different world, and one that would bring permanent transformation to life as we had known it. RAF Bridgnorth imposed an abrupt termination to any lingering complacency or feelings of well-being. From tranquil Bridgnorth town, we were abruptly absorbed by a world of noisy discipline. Groups of young men marching, without any apparent destination, to the bellowed sound of stentorian instruction, with accompanying verbal abuse to any individual who succumbed to rhapsodic interruption. There were yet more groups on parade squares, intent upon physical training to similar strict regimes. Others were rhythmically pounding the roads to the same tune, though at a more rapid tempo, and sweating profusely in the June heat. On leaving the trucks that had served as transportation from the railway station, we huddled together like alarmed chickens as we awaited our next call to purpose.

Randomly divided, we made our way to the small corner of the planet that would be ours for the next six weeks. The domestic portions of the camp comprised serried ranks of wooden huts, in which a bed space and storage locker had become life's abruptly reduced allocation, and even that was to be shared with twenty-three other trembling and apprehensive inmates. Allocated to each hut was a corporal drill instructor, whose rule was the law, and who presided with a verbal rod of iron over his appointed flight, as each group of two or three huts was entitled. His principal role and function was to ensure that the ensuing six weeks of our lives were to become as uncomfortable as the Bill of Human Rights would permit. Daily life henceforth, and for that period, was to be dominated by noise, from vulgar reveille to the relief of last post; by boot black and blanco; by bedpacks and kit inspection; by queues for food; by queues for pay; and by queues for the toilet. The DI corporal was a being in human form that had been robotically programmed to deliver high volume verbal abuse, which was graphically embellished by the inclusion of threats of unimaginable anatomical horror. It questioned parentage, it challenged our assumed membership of the human race, it poured contempt upon our gender. His indoctrination had transformed normal logical consideration into an all- consuming need to humiliate, to debase, and to reduce the more vulnerable to quivering submission. For some of his more susceptible victims, this onslaught became manifest, with outcomes ranging from service discharge to attempted suicide. He reminded us frequently that whatever the question, whatever the doubt, whatever the validity of the answer, however reasonable or unreasonable the reason, he was always, ALWAYS right.

He resided in a separate room at the fore end of the hut. Billets were allocated, though in no particular discipline, which allowed the retention of some of the new familiarities of Cardington. Immediately after taking up residence each flight was called to attention outside to receive its welcome address from the presiding corporal. It was terse and stern, and left us in no doubt that we would not find too many echoes of a holiday camp.

"It is my job to transform you rabble into a tidy bunch of airmen and a fighting force, and to provide your adjustment from boys to men. If we travel this path together, and in my chosen direction, our brief lives together will be peaceable. However, if we do not, I promise that your next few weeks will be absolute misery. At the end of your six weeks of training, this flight WILL pass out as the best of the intake. Do I make myself clear?", "DO I MAKE MYSELF CLEAR?"

"Yes corporal."

Thus the tone was set for this portion of our National Service holiday. As a concept or as a practice, it would make you, or it would break you, and there were many for whom the latter resulted in an early return home.

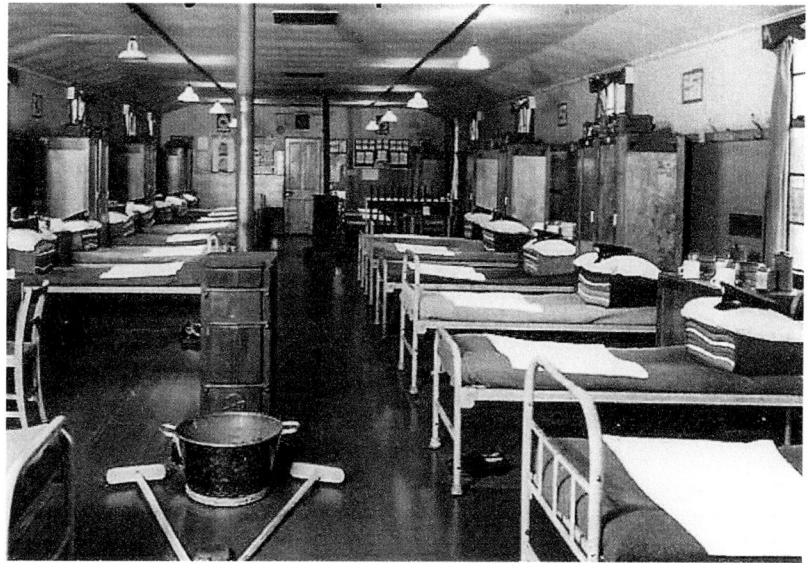

The tone of the following six weeks became indelibly set at six o'clock the following morning, as it did on every subsequent morning. The door into our snug little world burst open with a fearful concussion, our corporal strode the length of the billet and back, banging on the tail of each iron bed with a club and bellowing a discordant and unwelcome reveille.

"GET MOVING YOU IDLE BUNCH. HANDS OFF COCKS, FEET IN SOCKS. OUTSIDE AND ON PARADE IN THIRTY MINUTES, WASHED, DRESSED, SHAVED, SHAT, HUT READY FOR INSPECTION."

"Oh dear look at that. Someone has left dirty footprints from end to end and back again. How could that have happened?"

Within a few days, talking points made increasing use of the term 'assassination'.

This first of the daily outbursts set a scene of increasing familiarity. Cleanliness was to become one of the vital maxims of our very existence. Personal cleanliness, immaculately turned out uniform, dust-free bed space, hut purged to the point of sterility, boots as reflective as diamonds, life without blot or blemish. The hallowed ground of judgement in the hut was the floor. Covered in linoleum and burnished to iridescence, it was intended never to find contact with the soles of outdoor footwear. The occupants of the hut avoided this appalling prospect by sliding inelegantly across the surface on pads of old blanket cut especially for the purpose and wrapped around the potentially criminal boots. The rule, of course, did not apply to the uncaring NCO, who pursued his morning march with gleeful and vindictive deliberation. Each day, any lost sheen was restored by vigorous use of the bumper. This bizarre instrument took the form of a long-handled, broad-headed brush, to which had been added weights above and a cloth below. Applied with vigour this ponderous item could accommodate most of the blemishes of trespass, and transform their intrusive vulgarity into a creditable shine.

Hut inspections were carried out daily, weekly, and spontaneously. Daily inspection required that every bed space be prepared and presented in identical fashion. Bedding was stripped, neatly folded and presented as a sandwich pack of alternate blankets and sheets, all wrapped in an enclosing blanket, and all done in a manner that was to deny the exposure of any offending edge. This pack was placed at the head of the bed, surmounted by a pillow, and with other items of daily use arranged in the approved fashion. If this found immaculate approval, it would survive with no more than a glance, if not it was liable to noisy, abrupt, and wide dispersal. The distance to which carefully and lovingly placed items could be projected by the mere flick of a blanket corner was impressive. Weekly inspection added the complication of the demanded addition and presentation of every other personally issued possession, once again in the strictly approved manner. The unruly dispersal of disapproval during weekly inspection added the extra dimension of complex retrieval of collectively confused items from every corner and crevice of the hut. Spontaneous inspection caught out any of the unwary and the unprepared who had failed to arrange his effects in the approved manner, and had departed the hut in pursuit of duty or pretext.

Immaculate was a mere misnomer. No such condition could be permitted to exist, and any such illusion was hazardous in the extreme. Neither speck nor, smear need be present, nor miniscule displacement apparent, to induce the retribution of the fault seeking imagination.

Not infrequently, kit inspection provided a platform from which to remind us of our status. For the foreseeable future, your lives are merely on loan to you from the Royal Air Force. Everything that has been issued to you, is merely on loan to you from the Royal Air Force. Anything that is broken or lost will be reported and justified, and if your justification is upheld you will be able to apply to the stores for a replacement. Our issued equipment included that essential knife, fork and spoon trio of eating irons, and a large white porcelain mug. It was the common, and acceptable practice to decorate the white mugs. This served to provide identity, to allow freedom of expression to introduce a little colour, and to permit demonstration of usually limited and frequently dubious artistic skills.

However, kit inspection frequently exposed the vulnerability of the humble mug. Perched centrally among the carefully arranged personal items, and situated appropriately with the cutlery, the mug was ever prominent, and thus, subject to the closest scrutiny. Whatever the collective lustre of the assembled mugs, one would become singled out as a bearer of blemish, real or contrived.

"Is this your mug airman."
"Of course it is you stupid sod. It's on my bed." A sentiment oft thought but never expressed.
"Yes Corporal."
"Do I detect a tea stain?"
"I don't think so Corporal."
"Well, perhaps you can tell me what this is…"

Words spoken as a hand seized the allegedly offending mug, sweeping it upwards in an arc, and smashing it 'accidentally' into the bedstead as it did so.

Silence! Except for the rattle of shards as they hit the floor.

"Oh dear! That was an unfortunate accident... but here is the handle."
"Now clear up that bloody mess!"

Each flight comprised a complete cross-section of normal civilian human society, and somehow this disparate and grossly asymmetric group had to be forged into a cohesive synchronous unit. Very few days were to pass without the demand that we muster on the parade ground, and endure the relentless bellowing of marching orders. These directed our pursuit of the interminable practice of quick march; slow march; slope arms, present arms, reverse arms; saluting, wheeling, turning, halting, marking time; all of the movements performed so fluidly at an international tattoo, and all to the accompaniment of the stentorian tones of a personal, latter-day executioner. At first it was an utter shambles. Failure to keep in step resulted in half of the platoon skipping as they attempted to return to the rhythm. A stumble could result in several members hitting the deck. Arms and legs in continuous but totally uncoordinated motion, elicited high decibel apoplexy from the corporal instructor. Perhaps the worst offence was a dropped rifle. Though the noise of the fallen weapon shattered any fleeting moment of parade ground peace, the noise that followed was primeval in its quality.

"You 'orrible little man, did you just drop that rifle?"
"Yes corporal."
"One more time. DO YOU HEAR! One more time and I will tear off you arm at the shoulder and beat you to death with the soggy end?"
"IS THAT PERFECTLY CLEAR?"
"Yes corporal!"

The marching continued, day on day, the mistakes were proliferated, though fewer as the days progressed, and the threats of unimaginable fate continued to be received with penitence.

"One more time. JUST ONE MORE TIME. DO YOU HEAR ME? ONE MORE TIME AND I WILL SHOVE A PINEAPPLE CLEAN UP YOUR ARSE. DO I MAKE MYSELF CLEAR?"

"Yes Corporal."

"PLATOON, QUIIIICK MARCH." "EYEEEES RIGHT." "SAAALUTE."
"PLATOON HAAAALT."
"I TOLD YOU TO SALUTE NOT SCRATCH YOUR BLOODY EARS."
"YOU, AIRMAN, HOW DO YOU SALUTE?"

"Longest way up and shortest way down, corporal."

"WELL DO IT! YOU ARE SALUTING THE QUEEN'S COMMISSION, NOT ASKING TO GO FOR A PISS."

Day on day, improvement was perceptible. Fewer stumbles, more cohesion, less shouldering arms on a neighbours shoulder. However, just a few people lack natural coordination to the extent that keeping time in any context is beyond their natural or induced capacity. Our unhappy soul, was a man of small stature, whose civilian persona had been that long since extinct species, the Post Office despatch rider. On their little red motor cycles they had been a colourful feature of city life. Our man had pursued his calling in Newcastle upon Tyne. For him, coordination was not simply a difficulty, it was a calling far beyond his aspiration or his ability. Left and right seemed to have no meaning, be it applied to turning, shouldering arms, wheeling, eyes, or dress. Arms and legs moved at uncoordinated random, his own with his own, with anyone else's, or in time. When his randomly flailing limbs were located anywhere near the centre of a marching platoon, it became equally impossible for those at each side, or those to the rear to maintain their own rhythm, a disorder that quickly spread like a virulent disease, or a bad smell in a confined space. The shouting, the threats, the promises of paradise or an early and horrible death made no difference. Sadly it was no less distressing for the afflicted, it was simply beyond his capacity. Eventually, he had to be removed from the flight to other allocated duties, and may now be back in Newcastle, reflecting on his career on a little red bike, a calling that had permitted a more sedentary approach to his daily perambulation.

Throughout our period of basic training we were encouraged to make full use of the available sporting facilities, and to be competitive when any opportunity arose. As we were compulsorily confined to barracks for the first four weeks of our residence, there were few alternative avenues that would lead to any form of social or moral disarray. So, on these warm summer evenings it was the football pitch or the NAAFI. Sports activities, however, did provide another outlet. Physical training was compulsory and swimming was strongly encouraged, and as RAF Bridgnorth enjoyed facilities for neither of these activities, participants were taken to nearby RAF Cosford. This involved no more than a modest journey in a bus, but it afforded a glimpse of an outside world presently denied, and just occasionally, accompanying participants of the fair gender at our destination.

Though not compulsory, short course education in pursuit of improved literacy and numeracy were also available. Religion, carrying as it did, far fewer complications than today, also enjoyed a generous approach. C. of E, R.C, or 'other', seemed to be the only recognised and acknowledged doctrines, and thus, segregation was easily facilitated. Good fortune also permitted these activities to provide some good reason to be excluded from some of the less attractive tasks.

Everyone was required to take part in station duties - fatigues by any other name. Never particularly onerous, and usually conducted at a pace set by a blind eye or a turned back. Gently tending the verdant borders was a pleasant enough task in the summer sunshine. Shifting refuse bins, especially those associated with catering was somewhat less attractive. Any duties inside the cookhouse or its annexes were probably the most reviled. With the best ventilation working at full blast, the temperatures could be almost beyond endurance. Somewhat less overheated, but a prospect no less daunting, was the overwhelming task of peeling potatoes for several hundred men, but even this paled into relative insignificance beside the unparalleled horrors of the tin room. It was to this fearful placed that all of the vessels used for cooking were despatched for scrupulous cleansing. Grease, old cooking oil, burned fat, blackened concretions, and indescribable substances that enjoyed an incredible capacity for adhesion to any surface. All had to be chipped, scoured, scrubbed, purged and restored to glistering condition.

"How have they got to be lad?"
"Shiny Corporal."
"How shiny lad?"
"Er!"
"SO YOU CAN SEE YOUR BLOODY FACE IN IT, LAD."

Personal hygiene seemed to command a degree of occupational obsession, perhaps not without good reason. The gross indignity of personal hygiene inspection, which was suffered by all on a regular basis, was conducted by the corporals, working necessarily in pairs or in threes. Not in any way qualified medically, they were looking for any signs of speck or blemish, real or imaginary, that could be construed as a lapse in bodily hygiene. As an assertion of authority, a scapegoat would probably be identified in each flight. Hands, armpits, feet, genitals, every pit and pimple of each and every anal wrinkle, all became subject to the visual inquisition. Our scapegoat was an unhappy young man who had seemed somewhat silent and shell shocked since his arrival. He spoke little to anyone, remained very solitary in spite of entreaty, and viewed these occasions with terror. Almost inevitably he fell victim. Some contrived sanitary imperfection, or alleged modicum of bodily encrustations had been the excuse for a forced march to the ablutions.

"We'll show you how to keep clean," was apparently addressed to the entire hut.

Some time later, the quivering unfortunate was returned. His reddened exterior clearly revealed the brutality of the bathhouse scrubbing that he had endured. He was in tears, humiliated, and very distressed. The following morning he could barely be roused, and was despatched to the sick bay. He did not return, and we later learned that he suffered undisclosed problems of mental health, and was later discharged.

For those who survived this regular humiliation with clenched jaws and stoic resignation, far more, far worse and far more embarrassing awaited. No-one escaped the utter indignity of the health inspection. All that had gone before was repeated, this time in minute detail. Each naked conscript stood before his jurors to await their ministrations and judgement. Small consolation in the belief, or perhaps just the hope, that these invigilators were medically qualified to pursue their unwelcome practice. Every externally visible bodily function from ears to feet was tested, each orifice was peered into, every personal crevice examined. For those for whom the non-intervention of religious intolerance, parental choice or medical requirement, had permitted the retention of penile integrity, came the final vexation. Examination demanded that each foreskin be peeled back to allow intimate glandular inspection, and if considered necessary, the retrieval of a specimen. This, in pursuit of any vestige of the scourge of venereal disease, and for any for whom this may have already been a risk, apprehensive trepidation pending receipt of the notice of good health.

As if to leave no lingering doubt in our minds, or perhaps to find relief from indignity, we became obliged to view yet another screening of 'VD for all'. Even more graphic than the last, we became the unwitting and somewhat unwilling observers of organs infected and pustulated almost beyond recognition, and as if this were not adequate deterrent, some of the alleged treatment practices of the day surely would be. One antibiotic and antiseptic treatment involves the insertion of a long narrow tube, akin in form to a very slender suppository, which is a fitting title. To this is attached a tube of salve, and when the end is adjudged to have penetrated sufficiently, the contents of the tube were introduced into the offending organ. To impose even greater deterrent, skin-crawling and lurid tales of the gonorrhoea umbrella were also deliberately circulated among our group of innocents. Only later was this exposed as an urban myth, and that no such urethra-scraping device is to be found in practice. All of this in glorious and vivid colour, and even more suppuratingly horrid than imagination could conjure. It left us with a clear choice - testosterone or abstinence.

Even now, the ministrations of the medics remained incomplete. Regulation demanded that we all be rendered immune from several disorders. Apparently Typhoid, Tetanus, and Smallpox were the medical scourges of young men everywhere, and to ensure that we became immune to their ravages, the appropriate prophylaxes were to be implanted into our tender bodies. To these ends and purposes, we were ushered like sheep to the abattoir.

The purposes and principles of medical prophylaxis have remained unchanged since Pasteur, only the nature of the vaccine and the method of delivery have evolved. A controlled dose of live but impotent pathogen is introduced to the body, and the recipient endures a mild bout of the disorder. This induces the bodily immune system to spring into action with the agreeable outcome of long term or even permanent immunity. Today's filamentous needles, delivering tiny doses of aqueous vaccine can pass through the flesh without sensation, and in a deft hand the entire delivery will be momentary and will remain undetected. Not so the military equivalent of the nineteen fifties.

The instrument of delivery was a substantial glass tube and internal plunger. The exterior of the tube had been clearly marked with the quantities required for each delivery dose. To its business end was attached a needle that was, in description and design, a sharpened tube. By the standards of today, the dose delivery quantity was huge, and in consistency the vaccine was closer to gel than aqua. Thus each dose was delivered painfully and slowly into an inadequate crevice just excavated in the unwilling flesh.

The sheep were herded into single file, and the column shuffled unwillingly along the length of a corridor in the direction of the small execution chamber. Each line of confined but resigned victims, patiently awaiting their multiple puncturing, were unhappily obliged to pass the pale, vomiting, dribbling, evacuating, immobile or gently twitching forms of those who had passed before, or even some who had succumbed in advance of the ordeal. Some simply failed to reach the exit before passing out on the floor, others vomited as they passed, and the majority, looking haggard and deathly pale wobbled unsteadily toward the fresh air and sunshine outside.

At the point of delivery, three medics sat behind a table, each armed with the instrument appropriate to his calling. At the opposite side of the table, three temporarily empty chairs awaited each patient, who would progress from one to each of the others. At the first, and to the order 'present arm', the business end of the syringe was delivered into the upper bicep and the marked dose discharged. The recipient moved on, and his place was taken by his production-line successor. It appeared that the needle would be changed only when the syringe became empty, or presumably when it had become so blunt that it would no longer penetrate the epidermis.

At the second port of call, the upper opposite arm became subject to a scratch imposed by an unpleasant little instrument, and the wound thus caused was infected by the attachment of a prepared sticking plaster. The third port of call involved an even more bizarre procedure. In the centre of the soft inside of each forearm, a needle was used to raise a bubble of skin, and it was into the subcutaneous hollow thus created that the vaccine was insinuated.

Outside, the scene was one of impending mass extinction. Groaning bodies lay scattered on the grass embankments; others, white-faced and unsteady, were in evident danger of collapse; and many were already exhibiting the grossly swollen upper arms that would later affect us all. Our ever sympathetic corporal had the answer.

"Back to the billet, lie down until lunchtime, then on to the parade square for an hour of PT. Fall in at 14.00, we'll soon get those arms moving and back to normal."

Those still capable of an upright position, and not yet consumed by choleric fever attended as instructed. Grossly distended, and still swelling upper limbs were thrust unmercifully and painfully into positions familiar only to a gymnast, until a hitherto unseen spark of human kindness permitted the termination of the gruelling toil. The benefits of the enforced exercise were not evident at any time, and indeed some of those afflicted retained their symptoms through the following day, shivering uncontrollably in bed, or heading rapidly to the toilet for any one of a number of reasons.

We did, of course, recover, and training continued inexorably towards its conclusion. As the weeks had passed our relationship with our flight corporal had mellowed from aspired assassination, to muted respect. Our daily performance had improved from stumbling disarray to a respectably cohesive marching unit. Our collective thoughts began to turn to the challenge of the passing-out parade, and even the earlier unlikely possibility of earning the accolade of best flight.

While our final couple of weeks were to be no less intense, a new dimension had become included in the daily routine, and this had added interest and diversity. The battered remnants of the .303 rifles that we had abused so frequently on the parade ground were replaced by weapons that functioned as intended. Issued to us as battlefield best friends, we learned care and respect in every aspect of their use, care, cleaning and maintenance. We learned accuracy on the firing ranges, we practised the noisy use of fixed bayonets and we bellowed obscenities at straw filled sacks suspended from their corners in a wooden frame as we stabbed them to death, in-twist-out, in-twist- out. the greater the volume and the more obscene the vulgarity, the more the sack trembled in its fearful frame. We learned to use the bayonet as a hand weapon, and we found introduction to other kinds of firearm, notably the Sten gun, the Bren light machine gun, and side arms.

A battlefield best friend indeed, and perhaps the one to save the bearer's life. These were the real deal. They were a personal issue, and were accompanied by the stern instruction that they were to be maintained in pristine condition at all times. This was our adopted duty of care to our battlefield best friend. They were handled and cared for with a dedication that bordered on reverence. They were presented for critical scrutiny on spontaneous demand and were presented at every kit inspection. They were cleaned, oiled, polished, and purged of every blot or smudge. We learned and practiced the skill of dismantle and reassemble, and then honed that skill until it could be achieved in seconds. Then we did the same thing while blindfold, thus ensuring that our battlefield best friend would be ready and prepared for his life-saving purpose in any circumstance or condition.

We were obliged to prepare for some of the other perils of the battlefield, and no-one escaped the horror of the gas chamber. After instruction in how to do what, we entered the gas chamber in small groups wearing gas masks. At a signal, the gas pellets were released, and as instructed, we removed our gas masks and danced around the chamber shouting, singing, and making as much noise as possible, thus ensuring the unavoidability of our maximum exposure to the toxin. After a few minutes of choking exposure and inhalation, we were released, coughing, eyes streaming, sneezing, and gasping for breath. Horrid! Though as it happened, a lesson learned for me when exposed to gas once more and much later in a riot situation in South America.

We learned fire fighting, navigation, self sufficiency, and survival. We tested our stamina to breaking point on assault courses, and in the gymnasium. We enjoyed slightly greater freedom of choice in our approved group activities, as we slithered gradually towards our final days at Bridgnorth.

We headed for our passing out parade, and thanks to six weeks of bullying and threats, we were a credit to ourselves, to our training, and to the corporal who had been our persecutor, our oppressor, our tyrant, our authoritarian, and ultimately our respected guide and trainer, and our friend. It was he who had led us and directed us, along every step of our painful journey to this final moment. Passing out parade was a smart occasion, a proud occasion, an occasion that afforded us the rank of Aircraftman Second Class, and perhaps the feeling that we had finally earned the uniform that we were wearing. While each and every one of us would take our leave of RAF Bridgnorth without a single hint of regret, later reflection would concede that we had matured immeasurably, that we had learned to work as members of a team, that personal confidence had been hugely enhanced, and that six weeks of strict discipline had induced the final metamorphosis into manhood.

This moment however, marked only the half way point in our training programme. Our next essential step was to learn how to do something useful. In our final moments at Bridgnorth, we were to discover what trade or temporary profession each of us had been allocated. It seemed most likely that the principle purpose of trade selection was to serve the manpower requirements of the service, and not the earlier choice of the individual. I learned that I was to become an Air Defence Operator, a newly created craft that had evolved from the former twin tasks of radar operator and fighter plotter. In order to master the mysteries of this vocation, I would be required to spend the next six weeks at RAF Compton Bassett in Wiltshire.

Almost two months had elapsed since a large unruly bunch of strangers had arrived nervously at the gates of RAF Cardington. During that period, individuals had aggregated into groups of familiars, and for just a few, into comradeships that were to continue to the next stage, to the stage to follow, and for some, to friendship that would endure. Sixty years later, notwithstanding the passage of time, profession, family life, and emigration to distant locations. Beyond individual indulgence in a vast diversity of personal interests and pursuits, the entire panoply and complexity of lives and times, and mostly with complete absence of interim communication, small numbers would aggregate once more, would reunify, would revisit those lost moments, and would remember the innocence of youthful custody.

After the tumult and the tribulation of Bridgnorth, RAF Compton Bassett provided entry into a relative haven of peace. While the beasts of Bridgnorth, no doubt continued their reign of terror among another group of innocents, we who had survived the earlier onslaught found a relief in gentle, leafy, Compton Bassett that was almost unbearable. Hardly substantial enough to be called a railway station, the poetically named Black Dog Halt was our terminus to a waiting bus, and to the comparative tranquillity of the camp. The lines of huts were uncannily familiar, the grassy surrounds and open spaces were neat and tidy, the entire camp enjoyed an aura of orderliness, but without the urgency of bellowed command or the ordered tramp of a score of boots. A little music accompanied the breeze, conversation was audible as people strolled in the sunshine. More a college campus than a military barracks.

No longer the need to evade the verbal cannonade, no more parade ground sores, and no more crucifixion for misdemeanour that would barely rank as trivial in any other theatre. In this DI-free zone, reveille provided a more compassionate start to each day, relaxed and regular hours of work allowed the freedom of personal space, and the open door of camp security permitted the pleasurable exploration of the local licensed premises.

Discipline, of course, was dictated and demanded by rank and by protocol, but we were back at school, and it was at school where we were to become prepared for the remainder of our military careers. My first few lectures were a maelstrom of mystery and confusion. The principles, purposes, function, and operation of radio, radar, and electronics were far, far removed from my career calling into the world of biology. However, with the application of maximum self-discipline and diligence, the fog of incomprehension slowly coalesced into a clearer picture, and conviction replaced the faltering confidence of uncertainty.

Radar transmitters, and their aircraft tracking functions, came in many shapes and types, each one serving to detect range, altitude, speed, aircraft type and, inter alia, national identity. The mysteries of their electromagnetic waves, broadcast invisibly into the ether, and returning in the form of visible on-screen strobes in lurid orange or green, were alien to my perception. My youthful experience of looking at screens had been limited to very rare glimpses at the black and white flickering panoramas of the television of the day. These utterly unfamiliar, revolving, rising, falling or oscillating images were nothing if not perplexing. Here and now, I had become abruptly exposed to the mysterious world of PPI tubes, azicators, 'nodding neddies', and the ever scrutinised plotting table.

However, we were to be operators, and if operators are to be successful, they must learn how to operate. The mysterious world of radar and radio operation makes maximum use of the phonetic alphabet, utilises a mysterious phraseology that is unknown in any other human circus, and it demands absolute clarity of the spoken word. Operators may be speaking to someone in the next room or to the pilot of an aircraft that is many miles distant. Repetition and duplication are to be avoided at all costs, and thus, speech must be delivered slowly, with precision, and without embellishment.

To realise this purpose we were also obliged to become telephone operators. Cinema presentations that depicted hotel and exchange functions of the previous couple of decades, often included lady switchboard operators sitting in front of a large panel full of individual electrical sockets, which served to connect with the outside world via a corresponding electrical plug. Who can forget the familiar, dulcet, "Number Please!" Though our connection did not require the socket arrangement, we were adorned with equally fetching, breast hanging, inverted cornucopias that were our speaking tubes.

A significant and important part of our early training required some translation of familiar local dialect or intonation into dialogue that could be instantly recognised and accurately interpreted often by multiple recipients. Our student body had been drawn from many, varied, and linguistically diverse parts of Britain, and this sometimes posed a challenge to our endeavours. One of our group, was a softly spoken young man from rural Norfolk. He spoke with an accent so drawlingly slurred, that interpretation presented a real obstacle to comprehension, and presented a potentially serious risk that multiple recipients could make equally multiple interpretations of his speech. Though every effort was made to train him to reduce the duration of his vowel sounds and to clip his consonants, his vernacular proved more than a match for the accepted and required lingua franca, and his National Service had to be diverted toward an alternative purpose.

To our delight, our hours of toil had become those of a working day and these within the confines of a working week, thus allowing the freedom to seek leisure pursuits, or even to roam more widely for those closer to a home base. Restrictions were few, the local licensed premises provided a worthy drop of local ale, and the local townships of Calne and Chippenham were well within easy reach if more cosmopolitan delights were required. Though we were not without kit and hut inspection, and we were required to maintain acceptable standards of 'neat and tidy' around the camp, in comparison to Bridgnorth, life, as we learned our trade, enjoyed a reasonably leisurely pace. Our time at Compton Bassett drew to a close, we became elevated to the rank of Aircraftman First Class, and we awaited the instruction that would identify our individual relocation to a permanent base.

On our penultimate day at Compton Bassett, we assembled in orderly ranks on the parade ground to receive our postings and the likely destiny of the remainder of our two years of service. We waited in fidgety patience as one by one, names were called, to each of which was added a station identity for home postings, or geographical identification for those destined to head to a foreign port. No frills, no pack drill, just name, location, and foreseeable destiny. Mine, it turned out, was to be an unspecified base in Cyprus.

At the conclusion of the roster, the assembled company were preparing to shuffle off to ponder what had just befallen their lives.

"Wait for it!", "WAIT FOR IT!"

"All those who have received overseas postings will report to the MO at 09.00 hours tomorrow morning for necessary inoculations."

The groan was audible. More jabs!!!! In the NAAFI that evening, speculation and wild rumour mongering were rife. We were to be inoculated against Yellow Fever. The vaccine was akin to treacle in its consistency, and delivered in huge quantity. It had to be injected directly into the base of the spine! From the front???

In the event, none of these horrors were to become reality, and we headed for a final home leave before embarkation.

During my couple of home leave journeys since Cardington, I had shared the long-distance coach journey to Leeds with a fellow recruit whose family had been driven from the Sudetenland in 1939, and who had settled in that city. I continued my journey, by bus or train to Scarborough, from where a long hitch hike through the night would bring me to Whitby, usually at a grossly unsocial hour. We would meet once more in his home city to take the return coach, which departed Leeds at midnight. His mother baked the most memorable apple strudels, still hot from the oven when he embarked, we gorged ourselves on these delicacies as the southbound night flitted past the darkened windows.

RAF Innsworth was the transit location in which those sufficiently fortunate to have attracted an overseas posting reassembled before becoming cast like the seeds of a dandelion into the many corners of the map that were still coloured pink. It was a carefree place. The discipline that should have prevailed was totally ignored. There were no imposed duties from which our future lives as Air Defence Operators would have derived benefit. We considered our few days as mere extensions of our embarkation leave.

However, duties of a more tedious and unwelcome nature were imposed, and avoidance of these required some finer honing of embryonic skiving skills, together with a degree of guile, valuable qualities as it turned out, for the remainder of our service. I was one of a small group assigned to the task of tending the flower beds and the grassy borders, under the direction and supervision of an elderly, kindly, but gullible corporal. This gentle, unassuming man had spent his entire career in the RAF, was not too far from retirement, and had almost certainly received his promotion to corporal by default. He was an easy victim to indifferent duplicity. Each morning we assembled at the appointed location, he with a wheelbarrow full of tools of the horticultural trade. The title, 'Corporal Wheelbarrow' was an early irreverent endowment. On arrival, tools were distributed, the task was explained, and the work of the day was commenced. One by one, the members of the squad contrived some feeble excuse to be elsewhere, bogus prerequisites that the hapless corporal never found the dominion to challenge. Mid-morning brought the arrival of the Sally Army tea van and a welcome break from our skiving. None ever returned and the unfortunate 'Corporal Wheelbarrow' had simply been abandoned, with his wheelbarrow and tools, to continue his solitary chore. To my knowledge he never complained of our conduct, and my later reflection on these few days, did impose a pang of conscience.

The few days of smoking behind the roses quickly came to a close. We had been kitted out with khaki uniforms, tropical pyjamas and lightweight underwear, and our medical and travel documents had been checked and verified. We had boarded a train to London, which, in truth, was taking us, in some apprehension, toward a destination unknown to us all. My friend of the strudels, from Leeds, was taking a different route, to RAF Changi in Singapore. I never saw him again.

Late in the evening, we arrived at Blackbushe airfield, then an airport of entry and exit principally serving cargo and charter services. As we hung around expectantly in groups, apprehension rapidly evolved into anticipation. Our kitbags were removed for loading, and we learned that we were to be transported by Air Charter of London in a Bristol Britannia aircraft - the Whispering Giant. For me, the ensuing few hours would embrace two firsts. This would be the first time that I had taken to the skies, and the first time that I had left my native soil. An appropriate mode of transportation for one of the most recent recruits to the Royal Air Force.

We boarded the aircraft at a little after midnight. The airfield was shrouded in dense fog, and as we approached the speed for takeoff, I was afforded a view from my window seat of the slightly hazy runway lights, each one passing with greater speed as our velocity increased until we became absorbed by the night sky.

Our non-stop flight of a little more than eight hours duration, was uninterrupted by atmospheric turbulence, and for a time provided splendid moonlit views of the snow capped Alps below. We arrived in Cyprus at RAF Nicosia, tired, hot, into the brightness of the early morning sunshine, and into a new and bewildering world. On disembarking the aircraft, we were first directed to one of the airfield buildings to await our baggage. Still in our heavy blue uniforms, and unwilling to adopt shirt sleeve order until permission so to do had been granted, discomfort increased steadily in tandem with the rising morning temperature.

The first trolley load of kitbags had just arrived, when everything became reduced to mayhem. A loud explosion somewhere out on the airfield, quickly transformed order into chaos, as every alarm on the station sounded, and all personnel made haste to their appointed emergency locations, bringing our progress to a halt, where it remained for most of the morning. In the building, the sensation had been more akin to concussion than to detonation, though it had been sufficient to shock us all into temporary silence. At length, our off-loading continued, and we received the instruction to retrieve our bags, to remain inside the building, and to await the arrival of a truck that would take us to the transit location. We were later informed that an explosive device had been concealed in or on an empty Comet aircraft, and that it had been extensively damaged in the explosion.

"Welcome to Cyprus!"

A small fleet of trucks ushered us to the transit camp, and to some welcome lunch. However, the airfield emergency was to dominate the entire day and the entire function of the station, leaving we utterly bewildered new arrivals in limbo and confusion. Eventually we were informed that we would be going nowhere that day, and that we would be allocated accommodation for the night. The transit camp comprised a small village of wooden buildings and several rows of two-man tents. The latter were to serve our purpose, and I shared that billet with my companion since Cardington. The station would provide all that we required, there was a mess hall and a NAAFI, between which we would shuffle without purpose for the ensuing three days. For the remainder of the current day we were left to our own devices.

The tents were minimal, two beds and locker storage, but as we anticipated only very temporary residence, little point in unpacking all of our worldly goods. Very low tent walls allowed a sleeper almost no free space between his sleeping form and the sloping tent roof, a situation not for the claustrophobic. However, two long days and a long night flight ensured that sleep should not readily elude.

It was a hot night, and I awoke early, with a start, and with my face almost in contact with the tent roof. Staring down at me, and in alarmingly close proximity was the largest insect that I had ever encountered. Shock, more than irrational fear dictated my next move. I issued a bellow that must have disturbed any neighbours still with Morpheus and jerked inelegantly away from this perceived threat. This precipitated my plunge from the bed, striking my head on the corner of the locker as I descended noisily and painfully to the concrete floor. During this pantomime, my imagined assailant had made his escape, and a trickle of blood made its slow descent behind my right ear.

The day was to remain dominated by the aftermath of the emergency, and most of the morning had passed without progress, before information about our prospective future became known. We had to be registered, processed, recorded, and documented. Each of us would be allocated a unit, and with all of this complete, we would be transported. Once they had been set in motion, the administration and procedures would take some time. They did, but not on that day.

As the ponderous process proceeded stage by tedious stage, we made some attempt to seek a little enlightenment, about our likely locations and their character. Little was forthcoming, except one small snippet that came in response to enquiry.

"You see that white structure on top of the mountain? That is Ayios Nikolaios, and that is where you will likely end up. Believe me, it is rough. Tents, food not fit to eat, cockroaches and bugs, dust and heat, no running water. It is bloody awful, so be prepared."

Well, there was an endearing prospect. I almost regretted the enquiry.

The day was to become dominated by a succession of slow processions as we queued for each of the stages in the processing, satisfied the invigilator, and moved on to the next shuffling progression. However, and to our relief, most of the procedures had been completed by the end of the day, and we found some assurance that we would be moving on at some time during the following morning. Even at this stage no unit allocations had been forthcoming, and even if place names had been revealed, they would have enjoyed little meaning given our limited knowledge of the geography of the island.

The transit camp was a place that enjoyed all of the charm and character of a busy goods yard, and in human terms, it served precisely that purpose. We had no desire to linger longer in its impermanence than was necessary, and we hoped that our next dawn would herald our emigration to another place. After our shuffling to and from breakfast, the sergeant who had been allocated the task of transient patronage brought us to some measure of attention.

"Alright, you 'orrible lot. Get your things packed, and be ready to leave at eleven sharp! Got that?" "Eleven sharp. Anyone not ready will spend the rest of his life in this place, cleaning the bloody latrines."

Whether his words had conveyed inducement or repellent, we were indeed ready to leave at eleven sharp.

Our first view of the convoy in which we were to be travelling, quickly dispelled any lingering naivety. Our bus was to be preceded by an armoured Land Rover and a three-ton truck, each carrying members of the RAF Regiment and assortment of arms from the Bren light machine gun to side arms. A similar escort would follow. Our route took us first through the outer suburbs of the city of Nicosia, before turning south and later west, heading, we were informed, for RAF Akrotiri.

Not too long after our first view of the blue Mediterranean, we briefly traversed the environs of Limassol before heading south once more, past the splendid Kolossi Castle, and through a labyrinth of orange groves and tall Cypress trees.

In spite of the evident potential threat, our journey had been uneventful, and we made our safe arrival at the main gate and guardroom of RAF Akrotiri. At this point all of our documents became subject to scrutiny, a routine that was becoming increasingly familiar. On this occasion however, it was without the frustration that had prevailed at earlier arrival destinations. This time we had arrived. We had finally reached journey's end. Around and ahead of us was the reasonably agreeable campus of our living space and place of work for the foreseeable future. At least that was our perception at that moment. Another bus and convoy arrived, and we enjoyed the sunshine as they too received authority to enter. We had become quite a large crowd, and as we mingled, it became clear that we were in pursuit of a range of trades and professions. Several three-ton trucks arrived, that ever-present and highly ubiquitous form of military transport that carried everything everywhere. Names were called, which seemed to relate to professional designation, we heaved our kit into the indicated truck, heaved ourselves after it, and looked forward to arrival at our living quarters.

Our journey seemed to follow a meandering route, but it afforded us a tour of the station, and a moment or two of welcome familiarity. It was, of course, very orderly, and seemingly relaxed, as we noted the many facilities that were available for use, purpose, or entertainment. Particularly impressive were the neat lines of single storey cabins that were clearly the living quarters, and to which we were fully expecting an early introduction.

"This doesn't look too bad! Plenty going on here, and hey, look there! Even some female company."

"Those guys in Nicosia obviously fed us a load of old bollocks."

Our approbatory musings were abruptly interrupted as we passed through another boundary fence and into the somewhat desolate adjacent hinterland. Ahead of us now a dirt road extended into the distance. Around us a squat, spiny forest of low scrub extended in every direction, except the one fast receding behind.

A couple of chokingly dusty miles later we came to a halt once more. A pole barrier from which was suspended a coil of barbed wire prevented our further passage. Several forty-gallon drums painted in red and white formed a second barrier to any prospective unwanted intrusion. Against an adjacent wall of sandbags lounged a somewhat languid airman. He was dressed in untidy tropical kit and wielded a Sten gun. Behind the barrier, a wooden hut bore a sign proclaiming this to be Royal Air Force, 280 Signals Unit, Cape Gata. We dismounted for the mandatory personnel and paper check, and took this first opportunity to view our surroundings.

Ahead, dominating the immediate view, were two buildings, later, and very evidently, identified as latrines. In the near distance, row upon row of tents dominated the visible horizon, and beyond them, some taller structures that did little to further enhance the view. The dirt road continued beyond the barrier, and served as a physical boundary to this untidy and unappealing village. No sign of immediate life afforded any vibrancy to this somewhat desolate panorama. To our right and behind, the spiky 'bundu' scrub extended to the limits of visibility and no doubt beyond. To the left the view was dominated by the self same ecosystem, though in the far, far, hazy distance, way beyond the end of the Akrotiri main runway, glistened the blue water of Limassol Bay

As the remaining new arrivals pursued the process of registration, I stood slightly apart from the group. Through the heat haze of late afternoon, and the dust devils kicked up by the breeze, I pondered the barren and apparently unloved prospect ahead of me.

One of the guys on guard duty came up behind me. "Welcome to your new home!", he said quietly.

Chapter 3. Those early apprehensive days.

… "Life presents a dismal picture" …

*

*At the conclusion of your luxury cruise,
or your relaxing eight hours in a Whispering Giant from Blackbushe Airport,
a pleasing ceremony of reception and welcome will provide
invitation and introduction to your new surroundings.*

*A transit pause in lavish accommodation will be followed by
a short and comfortable journey by road through the verdant countryside.*

*This will bring you first to the principal resort,
though not yet to your idyllic retreat.*

*A further couple of miles along the highway remain,
to your final destination, whimsically entitled 'Hell on the Hill',
and to the domestic comfort and luxury that it offers.*

*Early in your long residence in the 280 Home for the uncertain
and perpetually bewildered,
you will encounter comradely banter from the guests in residence.*

Bloody 'moonies'- getcher knees brown.

*

The appearance of a cheerful countenance served to elevate the prevailing spirit of doom and desolation. A corporal approached! He was no less scruffy than the guys on guard duty, but he bore a smile and a sense of welcome. His unenviable duty was to afford a greeting to our bewildered group, and then to find somewhere for us to live.

As we shouldered our bags and followed him towards the tent lines, he explained that we had arrived at a period of some seriously confused overcrowding, and just in advance of the expected repatriation of a significantly large group of individuals who had completed their tour of duty. Thus, and for the time being, we would be doubling up, or worse, at least until the impending evacuation had liberated tents from their present occupancy. When that time arrived, he warned, available tents would not be allocated, but would subject to first claim.

These tents were of a size for ideal shared use by two persons, and were indeed designed to satisfy this objective. This would have permitted essential bed and locker space, and accommodation for personal effects or the pursuit on individual interests. However, in view of possible implications of covert sexual shenanigans, the current regulation stated that each tent would be occupied by three men. In any case, the current overcrowding had dictated that almost all of the tents were presently in three-man occupancy, and only those individuals whose trade or profession put them into a 'special' category, enjoyed the rare privilege of twin-share. This 'special' designation remained unexplained.

Tent by tent, person by person, we were allocated a billet. For most, if not all, this was to result in housing a fourth individual in a tent that was already overcrowded with three and their personal effects. There was no practical possibility of introducing a fourth bed into such a confined space. In consequence, I became obliged to endure my first few restless and sleep deprived nights on a canvas hospital stretcher, in singular discomfort. The available alternative was a collapsible wire and canvas camp bed, but this provided very little more in terms of comfort and nocturnal facility. Moreover, these makeshift truckle-beds were of design and construction that afforded guarantee that the occupant would be capsized instantly on to the floor if he or she made any nocturnal attempt to turn.

The three guys whose relatively comfortable lives I had usurped were reluctantly, but understandingly tolerant, in the confidence that this would be a temporary intrusion. The simple requirement was to proceed with daily life, to try to avoid any tension that would be the inevitable outcome of uncoordinated juxtaposition. This was difficult. I was totally without furniture or any other storage space, and thus, all of my personal effects and clothing were destined to remain in my kitbag until living circumstances enjoyed a change for the better. Daily life became an exercise in the avoidance of any violation of my three adjacent personal kingdoms.

It was to relief all round that this state of affairs persisted for only a modest number of nights. In recognition of the fact that four person occupancy was an impossible and intolerable situation, every effort was being pursued by the camp administration to rectify the embarrassment. Some were found temporary sleeping quarters in a spare marquee, which relieved the spatial problem but did little for comfort, security, or peace of mind. For a time, so sparse was the availability of beds that the guys in the marquee became obliged to adopt a 'hot bed' system. Those for whom night duty had concluded simply occupied the bed vacated by his duty successor. To my relief, my quadruple living came to an early close, and my small good fortune afforded me a significantly more spacious and practicable living space. Perchance, I became billeted in one of the rare, currently two-man, 'special category' tents, where I could find repose, at last, on a bed and mattress, and with storage and practical facility for my personal goods and effects.

 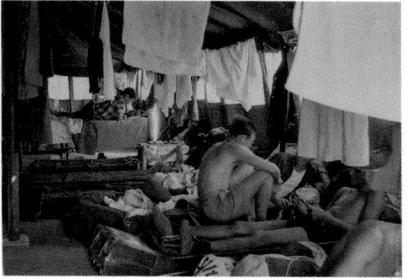

Two-man tent dwellers guarded their spatial and relatively spacious privilege with intense zeal, and my two companions made it clear they would tolerate this intrusion into their kingdom for no longer than was imperative. As it transpired, I also quickly formed the preferred view that my tenure of their bailiwick should become as brief as I could possibly make it.

This was a cook's tent, and cooks, it turned out were one of the few groups to qualify for the 'special' residential category. The reason for this is simply because a cook's tent is totally uninhabitable by any known life form, except of course, cooks. The nature of their profession dictates that they are perpetually exposed to all of the odours that accompany their daily lives. These olfactory assassins penetrate fabric, clothing, hair, skin, and perhaps over time, even deep into the epidermal cells that protect us from the ingress of anything else. Thus, cooks live in a kind of atmospheric cocoon. Fresh air seems only able to purge the more volatile, aromatic, ambrosial odours, leaving behind the malodorous, fetid, cumulative reek that clings to every part of every long-term, commercially oriented, mass-producing kitchen.

A cook's tent absorbs these odours, and stores them in every item of clothing, in every fragment of bedding, in and on every item of paper, dust or debris, on non-absorbent surfaces where they accumulate greasily, and even into the very fabric of the structure of the tent. They cannot, and will not be expunged except by the use of caustic or chemical means or in extremis, perhaps by incineration. A cook's tent enjoys the malodorous aura of an abandoned galley or deserted 'chippy' that has witnessed the sustained, long-term, and frequently repeated use of the same rancid, repeatedly congealed, and regularly reconstituted cooking fat.

While I had no wish to linger in this turgid atmosphere, living in a cook's tent did bestow benefit not generally shared by the rest of the camp. True to their calling, cooks conduct their craft and trade in the cookhouse, or perhaps the galley to the more sophisticated. The end product of their endeavours is their dietary delivery, proffered in the mess to the assembled airmen. The cooks do not eat in the mess.

Cooks enjoy access to the more select portions, the fine and prime cuts, and the pick of the incoming rations. These enjoy the kind of careful and practiced preparation not detectable on the daily production line. When at the peak of culinary perfection, they are concealed within swaddling napkin and transported to the secrecy of the cooks tent for the purpose of very exclusive dining Cooks are well nourished, jolly on the outside, and well satisfied within, and though their contraband practices were no mystery to anyone, theirs was a very open secret that must be protected at all costs. Thus it was, when I found entry to their hallowed ground, that I too became part of the mystique. I became obliged, upon pain of dietary inexpedience for the rest of my time at Cape Gata, to swear that I would uphold the illusion.

While this arrangement greatly enhanced my daily diet, it also required that I sustained the pretence of the normal procedure, three times daily in the mess. Uncomfortable engorgement was the occasional outcome, but perhaps a price worth paying for the short-term benefit of relatively fine dining.

These first few days became largely dedicated to familiarity, and the reduction of bewilderment. The domestic portion of the unit was not large, and it took but little time and effort to become familiar with layout and location, to become aware of the time and place of the lamentably few facilities, and to commit to habit the daily routine that was to dictate every aspect of life for the months that lay ahead. We discovered the delights of the nearby ocean and of the secluded lido that would provide a vital and essential outlet to frustrated energies. It would become the focus of our free time activities. On the technical site, we became introduced to the complexity of the machinery, of who did what, and how we, as Air Defence Operators, would finally be putting our training into practice.

But why were such a large body of Air Defence Operators, operating air defences in Cyprus at this time, and from seven stations distributed on coastal promontories and in the high Troodos Mountains?

Though Cyprus had become a British Crown Colony in 1925, for much longer than that its location in the Eastern Mediterranean had afforded the island a considerable degree of strategic importance.

However, it was not until the Suez crisis of 1956, the subsequent invasion of Egypt by Israel supported by France and Britain, and the short-lived threat of war in the region, that Cyprus adopted the additional mantle of military strategic primacy. The UK military withdrawal from Egypt had emphasised and considerably expanded the strategic consequence of the island, which had become the United Kingdom's only military presence in the Middle East.

However, though the British had made their Egyptian withdrawal to their annexed Crown Colony, they were not destined to enjoy a comfortable or easy occupancy. The Cypriot population comprised an ethnic mix of Greek and Turkish citizens. However, severe cultural and religious differences ensured that neither Greek nor Turk enjoyed their residence in equal or comfortable proportions. Of the total population, those of Turkish descent were numerically fewer than one quarter.

Since the end of the Second World War, the Greek majority had become increasingly vociferous in their demand for greater political, social and ethnic union with Greece. A movement entitled 'Enosis', which simply means 'union', had been active since the nineteenth century, originally to impose pressure for liberation from the sovereignty of the Ottoman Empire. Its governing principle continued into the twentieth century seeking that those Greek communities living outside of the Greek State, should become incorporated within its governance. It became rekindled in the early 1950s, and imposed increasing pressure upon the British government to relinquish their governance, to remove their colonial status, and to initiate and permit union with Greece. It follows that the Turks were less than enthusiastic about this prospect. To exacerbate tension, as the Turkish government had aligned with the axis powers during the Second World War, there was little aspiration for any closer links or relationship with the Turkish homeland. The Turkish population remained a significant minority.

While Turk and Greek remained at loggerheads about most matters political, and with no support from Britain for the principle or proposal to move toward 'Enosis', it was Britain that was considered the wolf in the fold. Thus, in 1955, and still under the banner of 'Enosis', a terrorist group came into being, and adopted the title 'Eoka'. Initiated, founded and led by 'General' George Grivas, it commenced a programme of guerrilla attacks on British installations, convoys, personnel assassinations, ambush, the planting of incendiary and explosive devices in buildings, aircraft and highways, in short, the application of the many and varied aspects of terrorist harassment. In this endeavour, General Grivas was ably aided and abetted by the Greek cleric Archbishop Makarios, who was later to become the first president of the newly independent Greek Republic of Cyprus. Many of the monasteries under his jurisdiction had become guilty of harbourage and the concealment of armaments, behind the considered immunity of an ecclesiastical cowl. Far from the benign support of a policy and practice of peace and love, this man of the cloth proclaimed unconcealed support for the terrorist policies and practices of General George.

So here we were. Innocents abroad. Removed abruptly from the comfort of familiarity, and thrust, perhaps somewhat unwillingly, into a world of technical confusion for some and into a role and function that was desperately in need of practical application and the benefit of experience. We had become shoehorned into a conflict that was little understood, and which had hitherto been no more than peripheral to our consciousness and awareness. Confused? Mystified? Apprehensive? Initially, all of those emotions and more, though with the benefit of the increasing familiarity of those introductory and extraordinary few days, the fog of bewilderment slowly began to clear.

Familiarity in and around the home is a fairly important asset. At home, as you are aware of the location of the toilet when you need it, you are significantly less likely to fall down the stairs while seeking relief in the middle of the night. Our home was large, ill-lit, and endowed with more obstacles and pitfalls than an abandoned junk yard.

280 SU was an encampment of two parts, and was situated on the bleak, treeless and exposed peninsula of Cape Gata. The name translates to 'Cape of Cats', and legend has it that when St. Nikolas moved to found a monastery on the cape, he discovered, no doubt to his discomfort, that the scrubby vegetation was infested with a huge number of snakes. Thus his endowment to the local geography is the legacy of his introduction of cats as a means to control the reptilian population. The monastery still exists, as do the cats, and so far as the biological records are aware, the snake population, whatever its threat to human kind or to cats, continues to thrive in the bundu.

The smaller, technical or working area of the encampment, accommodated the radar transmitters (revolving, nodding, or oscillating), the mobile cabins containing screens to translate incoming signals into readable traces, the control cabin where the readable traces were translated, plotted and recorded, radio transmitters, a well appointed motor transport section, and offices for day to day administration. This was the workplace for everyone on the unit, with the single exception of those earlier mentioned, whose sole function was the daily preparation of culinary delights.

The domestic portion of the encampment was considerably larger, singularly more complex, and provided for every other aspect of living at Cape Gata. The encampment was dominated by the serried ranks of tents. The provision of accommodation was designated by rank, with separate lines for commissioned officers, non-commissioned officers, and airmen. As dictated by custom, practice and status, the ablution facilities were equally segregated. Officers, commissioned and non-commissioned, each enjoyed their allocated facilities, while a larger unit satisfied the ablutionary requirements of the common herd. Our primitive conditions dictated that the differences between these units were few, and indeed, it was the very restricted supply of water, and not the geography of the location, that had dictated their establishment in a cluster. The entire supply of water to the camp, for any purpose, was trundled daily from Akrotiri in an ancient bowser. After supplying the requirements of the culinary departments, the vehicle was parked close to the ablution blocks, for use by all hands as the only source of water for washing or drinking.

For our only leisure and pleasure activities, a large marquee provided our NAAFI facilities, and a boundless supply of Keo, the local beer. To huge inmate delight, the dusty marquee was later replaced by a permanent building, one of only four such structures on the encampment, the others being the officer's mess, the airmen's mess, and the partly constructed cinema.

280 Signals Unit was contained, in its entirety, within an enclosure, the perimeter of which was a constructed barbed wire barrier of the Dannert or concertina type. This comprises coils of wire that are extended to become long rolls, and these are placed one upon two, or two upon two, and contained within by yet more barbed wire that is strained between metal posts. A similar structure separated the two site locations, each of which was served by and protected by its own guardroom. Access to the technical site was through the domestic site, and therefore through both guard posts. At least two guards manned these stations night and day, and they were armed, and ready to repel any unauthorised incursion, be that of pirate or insurgent, with .303 rifle and Sten gun.

Though designed for and effective against anyone sufficiently foolish to aspire to make illicit and unseen entry, the concertina coil barrier could also reduce the unwary to a sorry mess of entanglement. Any nocturnal wanderer, and especially one not in full control of his awareness for whatever reason, Keo induced insomnia, narcolepsy, a catastrophically replete bladder, or lunar compelled psychopathy, could endure many hours of suspended discomfort, pending discovery and assistance. This, perhaps only by chance, if the unwelcome perambulation had directed the perforated victim to a particularly remote portion of the perimeter.

During these introductory first few days, our presence attracted volumes of derisory comments. We were new boys, and true to schoolboy form and tradition, the older boys did everything in their power to ensure the maximum discomfiture of the new boys. There could be no disguise. While their well-burnished skins toned well with the colour of their tropical uniforms, our pallor reflected the sunlight like a freshly painted wall. At each and every location, and at all hours of the day and night, the call 'Moonies', and 'Get yer knees brown', reminded us of our unfledged status. It would pass, and we would echo the same superior mantra to the next and to every subsequent incoming group.

Though we had learned to live and breathe the need for the highest level of security at all times, one familiar aspect of this function was absent from the unit. Unlike every other station of our journey so far, 280 was almost completely without the presence and influence of the RAF Police. Only two were permanently resident, and their function were dedicated entirely to the task of camp security. These masters of bullshit, overbearing discipline, assumed authority, and occasional brutality, were much despised. Instantly recognisable by the white livery that adorned their uniform caps, they were universally referred to as Snowdrops. They strutted, they barked unreasonable instructions to the more timid, they were permanently armed with sidearm and truncheon, and they intimidated. Their absence at 280 gave no cause for lament.

However, and like every other unit or station on the island, security at 280 was at the highest level of permanent alert. At most stations, security was customarily the responsibility of the Snowdrop, and in the absence of the Snowdrop, their duties must be delegated to others. These would include guard duties, patrols, escort duties, and occasional forays into more public places to ensure that the rule of law and order was being maintained, or perhaps to root out the occasional miscreant.

For the entire station complement this situation imposed duties beyond the immediate calling of the individual. In addition to the function for which each of us had been individually trained, we would all be allocated the additional duties that were required to maintain the non-specialist aspects of the running of the station. As we were to discover, this policy and practice of, 'Everyone will do a little of everything', was to add considerable diversity to daily lives. Working as Air Defence Operators could be stupefyingly boring. We watched green and orange strobes, revolving, going up and coming down, and oscillating us into unintended slumber. We plotted the passage of every passing aircraft, military or civilian, on the table and on recording sheets. We retreated into an interconnected world through our headphones and speaking tubes and we longed for the end of each shift, and the attendant liberation from electronic bondage. Thus, the added duties of the Snowdrop, the janitor, the odd-job man, and the role of general factotum that provided assistance to anyone and everyone as required and imposed, were generally welcome.

Paramount among these additional functions was the security of the unit, of its installations, and of the couple of hundred or so of individuals who were confined within its concertina coils. To achieve this first line of defence, we would require additional training. Back in distant Bridgnorth, we had learned how to make a great deal of noise when making a bayonet charge, and how to use the same piece of equipment as a hand held weapon. We were never likely to make use of either. We had spluttered our way into and out of the ghastly gas chamber, another unlikely encounter. We had learned in which direction to point a .303 rifle, and had pulled the trigger with various and often questionable accuracy. We had been afforded the brief opportunity to try our hands with the Sten gun and the pistol, and generally speaking had made a hash of both. We had made our departure from Bridgnorth with little or no anticipation of the need to make use of any of these practices at any time during our period of service. Abruptly, or so it seemed, our lives, and the lives of others may have come to depend upon our individual ability to use these weapons to their intended purpose and effect.

Our onward training required visits to the cliff top firing range at Dekhelia Barracks, in the south east of the island. This venue would not only provide facility for the enhancement of our dubious skills, it would also furnish welcome future reasons or excuses for the occasional skiving day out. Initially we were to receive professionally directed training, and thereafter were encouraged to make application to make use of the range for supervised practice. Here, we learned to master and control the recoil of the .303, and to make little holes somewhat closer to the centre of the target. We learned how to release the sidearm from its holster in a smooth and efficient action, and without the unintended removal of part of a foot. We attempted to master the inherent inaccuracy of the Sten light machine gun. Using this cobbled together assemblage of scrap metal, to strike the proverbial barn door at thirty paces could be considered an achievement. However, this was the weapon of issue, and the one that we would carry on every occasion that involved security, defence, or protection. We needed to ensure that we could use it to good effect, if only to spread alarm.

We practiced with the Bren gun, a much heavier light machine gun. Fired from a sitting or lying position, when this weapon was propped on its bipod front legs, it enjoyed all of the power and accuracy that was totally absent from the Sten. Our principle target when using the Bren were twin offshore rocks that protruded prominently from the ocean surface, at a challenging range. This objective provided hours of fun as we watched the rocky fragments fly at every successful strike. Equally, the target afforded clear illustration of our inaccuracies as shots fired short or wide splashed into the water.

One additional competitive challenge involved the speedy exchange of the gun barrel. During sustained firing, the barrel of the Bren gun will become red hot, thus causing the firing mechanism to expand and to become jammed. In a critical situation, life could depend upon the speed and efficiency with which the barrel was changed. In practice, many fingers became seriously scorched in competitive haste as the gunners mate forgot to use the swaddling cloth before seizing the glowing barrel.

As this brief period of honeymoon drew to a close, we faced the prospect of full integration into daily life at 280, and the many months that lay ahead. Having been thrust into a conflict of which few had little understanding, we were far, far out of our personal comfort zones, a situation that insinuated and imposed a profound influence on some.

Ours had been a brutal introduction into a somewhat mystifying role and purpose. Slowly, slowly, the cloud of bewilderment was beginning to disperse.

The new boys had been listening to the whispers on the wind. The anticipation of impending repatriation had become a more regular topic of conversation in the NAAFI, and it had become clear, that those for whom a tour of duty was reaching conclusion, departure was becoming ever more imminent. I learned of a tent that was to be evacuated, and with my companion from the start, we staked our claim. For me, whatever somewhat dubious advantage had been bestowed by the unfair, gastro-diversity of these early days, destiny to join the mainstream of 280 daily life was almost upon me. As the occupants of tent number A12 vacated the premises, we made indecent haste to move our goods and chattels in through the door. I was pleased, at last, to find the facility to make my departure from the place where prime steak had been an occasional delight, but where the greasy aura of the fat in which it, and many, many before it, had been cooked, lingered in festering brown festoons from every crevice and protrusion in the tent.

The abruptly evolved condition of culture shock, was slowly becoming replaced by the excitement of the unknown. Suddenly, I seemed to be a world away from my tiny North Yorkshire hamlet of thirty souls - and still not certain why.

Chapter 4. The Quest for Elysian Domesticity.

... "Cats on the Rooftops" ...

*

*At our charming and exclusive resort, you will share luxurious accommodation
with companion guests, and you will enjoy the many facilities
provided for your comfort, leisure, and enjoyment,
and in pursuit of the collective and diverse interests
of your new-found and hugely enhanced family.*

*Maximum comfort is our enduring motto, and no expense has been spared
to ensure that our facilities provide for your every comfort
at all times of the day and night.*

*Each room, set in its own carefully and delightfully managed surroundings
commands magnificent views of the adjacent areas of the resort,
and provides facilities of quality unparalleled elsewhere in the region.*

*The high class team of chefs in our gourmet restaurant
have been recruited from some of the finest shebeens and flop-houses in the world,
they are on hand to provide quality fare at any time of the day or night.*

*Our toilet and bathroom facilities are so hygienically maintained
that they provide a home for a wide range of habituated wild creatures,
each of which will provide you with endless interest
and daily squatting fascination.*

*The ostentatious and extravagant management
of the stately lounges provided for your recreation and relaxation
is truly the stuff of legend, and will ensure, in tandem with the restaurant,
that the aforementioned comfort facilities quickly become
a regular, communal and social feature of your daily routine.*

*

'Hell on the Hill'. A term of endearment? A representational description that afforded accuracy to reality? A fanciful notion that served merely to exaggerate nominal discomfort? An emblematic term, worn with boast and pride? A figment of the collective imagination of those who were confined within its bounds? A veritable stockade from within which inmates gazed upon an outside world with envy and resentment? A diabolic place of pandemonium, shunned and reviled by the condescending and the self-righteous? Merely a place of three hundred or so lost souls condemned to shamble its dust and disarray until, purpose spent, they were discharged from its carbuncular agglutination?

Or, for those obliged to live within its bounds, perhaps a modicum of each of these characteristics dominated daily life. For some, it was true, every moment spent in this place was one purgatorial moment too many. These unhappy young men lived in a world that was completely alien to all of the sensibilities that had evolved during their more tender years. They lived their daily lives in abject terror of the unknown and the highly unlikely. Every waking moment of every day and night was filled with utter loathing and disaffection for the imposed obligation to live in conditions with which they were unfamiliar and which they found wholly unacceptable.

Their burgeoning prejudice precluded their involvement with any of the social, sporting, or leisure activities of the unit. Not for them the pleasures and the perils of a private patch of crystal ocean. Not for them the football pitch, the rugby field or sport for leisure. For them, not even the temptation of the near oblivion that could readily be achieved by modest over-consumption in the only available place of recreation. For these deeply unhappy mortals, daily life involved only a series of short walks, to the ablutions, to the mess, to the latrines, or to the technical site in pursuit of their elected task, or perhaps occasionally to the cinema. They lived this period of their lives in a dream of the familiarity of home, drifting meanwhile through a fog somewhere between despair and the cusp of suicide.

For the more optimistic of character, life at 280 provided prospect of an extended period of holiday. In the few fleeting moments that had brought us to this point, we had become liberated from stern parental gaze, from the daily drudge of the factory floor, from the required diligence of studentship, from the anxiety of future uncertainties, and from the daily peer pressure of youthful gamesmanship. Of course we would be required to bow to the need for compliance with the regime that had become the directing force of our daily lives, but as some of us were quick to learn, this could readily be manipulated to personal advantage and without evident detriment to the dictating system.

One prominent feature of camp life quickly became evident. Necessary protocols were observed. Rank and order were always afforded the respect that they commanded. Consequently, the machine that was 280 Signals Unit functioned smoothly, and performed its vital role in the military defence of the region with due efficiency. A long-established system of shifts and watches allowed the proficient pursuance of this function during twenty-four hours of every day of the year. Thus, in relatively equal proportions, the entire complement of the unit, at any given moment, was working, sleeping, relaxing, eating, or were in pursuit of other appointed duties that were vital to the self-sufficient survival and the integrity of the station.

Our commanding officer was a gentleman, was fair to the point of generosity in his running of the station, and was respected by all. He was kind, thoughtful and considerate. He recognised that the demands of a twenty-four hour function within the restrictive confines of a crowded encampment, where peace, quiet, and privacy were seriously limited facilities, would induce stress and tensions. To compensate, he permitted and encouraged a relaxed attitude toward daily discipline. Relaxed but not lax. Easy going but not disorderly. Tolerant but not negligent.

The strict dress codes with which we had been familiar were no longer strictly enforced. While uniform remained obligatory when on duty, the prevalence of the ever-present dust precluded any mirror-like glitter on the toecaps of boots. In acknowledgement of the basic nature of living conditions, the requirement for a strictly geometric approach to individual space was no longer required. While the bed-pack continued to dominate any temporarily vacated bed space, tidiness and not exactitude was the expectation. Regular tent inspections ensured that standards were maintained, though these events served equally to check on any other violations of the rules, or of the presence of items of dubious ownership.

280 was a relatively Snowdrop-free zone. Not three miles distant, the relatively huge airfield and station complex of RAF Akrotiri gleamed in stark contrast to the dust and the primitive living conditions of Cape Gata. Here, strict order dominated. Everything green was neatly trimmed and everything white was regularly afforded a fresh coat of paint. Impertinent litter was instantly expunged, and any surface not bearing regular traffic was swept to antisepsis. Inside each of the neat and tidy bungalows, neither speck nor blemish were permitted, and each utensil and artefact was made secure in its properly appointed location. Those engaged in the commerce and the enterprise of the day, went about their business in the fashion of Stepford wives, buttons, buckles and boots all blindingly agleam in the sunshine. An infestation of Snowdrops prowled the thoroughfares, scrutinised the hidden corners and chided those whose trousseau may have strayed from the acceptable.

It was from this stark contrast in presentation and practice, that the slightly more colloquial title became bestowed upon 280 Signals Unit, Cape Gata. This was not some veiled complaining reflection by the residents about their standard of living or their lack of facilities, but a title bestowed by the more salubrious and sophisticated mortals at the bottom of the hill. To them 280 was populated by lesser beings, scruffy sub-humans whose purpose was unclear, and which was, at best, merely ancillary to their own. Here were beings whose very tread on their hallowed ground was considered defilement. The rivalry thus induced was often challenged on more equal fields of endeavour, and rarely found wanting. Thus it was that 'Hell on the Hill' became inducted into the ancient and honourable register of stately homes. Our location on Cape Gata also provided our motto, 'Eyes of the Cat', and a somewhat alarming feline centrepiece for the unit emblem.

The familiar and jealously guarded 280 way of life did become subject to a single early challenge from within, and required the application of somewhat extreme measures in its defence. A young, eager, grossly inexperienced Pilot Officer, recently graduated from Cranwell, arrived to take up his duties among the rabble. He was dapper, excruciatingly smart, and full of brilliant ideas about how a unit should be managed. He arrived in a bright yellow Ford escort motor car, though just what he intended to do with it on a road that led to nowhere was a little unclear. His early self-appointed function was the imposition of a regime that would transform this untidy, slack, disreputable unit into a smaller facsimile of the immaculate station below. He pursued this misguided aspiration with a zeal and fervour that revealed the potentially disastrous weaknesses in his innocence and inexperience. He proposed more regular and more rigorous inspections of tents and tent lines. He suggested that full seasonal uniforms should be worn at all duty times. He suggested regular parades to ensure that standards were maintained. He went so far as to suggest that airmen should cease forthwith, the unworthy practice of attending breakfast dressed only in pyjamas and wellington boots. How unreasonable!

His unacceptable demands continued until morale reached a mutinous low. One dark night, someone etched the word 'HATE' into the rear bodywork of his yellow car. No culprit, of course, was ever likely to be revealed, and unhappily for all, this unkind action did nothing to reduce his headlong pursuit of permanent unpopularity. The next defensive steps adopted a slightly more subtle and less immediately damaging approach. Anonymous notes, stage whispers, words muttered in crowded places, all finally delivered the message that if the unreasonable campaign did not cease, and if the familiar were not restored forthwith, the car could readily and easily be relocated to the foot of the nearby cliff. We were soon back at breakfast in wellington boots.

The polite term that is routinely used to describe places of the kind in which we lived is 'under canvas'. This was no exaggeration. With the exception of the airmen's and officer's messes, the curious ablutions, and ultimately a cinema and a NAAFI building, every other function of the domestic site was conducted under a flexible canopy. Though the latrines were the remaining exception, human occupancy of these structures was only ever conducted as briefly as nature's alimentary processes would allow. Human occupancy, crowded as it frequently became, was thus a somewhat invalid term. Living quarters comprised first five, and later six lines of tents, totalling slightly in excess of eighty in number. For two occupants, as designed, long term residence could have been enjoyed in reasonable comfort. With the imposition of a third, each tent became an overcrowded tenement. Inject into this limited space, a fourth unwilling occupant, and the tenement has become a slum. Officers and NCOs fared somewhat better in their more exclusive occupancy of nine and five tents respectively, and of course, equally exclusive ablutions.

The tents were of conventional design, and in capacity, each one measured ten by fifteen feet and seven feet in height to the ridge pole, which was supported fore, aft, and centrally. Without additional superstructure, the lower edges of the roof at each side would have been suspended at a height little greater than that of the bed, leaving the sleeper with no more than a few inches of free space, and a claustrophobic decline into early morning insanity. To compensate, the construction of a low wooden wall afforded the entire structure an increased elevation of around three feet. This greatly enhanced the comfort of the occupants, but for the fact that the same elevation now separated the supporting poles from terra firma. Equally, all of the guy ropes now fell far short of the securing stakes. The application of a little ingenuity provided remedy for these problems. Recently, the dusty earthen floors of each tent had been replaced by concrete, and the timber from the duckboards that had carpeted the floor, had become the principle source of material for the construction of the walls. The three upright poles, now in suspension from the ridge pole, found support on bricks or blocks. The earlier tent pegs were replaced by long metal rods to which the free-flying guy ropes were attached and secured.

It is worth noting that none of the necessary raw materials for these or for any other adjustments or aids to comfort and facility, were provided. Nor could they be obtained by purchase, barter or bribe, or through any other socially acceptable exchange. The construction, camouflage, concealment and use of furniture, fixtures or fittings was achieved only by observation, guile, opportunism, cunning liberation, and ingenuity. Many and hugely diverse were the items of home comfort and domestic convenience that brought simple enhancement to lives that would have been intolerable without. The benefits to morale were well recognised by authority, and the source of the 'improvements' was almost never questioned.

The official provision for each occupant was a bed and bedding, a small bedside locker and a tall hanging locker. There was little or no provision for personal security, which depended, without failure or fault, upon honesty. Any additional furnishings, if space permitted, were either re-homed, or constructed from materials that had also been re-homed. A recently installed supply of electricity, and a single central, suspended, forty-watt bulb elevated the night-time tent from total darkness to mere gloom. However, on a technical unit that was awash with electrical fittings of every kind, purloined sockets, switches, pedestals and cables ensured that most of our dwellings could be illuminated in modest competition to a small football stadium.

Home comfort was dictated in fairly high degree by the climate. During the summer months the in-tent temperatures were sustained, day and night at an unbearably high level, while in mid-winter, temperatures at night could dip to zero or beyond. While the eighty or so electric fans that had materialised like ectoplasm into living space, helped to move the summer air though the maximum possible ventilation, nature's dusty furnace would not be denied. The provision of upright, paraffin-burning, 'Aladdin' stoves, provided some winter comfort, together with the attendant considerable fire risk, and a modest danger of asphyxiation.

During the summer months, dust pervaded everything and everywhere, and particularly so during October and early November when the hot, powerful Sirocco wind carried thousands of tons of red Saharan dust, a blanket of which embraced every surface, choked every breath, and filled every vessel. A heavy sleeper could rise from his sheet leaving behind a perfect outline of his body. We seemed to be first in line for this heavenly gift from Egypt, though the dreamy vision of having slumbered in the perfume of an Egyptian garden was quickly lost as we shook the soil from bed and pyjama. The late summer dust storms always preceded the autumn rain in mid-November and though imposing the quality and ferocity of heavy monsoon, they brought welcome, if temporary relief.

To assuage the heat and the constant thirst of the summer months the occupants of most tents had acquired a chatty bottle. These large unglazed terra cotta jars are in common use throughout the Mediterranean Basin as vessels in which to keep water cool. *Bojitos* by name in Spain. They function in much the same manner as a sweating body. Moisture passes through the porous terra cotta, is evaporated on the outside and thus, exterior heat does not pervade the water inside. One inventive soul took this principle to a greater and more adventurous level, and by making use of several jars, he devised and constructed his own beer cooler. This inventive device made multiple use of the cooling qualities of evaporation, by linking three jars through a slow siphon system. The first jar transferred its cooled water to the next which in turn cooled and transferred to the third wherein the Keo awaited its chilling influence. When the Keo was removed for consumption, the cooled water was simply returned to the first jar, a progressive process that enjoyed almost limitless repetition, and a steady supply of cool Keo.

The wise, the experienced and the best advised had taken remedial steps to avoid autumn's next little gift. Though the first rainfall brought welcome relief from the heat, and bore witness to naked men running around gibbering in relief and delight, the first heavy autumn rains were ferocious, and finding landfall was a mere brief interruption of their continued progress. In combination with the generous layer of fine dust, a fine slurry now pursued gravity's irresistible attraction. Precautionary measures were simple and effective. Those who had excavated a substantial trench around the entire perimeter of the tent with an outlet at the lowest point, escaped inundation. Those who had failed to undertake and maintain this task became overwhelmed while they were out looking for a shovel, a rare and coveted item at this juncture.

The trenches served a dual purpose. While nocturnal visits to the verminous latrines were to be avoided at all costs, an alternative depository, following the excessive consumption of beer, is a requirement. The trenches were ideal for this purpose, and in the full knowledge and confidence that the autumn rains would cleanse and purge. Alas, many months elapse between March and November, and continued deposition during this long period bestowed upon the tent lines, the all- pervading reek of used beer and urine. In extremis, attempts were sometimes made to rinse the offending trenches, but water for this, or for any other purpose was ever in perilously short supply, and wasting water was akin to selling state secrets. Supply of this most precious commodity was limited to the daily visits of the water tanker, and supply from this vessel frequently expired during the summer months under the pressure of more essential and less mundane demands.

The ferocity of those early autumn storms imposed a severe test of the strength and stability of our fragile dwellings. Not infrequently, the canvas material became ripped, and guy ropes were torn from the ground. Thus abused, fly sheet, roof and wall became transformed into wet, heavy, manically flapping tarpaulins. It required almost super human restraint to exercise control and to restore stability, at least until the storm had passed, or when daylight permitted an assessment of the severity of the damage. On occasion, the tempest would prove too great and an entire tent would be exploded from its moorings to become festooned across its neighbours, or tumbled across the soggy bundu, leaving the unhappy occupants with the task of attempting to secure the contents of house and home.

Between, and to the front of each row of tents, and interconnected at intervals, rough concrete pathways were essential features in preventing the mud of the rainy season from its otherwise invasion of every aspect and moment of daily life. Short sections of the same thoroughfare extended to a point a few feet short of the door of each tent, and the gap, which carried the all-essential trench, was spanned by a short drawbridge duckboard. The same grade of coarse concrete provided a floor to each tent. It was an inferior quality material and was thus an additional source of constant in-house dust. Floor coverings to prevent this problem, and to induce an enhanced sense of false comfort were in perilously short supply, though not entirely so. Tent canvas, coarse matting, linoleum, carpet pieces, all could be re-fabricated to fashion a bedside mat or even more extensive floor cladding. An unexpected encounter with a roll of coconut matting provided me with sufficient material to carpet my entire ten by fifteen concrete pad.

In spite of the deprivations, a combination of cunning, stealth, opportunism, and pride ensured that living standards were maintained, and however limited, that individual space was clean and tidy, and reflected the character of the occupant of that tiny domain. As already indicated, the crude wooden walls had been constructed from the original wooden duckboard floor coverings, with the addition of scrap timber and broken up packing crates, and were thus somewhat lacking in the quality required to compete in the International Interior Design Awards. However, paint was fairly abundant, and though limited in choice of colour, did not seem to appear on any regularly scrutinised inventory. As a commodity, its storage became fairly widely distributed.

Ornamentation and decorative enhancement were by no means restricted to a pot of paint. Ingenuity and artistic acumen were employed in manners many and divers, to ensure that interior decor matched the mood or character of the bed-space occupant. Among the smattering of pictures of wives, girlfriends, family, conquests, and the abundant unclad female figure, were small shelves for personal items or books, celebratory and greeting cards, or displays of empty beer cans nailed to the wall. Popular and sometimes ingeniously elaborate was the often highly illustrated 'days to do to demob' chart. The salvaged canvas from purloined tents, when stretched over the wall surface and nailed in place, became wonderfully rigid after a few coats of paint. In this condition, it became ideal for artistic expression, and murals of many moods revealed many a latent Michelangelo, Hieronymus Bosch, Lucien Freud, Salvador Dali, or latter day Banksy. My chosen wall adornment was the corrugated cardboard readily available from incoming cargo. This too provided a versatile surface for decoration, with the added advantage of easy and secure pin retention.

Tent availability remained at a premium for many months, and only became relieved when twelve were added to the dwelling complement in the form of an additional line. With my intending house mate, I had made my bid for the occupancy of the soon to be vacated tent, A12. To secure the bid, and to reduce the risk of a gazump, the twin operations of moving out and moving in were conducted seamlessly on the entrance duck board.

For a brief period of unaccustomed luxury we enjoyed the rare privilege of twin occupancy, and though carefully concealed from public awareness, this situation was destined to be short-lived. Though we defended our tiny protectorate against all-comers, we became obliged to share the bailiwick with a succession of transient individuals. One such was a particularly heavy and noisy sleeper, whose somnambulistic day and night ramblings frequently attracted an intrigued audience. He was difficult to wake, and on arousal, he adopted a rigidly upright sitting position, eyes wide, staring, and sightless before seizing the corner of a blanket. This, he proceeded to stuff into his mouth until absolute capacity had been reached, and his lower mandible had descended to the point of dislocation. An ideal model perhaps for an Edvard Munch masterpiece. In this incongruous position he mumbled through the often lengthy transition between arousal and awareness.

Tent A12, quickly afforded the name 'Paradise Lost' (with apologies to Milton), was to remain my home for the remainder of my service on Cape Gata. Of course, 'Paradise Lost' was something of a misnomer. Never exclusive to human occupancy, our Abraham's bosom was a shared dwelling and commodity. An occasional semi-itinerant cat, a gecko or chameleon to reduce the number of summer-time flies, or sundry other invertebrates that had elected to adopt temporary residence. More offensive than these by far, were the invertebrates that had elected to take up permanent residence, and in so doing had become an all-pervading, and singularly disgusting aspect of daily life.

Of all of the many millions of living organisms with which we share the planet, high on the list of the most repulsive must be the bedbug. While these hideous creatures are very fond of humans, I have yet to encounter a reciprocal sentiment. Their fondness for people drives them to live in human dwelling places, where they conceal themselves by day, and wreak havoc by night upon their unwitting and unfortunate victims, innocently dreaming of better things. They are small, and pass through five larval stages before reaching adulthood. On hatching from tiny eggs, they measure no more than two millimetres, and as adults they only achieve four or five. They are dorsally flattened when unfed, and are able therefore to conceal themselves in tiny crevices. Each larval stage requires a blood meal before advancing to the next, and adults will feed regularly as they commence breeding. When unfed they are greyish red in colour, and when full-fed they enjoy a healthy, rotund, rubescent glow, that gleams mockingly through their semi-transparent skin. The derivation of this globoid horror has of course, resulted from the ingestion of a small quantity of kindly donated haemoglobin, most usually that of the itching benefactor.

They are nocturnal, entirely parasitic, dependent upon mammalian blood, and almost impossible to eradicate, especially from dust-ridden dwellings constructed of broken up packing crates. Their feeding legacy is a red, raised, persistent lump that produces an extremely severe itch. In extreme attacks, the lumps coalesce to produce even bigger lumps, which frequently blister and become open sores. Hospital treatment was a not infrequent requirement. For the innocent and unfamiliar, waking at night to become aware of movement in the bed, neither of his own making nor that of a welcome or invited guest, and to throw back the sheets to reveal hundreds of crawling black invaders is akin to the dark product of an Edgar Allan Poe imagination.

For comfort and in the defence of sanity there had to be remedy, an eradicator, or a deterrent. Alas none was provided, nor was such a substance available. Any rescue or prophylactic mission required ingenuity. It had been discovered that the object of our collective detestation was intolerant unto death, of paraffin, an oil that was freely abundant as fuel for our Aladdin stoves. We sprayed the floors and the walls, and still they came. We used empty beer cans filled with paraffin in which to stand each of our bed legs. The bites were no less abundant so clearly they were not making ascent from the direction of the floor. We periodically stripped our beds, took the mattresses outside and sprinkled them with paraffin. While this did serve as some deterrent, it also served to asphyxiate the sleeper. Using abundant paper and cardboard, we even set fire to the bedsteads before reassembling our now charred and reeking sleeping quarters. On making the discovery and revelation that our pestilential companions also found residence in the seams and creases of our mattresses, these too were hauled outside, and lightly incinerated. Unhappy was the sleeper whose thus abused mattress had been paraffin treated within the last month or so. Mostly, a searing on a bed of crumpled paper imposed no greater damage than a few scorch and singe marks. It was all to no avail. Nothing, it seemed could halt this pestilence.

Ultimately, I was to discover my folly. My carefully installed and lovingly decorated corrugated cardboard wall covering was harbouring seething, breeding colonies of the creatures. Stripped off and layered on the path outside, we walked on them, we stamped on them, we raged and we jumped on them, and the appalling stench of our own pre-digested blood made us vomit. Though a final funeral pyre had us cackling like witches around the cauldron, our considered victory was to be short-lived, and however reduced in number, we remained obliged to share our living space with Cimex lectularius until the day of our farewell.

During my service at Cape Gata, I secured a short-term posting to another station. Perchance this was during a period at 280 when population levels were not excessive, and we had returned to two-man occupancy. My companion also found posting elsewhere and we abandoned 'Paradise Lost' and some of our effects and belongings in the hope that piracy would not prevail during our absence. It did not, and I was the first to return, relieved to find 'Paradise Lost', apparently just as I had left it.

Well almost!

I pushed open the door, and took the few short paces to my bed space. It was mid-summer and I was wearing shorts, and in those few seconds my lower legs to a point just above my knees, and advancing rapidly and alarmingly northward, had become black with fleas. Perhaps an animal had taken refuge in my absence, and its passengers had procreated furiously, but whatever the cause, the coconut matting had become totally infested. In those few moments of arrival, most of the squatters had just risen a couple of feet from the floor in warm greeting to their new-found friend and dining companion. Another funeral pyre prevailed.

At 280, we enjoyed only a fairly sparse laundry service, which dictated and limited the cleansing of just a single bed sheet each week. The nightly combination of dust, sweat, paraffin and bugs, not to mention spilled beer and the occasional sundry mishap of one kind or another, often revealed this to be a woefully inadequate service. It required little ingenuity to devise a remedy to this small disorder. Spare sheets, or even entire sets of bedding were not difficult to obtain, and served the dual purposes of instant mishap mitigation, and the rapid provision of a spare bed-pack in the event of unannounced and unexpected tent inspection. Limitations or even restrictions on the personal laundering of these, or of other items, was an imposition that was dictated by the permanent shortage of water on the unit. The spare bed-pack could serve to protect against retribution for untidiness when caught out by unheralded tent inspection. Stuff the current bedding into a locker, and simply replace it with the neatly folded and immaculate spare.

The southerly aligned Akrotiri Peninsula projects like a carbuncle from the south coast of Cyprus, and terminates in the twin promontories of Cape Zevgari and Cape Gata, the southernmost point on the island. The Troodos Mountains to the north exert a considerable influence on the climate, and ensure modest rainfall and irrigation on to the southern coastal plain. The rocky capes are separated from this celestial oasis by a broad, flat isthmus that is seasonally dominated by a salt lake. There are no natural irrigation channels or aquifers on to the capes, and the winter precipitation is quickly absorbed by the limestone substrate and lost. The rocky southern half of the peninsula is arid, and desiccated, and is supportive only of a xerophilous flora of low shrubs and grasses.

As a consequence, every drop of water required by the unit and its personnel, for drinking, cooking, ablutions, or any other purpose, was trundled there each day in a lumbering, 500 gallon capacity bowser. This dependency was one that was shared by every other peninsular unit on the island, and the ponderous nature of these heavy vehicles rendered them readily vulnerable to attack, either directly or by concealed explosive charge.

The ablutions block at 280 was a curious structure. A simple roof of corrugated zinc sheets provided a canopy, and shelter from the seasonal elements. There were no walls, and thus, privacy at any time was out of the question. Under the canopy, low concrete block pillars supported wooden benches, into each of which had been fashioned a series of equidistant circular holes. Each individual seeking to conduct his daily ablution claimed one of the enamel bowls provided for the purpose, filled it with water from the bowser, and awaited the vacancy of one of the holes in which to place it. There he washed, shaved, powdered his parts if he wished to, and all under the totally indifferent gaze of the other aspirant abluters. Necessity dictated that early embarrassment was quickly banished, as the only alternative was not to wash at all.

The shower provision was basic, and provided only a very limited supply of cold water. In the best interests of the collective requirement (and the winter temperatures), speed was essential. These facilities provided the only available opportunity for personal cleanliness. As consolation for this meagre provision, the authorities made weekly reservation of a shower block within the school on the main encampment at Akrotiri. The provision of this limited facility was restricted to weekends, when the school was not in use.

The risk of sniper fire was considered too severe to allow pedestrian passage between the two locations, and three ton trucks were used to provide a more secure and speedy ferry service. These were hot showers, luxury beyond daily imagination, and inevitably so popular that it proved necessary to introduce a system of weekly rationing to ensure the fair distribution of the provision, and time rationing to ensure that individuals did not linger in the warm caress beyond reasonable duration.

Relationships between the personnel at the two locations had never been particularly cordial. Indeed for the most part, it had been non-existent. Space, time and occupational hazard dictated that social interaction was restricted to furious encounters on the sporting fields of battle, locations where David was oft seen to slay Goliath. To the orderly and disciplined community at Akrotiri, 280 SU was populated by a bunch of slobs. Scruffy, untidy and unworthy, their presence on the hallowed ground was greeted with some resentment. While this only rarely erupted into anything more than taunts and catcalls, these were in particular abundance on shower days, as the unwashed trod the gauntlet before imposing their challenge upon the drainage system.

Perchance this required service was of relatively brief duration. A new structure was being fabricated, adjacent to and slightly more elevated than the ablution block. Four concrete block towers were to support a water tank, and for the first time, water would be on tap. However, the four 'Pillars of Hercules', as they became known remained naked and unadorned for many weeks, pending the arrival of the intended reservoir, a daily reminder of an unfulfilled promise of luxury. Though wash bowls remained a requirement, the partially improved facilities provided additional drainage and thus reduced the slop and carry distance. Finally, shower heads were installed on a hastily constructed wall, the long awaited tank was heaved into place atop the towers, and connection permitted the luxury of limited sprinkle. Limited, of course by the capacity of the tank, which still required replenishment from the mobile source. A measure of rationing remained. At this point in time, the Akrotiri shower service, and its hot water luxury, was terminated.

Some time later, and when the threat of guerrilla activity or intervention had become greatly reduced, an announcement suggested that a piped water supply was to be installed. This was an economy measure, designed to save manpower, the cost and inconvenience of constant bowser use, and the risks and hazards associated. The pipe was laid amid protestations that it was not being installed in a trench as would be the customary expectation, but was to remain on the surface. This was a metal pipe with a total length somewhat in excess of two miles. The protestations included simple explanation of the academic physics of the effects on pipe and contents of constant exposure to the elements. They fell upon deaf ears.

"Too expensive to put it under the ground."
"This way you will enjoy nice hot showers by day, and cold water at night."

Spring and autumn were not too bad, but winter showering was akin to standing under a waterfall in Iceland, while by mid-afternoon on a summer day the issue roared through the holes in the shower heads like superheated steam.

At the conclusion of my brief gastro-holiday in the cook's tent, the reality of the daily cookhouse fare came a something of a shock. Three meals were served each day, and were timed to accommodate the changes of watch on the technical site. While it must be conceded that catering daily for most of three hundred hungry young men cannot be an easy task, there are culinary methods that can transform the commonplace into a reasonable measure of palatability. Equally, there are culinary methods that can reduce the most promising ingredients to total and complete inedibility. While our contingent of chefs may have been trained to the highest service standards, perhaps that training had failed to transform the standards demanded by their training supervisors, into the mass production requirement of a small army.

It must also be conceded that the basic ingredients available to tempt our gourmet palates were limited, but we argued that this simplicity of provision should permit and encourage a measure of perfection, or even culinary ingenuity, especially with the benefit of daily practice with the monotonously familiar. This was clearly not the case, and the contempt in which the cooks clearly held the provided commodity was matched only by the contempt expressed by the clientele.

A measure of consistency would have provided some consolation, or even indicated a step in the right direction, but that simple achievement seemed elusive. Breakfast porridge emerged from a large container, either with the consistency of thin gruel, or of a quality more appropriate to bricklaying. The watch system dictated that the serving of most meals, and especially breakfast required an extended duration. Late comers to breakfast, perhaps seeking a bowl of nourishing porridge, were often to discover that the heavy duty variety had evolved a thick crust, and that this unwelcome encrustation enjoyed the resilience and elasticity of a child's trampoline. A carelessly dropped or projected spoon might adopt the character of a missile, while mechanical assistance might be required to access the gloop below.

How many ways can there be to totally desecrate a fried egg? While the occasional chewy stew or rocky pork chop provided an almost welcome diversion, heavy menu dependence was placed on the sausage and the corned beef. Even mass production will permit the preparation of a sausage in such a manner that it emerges from its final resting place still looking like a sausage and not like a dog turd that has lain in the sun for a week. Vegetables were mercilessly drowned in boiling water, from which they emerged with the appearance and the resilience of laundered underpants. When we enjoyed real potatoes, they were habitually transformed into chips, and thus into one of the more palatable items of our daily fare.

More frequently we were treated to the dubious delights of POM. It seems that vast quantities of this vile substance had remained in surplus at the termination of Second World War hostilities. We figured that this was probably because no-one would eat it even in those stringent times. It purported to have once been potato, a highly dubious claim. To achieve the consistency of cement dust the innocent Solanum tuberosum must have been brutally slaughtered, dismembered, sliced, diced, dismantled, fragmented, dissolved, dehydrated, precipitated, packaged and given a name. POM may have been an acronym for 'Product Of Maleficence', though I do remember a white fluffy substance that had been prepared in my mother's wartime kitchen that bore little resemblance to the 280 mash. It had been shaken from a packet that described it as 'instant mashed potato'. As no trace of the original could be detected in its Cape Gata cousin, all resemblance ceased at 'instant mashed', and before the ill-contrived reference to the noble tuber.

It was grey! Grey in colour, grey in texture, and grey in flavour. A shapeless blob of the stuff, in repose beside a couple of dog turds, with perhaps a baked bean or two to provide a little colour somehow lacked gastronomic appeal. Our saviour in a bottle was the camouflaging qualities of Daddies Brown Sauce. This marvellous condiment concealed every character of the mash, totally absorbed the turds, and mingled appealingly with the beans to produce a gentle puce gravy.

An additional ingredient was evident in every dish and culinary preparation. Cockroaches were ubiquitous throughout the entire cookhouse and mess. These despised and omnipresent Blattids were resident in huge numbers, were unavoidable, and lived in every crevice and cranny in the building. A suspended ceiling provided an undisturbed roof space in which they could enjoy unlimited and uninterrupted procreation, though the regular pattering of somewhat larger tiny feet suggested that resident rodents may be exercising some control of the cucaracha population. Alas for the diners below, the softboard panels that comprised the ceiling fabric had warped and twisted under the regular fluctuations of hot, cold, wet, dry, exposing generous cracks and gaps between. Through these, a veritable rain of careless cockroaches, rat excrement, and sundry effluent tumbled constantly on to the gourmands below.

Las cucarachas floated in the soup. They peered sightlessly through the gloop of the morning porridge. They submerged into the grey instant mash. They swam ineffectually through the custard. They were stewed, boiled, roasted, toasted, fried, scrambled and infused. They frequently provided an unexpected crunch when one was least anticipated. They pervaded every moment and every aspect of our thrice daily visits to the mess. To the more hardened souls, they simply became an accustomed ingredient in the daily fare, and joined the dog turds and Daddies sauce in a couple of hundred daily impervious alimentary systems.

They even provided an occasional moment of unkind amusement. Entry to the mess was through a narrow corridor of wooden walls that afforded the waiting and queuing diners with some protection from the sun. Visitors, or the recently arrived unaware and uninitiated, were treated to their first cockroach tempest when the wall sustained a hefty kick. Equally unaware, as they engaged with their meal, a bang on the ceiling with a broom handle released a veritable cataract of skittering cockroach.

Just occasionally rations and supplies became genuinely insufficient to feed the entire complement, and on these occasions, 'Compo' rations were issued as alternatives to those prepared to volunteer to undertake the gastro-substitute. Each 'Compo' box, many of which indicated preparation dates in the 1940's, contained sufficient food to supply one man for a period of twenty-four hours, and included breakfast, a main meal, and a sundry collection of biscuits, cheese, sweets, coffee, tea, and even cigarettes and matches. They were frequently sought after as a welcome substitute for dog turd and cockroach. Other packages, no less elderly in their vintage, bore labels bearing the unlikely claim that they contained 'Rations for one man for ten days or Rations for ten men for one day'.

Each day, the final act of generosity performed by the cooks before they retired to their private bistro, was to prepare a small repast known loosely as supper. Its intended purpose was to provide a snack for those returning from the late evening watch. Its character and content never deviated, comprising as it did, hard tack biscuits and cubes of cheese. It was left in a large cooking tray on the serving counter and was available to anyone in requirement. Few did. By late evening the cheese cubes had rendered down in the heat and congealed into a petrified flow, while the concrete tooth-breaker biscuits had slowly begun to disintegrate. La cucaracha again. An abrupt movement of the tray resulted in a red-brown eruption, and a tsunami of millions of noisily skittering spidery legs in the simultaneous propulsion of an ever widening circle of cockroach from the serving counter to every corner and crevice in the hall.

Tea was available at every meal, and was presented for self service, in a large urn at the serving counter. Alas for those who had ever encountered a worthy pot of rosy lee, this vulgar beverage would provide a new, unfamiliar, and singularly unpleasant experience. In addition to hot water, the principal ingredient of this pale beige liquid, was evaporated milk, and when stocks of this were running low, it was substituted by the even less appetising condensed variant. Tea, if present at all in the familiar leaf form, could only have been administered as mere afterthought, and in a quantity so small that it had little or no influence upon flavour or hue. To make it even less palatable, it was sweetened, not with the genteel 'one lump or two?' but in quantity sufficient to ensure an early onset of diabetes, and later years dominated by obese immobility. For the most part, no-one touched the stuff, and thus its most devastating effects were avoided. I used it to water my garden.

It was also widely speculated that the basic ingredients of this utterly vulgar beverage had been laced with bromide. Such an action must have enjoyed some kind of sinister purpose. If, as rumoured, its insidious presence in our morning brew was intended to suppress the basic and carnal desires of young warriors at the peak of their athletic and procreational prowess, it met with dismal and abject failure. Perhaps, as some kind of chemical pollutant, it was insinuated to serve as a prophylaxis by interrupting normal testicular productivity. As the closest anyone came to contact with members of the fair sex were limited to ceremonial occasions, when the assembled throng would leer uncompromisingly at the CO's gorgeous wife, testicular activity was denied facility, or if self-administered it was not the subject of open discussion.

These were gastronomically dire times, and for most of the happy campers, supplementary dietary arrangements were much sought after. Pilfering from the cookhouse was a near-capital offence, akin to the deliberate wastage of water, and the kitchen area with its refrigerators and larders was isolated, barred and locked. Ostensibly the security was to prevent intrusion, but it was widely considered that a principle purpose was to ensure that the carefully selected and separated prime portions, destined for an alternative restaurant, did not find public scrutiny.

However, breaching the outer defences required no especial cat-burglar skills, and provided that the inner sanctum storage units remained intact, a relatively blind eye was turned to the liberation of some stores. Eggs, bread, biscuits, and sauces were favourite, as these were reasonably short-term non-perishable, and could easily be toasted, fried, and garnished with the aid of an Aladdin stove. An adequate number of purloined eggs, a little margarine, and a container of sufficient dimension can bring about the manufacture of an omelette of impressive proportions. Though limited in productivity, and only occasional at best, freshly caught fish also provided welcome alternative to the regular fare.

Food parcels from doting mothers also brought welcome relief to the monotony of instant mash and dog turd. For some recipients some embarrassment accompanied the receipt of food parcels. Our senior generation had not been travellers, and some had little concept of distance and transit time for packages taking the sea passage. A package containing a parcel of Granny's home-made cookies, a fruit cake or two, or some tinned goods were abundantly welcome, but when perishables had been inadvertently included, the ceremony of opening the cornucopia adopted a somewhat different flavour. Perhaps the example that resulted in the most rapid evacuation was the carefully wrapped box that contained a dozen lovingly packed large brown fresh eggs, collected lovingly from the home chicken coop a month earlier.

While one or two had purloined small electric hotplates for their home cooking, the upright Aladdin stove was a faithful and reliable companion in this endeavour. The secret of successful culinary masterpieces on the Aladdin was to always ensure that the wick had been trimmed and set to maximum output. For really extravagant meals embracing three or more courses, multiple Aladdins can reduce waiting time and the risk that guests will be dining over a period of several days. However, this practice was actively discouraged for two points of sound wisdom, especially during the winter months when tents were more securely battened down. The heavy breathing of more than one Aladdin would impose serious risk of asphyxiation, and given the flammable nature of tent canvas, that the entire happy home could become reduced to a smouldering heap of ash.

However, notwithstanding words of wisdom or sound advice, it is my proud boast that the occupants of 'Paradise Lost' did indeed prepare a worthy, three course Christmas dinner. Our combined food parcels afforded soup, roast chicken, or more correctly, chicken boiled in its can, vegetables, and fresh potatoes nicked from the cookhouse. To claim that these purloined tubers had been roasted to golden brown perfection would have been bogus, but sliced and fried served as an adequate substitute. Christmas pudding complete with a fine rum sauce rounded off a meal of considerable merit.

Of course, no dinner of note can be enjoyed in comfort and finesse without a glass of wine appropriate to the occasion and to the ingredients, and more important, without a pedestal upon which the diner may sit, and a platform upon which the diner may place his plate, his glass, his cruet and his inscribed napkin ring, his tankard, and his candelabra.

If necessity is the mother of invention then ingenuity is surely her right-hand man. Chair bodgers were a rare breed at Cape Gata, and most of the chairs that were in regular in-tent use, had been purloined from elsewhere or from Akrotiri. They were generally small or folding, and could be readily concealed in nearby bundu when necessity dictated. Most tables that may have been available for misappropriation were simply too large for practical purpose, and were too difficult to camouflage or to conceal in a hurry. However, more rudimentary furnishings of this kind could be fairly readily fabricated from scrap timber.

The problem of available space in an already crowded tent precluded the use of a table, unless it could be included into the fabric and structure of the tent. This had become my conclusion, and in due course adequate and appropriate timber was gleaned from various sources, and a small but sturdy table took shape. The next necessary step might have been considered a little drastic, but in order to incorporate the table into the structure of the tent, the structure of the tent required a little modification. Each tent and frame was supported on three tent poles, one of which was precisely central. The installation of the table would require the removal of the lower three feet or so of the central pole, thus imposing an alarming measure of instability upon the entire structure. After careful calculation, and with two strong men and true to give temporary structural support, the bottom third or so of the central tent pole was removed. The table was slipped deftly into its place under the stub of the pole, which now rested comfortably at its centre.

This skilful installation had however, introduced a couple of potential hazards. The action would have been considered wanton damage or defacement to government property, and one that would, almost certainly have been rewarded with a formal charge to that effect. Equally, if during a regular tent inspection the order had been given to remove the table, there was a fair chance that the entire structure would have become subject to total collapse. Good early planning had secured some very natty curtain material which was wrapped around the table and secured. Thus concealed from immediate view was the fact that the central pillar of the tent now fell short of the floor by most of three feet. Making use of the under-table void as a storage location further concealed from any passing or casual view behind the curtain, the imposed deficiency in structural stability. The table remained a useful artefact for the remainder of our service at Cape Gata. In spite of many and repeated tent inspections, no-one ever questions the juxtaposition of pole end and table top.

Though the limitations of living provision by the military authorities continued to deny us the comforts of home, and while the restrictions imposed by General Grivas and his gang kept us mostly penned within our barbed wire compound, internal revolution was never a serious threat. The same conditions prevailed for us all, and the bonds of common comradeship dictated that we were all obliged to learn to live with it. There was, however, one exception to this superficially placid situation.

For a sustained period, and in spite of great tolerance on the part of the recipients, the quality of the food had deteriorated beyond acceptance. Direct complaints to the cooks had simply been retrograde steps, and had only resulted in vindictive retribution, while complaints to duty officers simply seemed to remain unheeded or ignored. In the face of poor quality evolving into inedibility, and the endless monotony of dog turd sausage, questionably reconstituted potato, baked bean, and cockroach, the entire camp populace adopted a firm stance and revolution was born. It came to a head in the wake of a period of six weeks or so during which time the ghastly dog turd sausage had been served, in one assassinated from or another, at every meal. The entire unit simply, and without broadcast warning, elected to impose a complete boycott on the mess. This small revolution was well prepared for, with hoarded stocks of pilfered rations, retained food parcels, coffee in abundance, and of course, the NAAFI continued to function.

There could have been little excuse for this lamentable state of affairs. The mess and cooking facilities were of comparatively recent construction and installation. Pre-construction diners had been obliged to carry their meals from an outdoor cooking facility to a provided dining marquee. While this was no great distance, in windy conditions less secure items of fare simply took to the air, and when the willie-willies raised the dust, everything on the plate became generously swaddled in a gritty garnish.

Thus it was that for a few days, almost no-one visited the mess. As food preparation remained a continued obligation as normal, huge quantities were spoiled and wasted, and the protest created a situation that could not be tolerated. In addition, the revolutionaries demanded to be shipped three times daily to Akrotiri main camp to receive their meals. Long standing rivalry between the station and the unit resulted in counter protest and profound embarrassment. The situation demanded action, and action was taken. A critical appraisal of the allegations and the complaints revealed ample justification. Improvement was ordered, much more regular surveillance of the product was imposed, and while cockroaches continued to peer from the porridge, we never again were obliged to dine upon the utterly unwholesome dog turds.

No known form of sanitation existed at 280 Signals Unit, and perhaps the chambers of horrors that invoked the greatest revulsion, and which might have justified complaint, were the ones for which improvement or change could never be a practicable proposition. So, while comment was frequent, formal complaint was never lodged. The latrines were appalling places, but in the absence of any permanent water supply, there was no way that they could ever enjoy any measure of transformation. Damage limitation was the only adoptable policy and practice, and visitation was undertaken as infrequently as bodily function would permit.

Some short distance from the tent lines (far too short when the wind was in the north west, and too far on a wet and windy night), had been excavated two huge holes in the ground. Around and above theses putrescent pits had been erected a timber frame that had been clad in corrugated sheets. The roof and the walls were separated by a gap of around two feet in order to facilitate essential ventilation. Over each pit, and completely enclosing it, had been fabricated a wooden structure a little like a huge upturned wooden box, into the surface of which (or bottom if the upturn is considered - excuse the pun), had been incised two lines of bum-shaped holes. With eight holes along each side of the pedestal, the facility afforded squatting room for sixteen persons. In the early days, there were no partitions between each of the parking places, so the morning rush hour was either an extremely social event or profoundly embarrassing, depending upon individual disposition.

While lack of privacy was an unfortunate and unhappy feature of our facilities, voiding the bowel of its waste products is viewed by all as an intensely private function, and for some, any comfort in making use of the facility could only be enjoyed when everyone else on the unit was otherwise preoccupied. This difficult imposition usually required an alimentary system that had been carefully trained to perform this biological function very infrequently or in the middle of the night. Protestations about this violation of human dignity did eventually find effect, and partitions were raised to screen each from his neighbours. However, this was without the added privilege of doors, which would have required some additional carpentry skills, as the knees and lower legs of those in residence protruded over and dangled from the edge of the pedestal.

The pedestal had clearly been designed and constructed by a craftsman. All of the holes, carefully, carved for the purpose of evacuation were precisely the same shape and size. This would have been fine if the rear dimensions of all of those making use of the utility conformed in similar fashion, which, of course they did not. In any body of men as large as three hundred or so, every physical shape, size, and example of bodily architecture will be represented. Thus those who were somewhat more corpulent of the buttock were obliged to perch uncomfortably, and probably somewhat ineffectually while taking some of the down-thrust on clenched knuckles. The opposite problem beset those who were unusually narrow of rump, and who may have harboured a fear of falling butt-long into the pit. When sitting, these slender persons descended far enough into the abyss to entertain the prospect of becoming jammed, creating a serious dilemma for those whose choice or whose alimentary systems had become nocturnal. There were no known fatalities.

These facilities were of the 'thunderbox' variety. The name derived from a curious appendage that was affixed under and inside the front face of the box and which projected downward and outward towards the centre of the pit at an angle of around forty-five degrees. This was a somewhat flexible metal plate. Any object of sufficient weight that dropped upon the plate, which of course every object did, caused it to flex downward until its increasing angle caused the object to slide off into the void. As it did so, the plate returned to its resting position with a noise very reminiscent of a rhythmic wobble board. I have never found explanation or reason for these curiously musical pieces of excremental apparatus.

A population of three hundred bodies will produce a remarkably large quantity of effluent in a remarkably short period, and while some may soak away, and some may evaporate, from time to time, the contents of the pit became alarmingly close to the original points of delivery. Thus, and from time to time, the facility to empty the pits became an issue of serious urgency. The first essential requirement was the dismantling of most of the superstructure and of the entire box pedestal. It followed therefore that only one of the latrine units could be accommodated at any one time. The timing and speedy execution of this grisly operation was of paramount importance. The increased burden imposed upon the remaining facility did incur a serious risk that the overworked pit would fill to and beyond capacity before the unit undergoing maintenance and cleansing could be restored to service.

As station units that were without plumbing of any kind were very few, there were no machines of the kind that slurp effluent into large mobile tanks and take it away. The substitute for such a service was a local company that was slightly less up to date in the provision of facilities. They made use of a four-wheel drive vehicle, an open trailer, some shovels, a bucket on a rope, and employees in the form of a couple of Armenian labourers. As always, when outside services entered the camp, they must be guarded, escorted, and observed at all times. Lives had been lost when this close surveillance had been relaxed and deadly explosive devices had been concealed. There was no less welcome assignment. However, the fearful prospect of a concealed cache of high explosive in the pit, and the terrifying potential of its entire contents heading skyward in a dreadful mushroom cloud, held in brief and temporary suspension over the happy home, perhaps provided some incentive to shoulder a ring-side Sten gun and demonstrate a willingness to share the malodorous burden.

The process was simple, crude, and utterly abominable. One of the labourers descended into the pit with a shovel, while the other lowered the bucket. Observation was endured only with abject horror lest the first to enter the pit should disappear, thus imposing the requirement for the launch of a rescue mission. The man in the pit, wobbling perilously upon an unstable plank, filled the bucket. The man on the rope hauled it up and emptied the contents into the trailer. The trailer was taken away when it was full. These were big, deep pits, and the whole ghastly process would embrace a period of several days. The stench that hung over the camp during these operations was indescribably atrocious, and pervaded everything and everywhere. Escort and guard duty were assiduously avoided, though in view of the unpleasant nature of the task, the duty was shared as widely, and thus as briefly, as possible. There were very few curious onlookers at any time, and avoidance of the immediate area provided distant, if only limited relief. Indeed only short term posting to an alternative location, Hong Kong perhaps, would have provided guaranteed relief from the foetid cloud in narrow orbit over the cape.

Job complete, bowser, pump, and hose provided a comprehensive sluicing, the pedestal and superstructure were reconstructed, and for some weeks the daily resonance from the thunderbox enjoyed a more sonorous tone.

Shortages and deprivations, some short term, some of longer duration, punctuated daily life on all of the more remote stations. Quite inexplicably, one of the commodities almost constantly in short supply, or unavailable for long periods at Cape Gata, was toilet paper. The irregular and intermittent delivery of newspapers provided substitute, and these were jealously hoarded. The most sought after was the overseas edition of the Daily Telegraph. This broadsheet was printed on paper that was significantly less heavy than any of the others. Lightweight without being excessively flimsy, it was a reasonably ideal substitute for the genuine article. Alas, much less frequently included in deliveries than Mirror, Herald or Sketch, it was frequently reduced to narrow sheets and felted away without being utilised as the publisher had intended. Indeed, visits to Akrotiri main camp were rarely concluded without a tour of NAAFI or other recreational buildings to pilfer any unattended copies and to whisk them in triumph toward a new and different facility.

However, the clear evidence that the use of large quantities of inappropriate paper did bring disadvantages to pit management became rapidly and progressively apparent. While newspaper may enjoy many qualities, and can be utilised for many purposes, its manufacture did not take into account any requirement to dissolve or degrade having been cast into an earth closet of gargantuan proportions. Here, sullied and crinkled, it merely rested where it had been cast, and in response to the daily requirement of three hundred or so alimentary systems, it steadily and alarmingly accumulated.

Down here, in among the putrescent horror of its foetid darkness, other life forms, adapted it seemed to pursue a coprophilous way of life, pursued their constant forage among the well digested outfall of our imperfect culinary art. To the unwary and the unaware, the short walk to each of the latrine blocks required no more than a brief stroll across the dusty terrain. However, among the sparse and spindly vegetation, an unseen black multitude, disturbed by any approach, darkened the sky as it rose into the atmosphere. Flies were a perpetual presence around and inside the latrine buildings, and though less visible, were no less apparent in the pit, unseen in the constant hum of their grisly mating pursuits. The presence of the offspring of this multitudinous coition, was readily betrayed in a beam of light only as a gentle undulating sub-surface ooze.

Our other cesspool companions made welcome third use of our fluttering paper offerings. Chewed and shredded, and carried deep into tunnels excavated in the pit walls, warm, snug nests afforded birthplace and nursery for a burgeoning population of robust and remarkably healthy rats. Normally nocturnal in foraging habit, the perpetual darkness of the stygian pit was ever alive with the rustling, squeaking and occasional splash of their incessant industry. To those human residents of a more intrepid or foolhardy character, a beam of light directed into the abyss, and especially in the silent hours of darkness, quickly revealed the magnitude of the rodent population. To those of a more timorous or retiring nature, the experience could initiate a firm resolution to adopt any alternative course of action or location in preference to taking a single further step into this chamber of nightmares.

There was of course no alternative, except to defile the bundu, and apart from short-term relief, this would serve only to amplify the problem. Thus, and on a daily basis, each Cape Gata resident was obliged to respond to the irresistible call for evacuation. It requires little biological knowledge, and even less imagination, to appreciate that during this function, certain portions of the male anatomy, normally protected and defended at the first threat of danger or harm, were thus pendant, in free suspension, and in the face of mortal peril. No mean hazard at any time, the daily use of Telegraph, Herald, Mirror or Sketch, exacerbated this alarming situation exponentially. As the steadily increasing stack of crumpled newsprint rose with alarming rapidity towards the upper parts, and even the rim of the pit, so did the scurrying rodent population, borne comfortably aloft on its luxurious mattress, and ever closer to those suspended tender items of male genitalia.

At this point, it would have been foolish to allow even a morsel of complacency to infiltrate awareness, however uncomfortable the daily reality. There could be little doubt that any omnivore obliged to endure an exclusive diet of selected human excreta, would relish a brief momentary lapse into carnivory if afforded the opportunity of a rapid and providential testicular dispossession. Remedial action to relieve this grave and threatening situation was a clear and urgent requirement. Complaint and demand seemed unlikely to enjoy outcome other than more regular evacuation of the contents of the pit, and thus the ever more regular imposition upon the entire camp of the ensuing atmospheric horrors.

A more expedient remedy was required, and a plan soon formulated that could rid the putrid grotto of both paper and pestilence. To ensure success, this clandestine operation required secrecy, stealth, and precision, and could only be undertaken during the darkest, quietest and least disturbed hour of the night. At around three of the clock, the domestic site slumbered, and the two perpetrators crept silently and unseen to the chosen latrine. To ensure optimum escape and minimum likelihood of detection they had selected the facility closest to their respective tents. They entered the chamber and took up positions at diagonally opposite corners of the pedestal. At an agreed signal, each ignited a rolled taper of the Daily Sketch, which had been afforded an ignition-secure soak in a little paraffin, and dropped them into the pit.

Alas, their most worthy intentions had lacked one small scientific element. They had overlooked the chemistry of putrescence, and the inevitable accumulation of methane or other inflammable gases in a large enclosed and unventilated chamber. The outcome was instant, and splendidly dramatic. There was no devastating explosion, just a huge, prolonged 'whump'. Tongues of flame of enormously satisfying proportion roared their way through each and every pedestal bum hole in the direction of the roof, across which they were flushed toward the ventilation vents. Alas for caution, the concussion had aroused that portion of the slumbering personnel closest to the conflagration, who were now emerging in curiosity. During this period of sleepy inquisition, the perpetrators had made best use of the shadows to make hidden return to their respective tents, and having cunningly committed the deed while dressed in their night attire, they were able to take an innocent place among the cheering and supportive audience.

The possible benefit of the deed quickly became clear and under some discussion, with the result that several minutes had passed before the fire service was alerted. The blaze was far beyond the capacity and depth of fire extinguishers, and as the only fire appliances were located at the main camp, several more minutes had elapsed before any extinguishing purpose could be pursued. By this time, the latrine had taken a destructive turn somewhat beyond original intent.

Daylight revealed the extent of the destruction. The pedestal had become charred beyond repair or further practical use, the structural timbers that supported walls and roof were damaged but probably still serviceable. As for the survival or destruction of the pestilence? For the moment, that remained an unknown quantity.

In the days that followed, the structure was dismantled, the pedestal removed, and the local company summoned its Armenian labourers to return bearing shovel, bucket, rope and plank to exhume the contents of the pit and its part-cooked livestock. Thus, the entire camp became obliged once more to endure the horrors of atmospheric profanity, if a little toasted on this occasion.

In practical terms, the exercise had been of negligible purpose, though the final outcome would await the conclusion of the Armenian cleansing department. However, it seemed quite probable that the evolving, and still larval generation of flies would be less likely to reach the puberty of pupation, and with luck, a significant proportion of the rodent population may have fled the conflagration or been roasted in their tunnels. The immediate post-Armenian benefit would be the greatly enhanced comfort and security of three hundred clusters of daily suspended male genitalia, and smiles of relief on the faces of their owners.

Chapter 5. In Defence of the Nation - the selfless daily toil.

... "If your azicator sticks, never mind." ...

*

Of course, no resort or institution will find success and satisfaction without a willing, cheerful, and accommodating workforce.

For the benefit, comfort, and safety of those in pursuit of a vacation, for those responding to a call to arms, or for those following a chosen path in the service of mankind.

Equally, for those merely making every possible endeavour to undertake as little as possible for two or three years of their lives, it remains the most urgent aspiration of the management team to ensure that the workplace is safe, comfortable and inspiring, and is a source of encouragement for every individual in every branch or profession.

Thus is daily workplace satisfaction our collective goal.

The occupational range of the 280 resort is broad and varied, providing as it does, the facility to find and to enjoy brief periods of mild interest in a hugely extended matrix of utter hopelessness.

*

Thus was domestic bliss and harmony lived out at 'Hell on the Hill'.

However, our principle purpose was not simply indulgence in the hedonistic delights of our dusty paradise, or the epicurean turpitude provided by our dedicated team of cuisiniers, nor even the heady, if imagined delights of maidenly forms as soft perfumed music serenaded the evening beach and the breeze whispered gently in the palms.

We were here in defence of the realm.

During our earliest days of training, we had been taught how to kill with a single blow, thrust, or squeeze of a trigger, and how to avoid the retaliation when that failed. We had learned how to move forwards, in unison and harmony, and when looking in another direction. We had practiced the art of sticking a bayonet into a straw-filled sack suspended by its corners from a frame, while bellowing mindlessly at nothing in particular (no reaction from the sack, but he had seen it all before).

We had been taught the theories and the complexities of radar, of electronics, of tubes and consoles and azicators. We had come into some understanding of maps and navigation, and how to transfer blips on a screen to monopoly pieces on a plotting table. We had learned how to write in reverse using 'chinagraph' on to a transparent perspex screen. We had become familiar with the mumbo-jumbo of communication jargon, and fluent in the mysterious abbreviations of the phonetic alphabet. We had learned how to interpret what we were seeing on a flickering screen, to translate this into something meaningful, and in order to avert a disaster, to pass this information accurately and meaningfully onward and up the appropriate chain of action.

We had completed all of this training, and on convincing our adjudicators of our competence, we had risen from lowly Air Defence Operators Second Class, to the same breed of fearless warriors in a first class capacity. Now we were in defence of the realm, and we had to emerge from practice formation and embrace reality.

The technical site at Cape Gata lay directly adjacent to the domestic site, was roughly circular in shape, somewhat smaller in area than its homely cousin, and surrounded entirely and independently by its own ring of barbed wire coils. One small step to the south of the homestead, and at a slightly lower elevation, its cluster of mysterious machinery nestled in a shallow depression. In conditions of dry tempest, when the wind hurled the domestic dust in every direction to deposit on, in, and under every surface, the technical dust was raised from the technical depression in swirling cyclonic towers. These collapsed in unruly clouds among the hapless victims of the slightly elevated model of unfortunate domestic urban planning.

The technical site was home to everything technical. Radar heads of many types revolved and nodded, casting unseen beams of electrons into the atmosphere, and collecting the images of passing aircraft on the reflected and returning beams. One such, a low level revolving structure, was the object of dire warnings, should the fragile human frame become exposed to the power of its electron death ray. Warnings verbal, warnings written, warnings dire, and warnings exaggerated to Machiavellian fantasy, but all striking fear into six hundred under-used gonads.

"A few seconds of exposure, and you will become sterile"

"Shrivel your nuts!"

"Scramble your scrote!"

"Blacken your bollocks!"

"Freeze your bloody gentiles!"

"Make your sperm swim backwards!"

Whatever the truth of these ominous threats, no-one was going to take any chances and we either kept our distance, a ludicrous gesture as its death ray was programmed to travel for many miles, or we assiduously avoided face to face confrontation. So far as I know, no-one required testiculectomy.

Tall masts supported aerials of many shapes and sizes that were integral to our radio communications systems. An intricate network of cables and wires that provided support for the masts and created an elegant interlacement between, them were all parts of the paraphernalia that permitted us to speak to passing aircraft, and to the rest of the world.

Several mobile cabins housed the screens, consoles, and various items of apparatus for gathering in the returning radar signals, and the telephonic systems for relaying this information to the control centre. These cabins were places of perpetual darkness, relieved only by the sickly green or orange glow that emanated from the screens. Places of punishment and banishment, purgatory for all lovers of sunshine, suitable only for the un-dead. Blisteringly, swelteringly hot in the summer time, with little or no ventilation, and doors that must remain closed to avoid the ingress of dust and its detrimental influence on delicate electronic machinery.

The cabins were mobile simply to maintain readiness for removal and deployment elsewhere should the need arise. However, without additional jacked-up support, from time to time these cabins became subject to mobility from an unexpected quarter. Protruding southward from the body of Cyprus, the Cape Gata peninsula intrudes the ocean immediately above an active tectonic zone. While mild tremors were fairly regular occurrences and raised no more than an eyebrow, a heavy duty wobble was a much more physical affair. The only point of cabin contact with terra firms were their inflated rubber tyres, features that induced a motion of cartoon quality. For those inside the cabin, it became a fairground rodeo bull, and evacuation was an instinctive reaction. The outside spectacle recalled the antics of the Keystone Cops as the cabins bucked and swayed and bounced until the tremor headed for Turkey and normal service could be resumed.

The control centre was housed in one of only two semi-permanent buildings on the site. A wooden hut contained all of the impedimenta of death by boredom. Around a large central table adorned with a map of the Eastern Mediterranean, three or four Air Defence Operators brandishing long rods, each terminating in a magnetic pad were arranged around the table. Deaf to the world save for instructions received through tightly clamped earphones, the robotic airman used his magnetic stick to seize and progress facsimile aircraft, changing location by location across the table, as instructed by the screen watcher in the cabin.

Adjacent to the table more airmen, also plugged in to earphones, were receiving additional information about each aircraft. Their task was to transfer this information to the rear of a large transparent screen, by making use of the ancient art of reverted writing. Another poor soul, tucked into a tiny corner of the cabin little wider than his shoulders, made permanent record of every aspect of this evolving scene on sheets of paper.

On an elevated stage, with a clear view of table and screen, and with their own battery of equipment, the officers of the watch adopted a directorial role, maintained contact with each passing aircraft until it was out of range, and communicated this information to the main airfield as and when necessary. Thus every aspect of the disposition of every aircraft within radar range, leaving, arriving or simply in aerial transit, aircraft type, nationality, elevation, bearing, speed, destination, point of origin was watched and logged. From Akrotiri, regular photo-reconnaissance flights using Canberra aircraft maintained regular vigil over much of the Middle East. On an almost daily basis, a Russian aircraft flew into and out of Alexandria. Its recognised regularity earned it the title of the 'Milk Run'. We delighted in regular visits by those most magnificent flying machines, the V-bombers, Victor, Valiant, and Vulcan, and even the occasional historic Shackleton on Wellington bomber, now relegated to the status of museum pieces.

This scene of frenetic activity also served an additional purpose, and one to which we could all relate much more closely. The grisly band of terrorist warriors under the direction of General George required regular replenishment of weaponry and ammunition. This service was performed under cover of darkness in small sea-going craft and to remote and lonely landing places around the island coastline. Gun running from mainland Greece was a serious business and posed an equally serious threat to our well-being, to sovereignty, to international peace and to unity on the island. It posed an equal threat to the diplomatic processes that were making attempts to unravel and resolve the more local ethnic, political, and ecclesiastical differences. Some of our radar, in tandem with that at other coastal locations, was trained upon the ocean. All sea going craft were recorded, identified and followed, and were apprehended if identity could not be satisfactorily confirmed or if there was any suspicion of gun smuggling.

A large marquee served to provide respite from the mesmerising influence of rotating strobes, nodding luminosity, or small metallic tokens moving slowly across a table. Here was consumed copious quantities of truly dreadful coffee or coca-cola, as a means to find the restoration of awareness, and its prolongation into the next session of world weariness. Those whose passions related to all things electronic may have exulted in this world of spark and radiation, but for the devotee of bugs, birds, blossoms, biology and the sensuous pleasure of sunshine, these electric caverns provided little delight.

The technical site also provided a home to the motor transport section. Here were parked a dozen or so three-ton trucks, our sole form of transport; sundry machines for generating electricity, pumping water, repairing roads, or emitting decibels in tumultuous fortissimo. This was an alien domain, populated exclusively by black shiny individuals clad permanently in black shiny overalls. They were a breed apart, and no form of social hybridisation would be tolerated or entertained. Their central citadel was the only other on-site semi-permanent building, and from its gloomy and secret depths emanated the regular heavy concussion of metal upon metal, the roar and scream of engines being tested to destruction, and copious clouds of acrid blue smoke.

Visitation to this tumultuous Erebus was never a welcoming occasion. Any polite enquiry or expression of casual interest met with a surly riposte and an expletive loaded invitation to return whence cometh. Few ever had reason to go there and so few ever did, and the vital business of this department was conducted in its own shiny black cocoon. That is not to detract in any way from the essential character of their daily function. Theirs was the task of ensuring that the lifelines shared by us all were maintained and functional at all times. The three ton trucks ferried our supplies and took away our waste. The generators provided power for our every function, and thus our every function was dependent upon the clamour and the fug that enshrouded the daily MT building.

However, this facility was located in a remote corner of the technical encampment, where it also served as a dumping ground for unwanted material, unserviceable equipment, broken domestic items awaiting removal, and a plethora of defunct electrical components. While most of these latter items were of no further value to their original and intended purpose, they were readily portable, could be dismantled with ease, and were very valuable plunder for purposes of a more domestic nature. Thus, to the inmates of the hill, this entire untidy area was a gold mine of material that, could readily be purloined during any watch period, especially during the hours of silent darkness, and which could enjoy a resurrection in support of the enhancement of living conditions. Against the regulations? Sure! But this embryonic recycling earned and deserved the non-seeing blind eye, of tacit but unspoken approval.

No functional workplace can conduct its business in an efficient manner without an equally functional administration. Cape Gata was furnished with this facility in an additional row of cabins situated to the rear of an open area of baked and dusty ground.

Though this bleeding piece of earth served little regular specific purpose, it was generally referred to as the parade ground. Parades were not a regular feature of life on the cape, considered as they were, a pointless extension to unwelcome bullshit. However, from time to time, the assembly was called to muster, to learn of essential changes to station standing orders, to receive collective admonishment, or for the occasional open air ecclesiastical service, though the requirement for regular worship could only be satisfied in Akrotiri. The cabins provided office accommodation for the Commanding Officer, his adjutant, and a number of conscripted individuals whose backgrounds indicated that they might be adept at filing paperclips.

Our efficient function demanded that that the station remained active and operational at all times, and this simple maxim took precedence over every other function or purpose, even if a more generous approach to other aspects of camp life were allowed. We were employed on a system of four watches to embrace twenty-four hour attendance in a five-day cycle. The first day required morning and evening duty, with an afternoon call on day two. Day three imposed the night vigil, and the fourth day was set aside for sleep and restoration. Day five provided a sabbatical, before the cycle began again.

The sleeping day occasionally provided the less scrupulous with an opportunity for mischief. Authority recognised that human reaction on abrupt awakening from deep sleep is often unpredictable, and can take many forms from uncharacteristic violence to deep melancholy. Tent and kit inspections were infrequent, and were normally afforded a short measure of advance warning. They were conducted by a duty officer and an accompanying NCO, who wandered the tent lines and selected tent entry at random for impromptu inspection. They could have no idea which personnel were currently on watch, or, more importantly which personnel had just returned from night duty and were sleeping. In recognition of the unpredictability of human condition, any airman whose legitimate slumber was thus disturbed, was permitted a few moments of verbal freedom without charge or retribution.

Thus, the unscrupulous would lie in wait, purporting sleep until the scrape of an opening door propelled them into a frenzy of verbal abuse. Less popular officers were the most frequent victims of this ruse. Anyone within audible range could only marvel at the linguistic dexterity of those skilled and capable of delivering such a huge and sustained tirade.

For a time, the third corner of 'Paradise Lost' was occupied by a burly young Brummie whose capacity for sleep was considerable, and profound. Day time, night time, standing up or lying down made little difference, and once well into the land of nod, he became earthquake resistant. However, daytime sleep in the heat of summer was difficult for many, and was frequently accompanied by vivid dreams, many of them of a most obscure and incomprehensible nature. Greater comfort was often more readily achieved by abandoning swaddling sheets and simply making use of the enshrouding capacity of a single loosely draped blanket.

My tent companion and I did not share the same watch, and by chance he normally returned from night duty as I headed for the 07.00 morning watch. As I returned one day at around lunchtime, as expected, my tent companion remained deep in the arms of Morpheus. Well! Deep in the arms of someone. Taking care not to wake him with noisy tent flaps and a scraping door, my silent entry bore witness the burial mound of his blanket, beneath which he was clearly enduring a somewhat torrid somnambulant encounter. However, it quickly became clear that this was no combat to the death with the demons of his personal underworld. Not only did his moans, and squirms, and whistles and sighs make it clear that his nocturnal crusade was of a much more lascivious nature, the physical and practical manifestation of his nocturnal fantasy was protruding proudly through a hole in the blanket like a wildly oscillating, pulsating and somewhat threatening Tower of Babel. This, the only visible portion of his anatomy, gestured and waved menacingly in unison with his bodily movements and his audible outpourings. Being a big lad, it seemed a shame that the comely subject of his nocturnal fantasy was not present to permit the enjoyment and the satisfaction of fulfilment.

This was an opportunity not to be squandered, and I quickly summoned one or two others to share a spectacle that might be heading for a sticky moment. The word quickly spread and it soon appeared that most of the encampment had sped off to seek cameras.

Common decency would not permit the indignity of mass embarrassment, so when the initial chuckles had died down, I spared his further blushes with an explosive cough.

While our principal daily duties involved all thing air defence operative, there were many for whom electronic wizardry had not been a lifelong passion. For them, duties of an alternative nature provided some welcome relief, though not without the imposition of hazard. With the exception of those few whose specialties directed them toward more independent daily duties, everyone at 280 was called upon to contribute to the full range of required tasks. In addition to the radar routine, this principally involved guard duty, site and perimeter patrols, and escort duty to Akrotiri and beyond. 280 SU was operative during twenty-four hours of every day, and thus, every essential function of the unit was awake and aware during the same period.

It takes little imagination to comprehend that duties relating to guard, patrol, and escort, were potentially the most hazardous that we were to undertake. Here, the firing line was precisely where you were standing, and for the most part, the enemy without enjoyed the upper hand. Training had unlocked the secrets of point and pull, but suddenly here was the real thing, and the realisation of vulnerability came as a serious shock to the system.

280 Signals Unit, Cape Gata, was fairly well protected against prospective insurgency by a confusion of barbed wire perimeter coils that surrounded the entire unit. A dividing fence of similar construction made separation between domestic and technical. Two guard posts provided the first line of practical defence, and both were permanently manned. Situated at the main entrance, the first of these stopped all intending incomers, and denied entry until identity had been established, and details had been entered into the daily log. The second guard post served a similar function at the entrance to the technical site, though recognised identity was normally the only requirement for entry. Two were necessary because a low hill separated the two locations, and no part of the technical site could be seen from the main entrance. Thus, if anarchic nocturnal entry had been gained through the wire at the quietest corner of the technical site, significant and damaging inroads could have been made before a major alarm was raised.

Each guard post was manned at all times by two armed guards and a guard commander, normally a corporal or sergeant. During the day this was somewhat relaxed with a single, somewhat peripatetic guard commander who divided his time between the two. Guard duty during the day was routine and fairly relaxed, though in theory the rules of engagement, night or day, remained the same. For the newcomer, the first few occasions of night guard duty, were hours filled with apprehension, mainly in trepidation for what could transpire, but which was most unlikely to do so. Each man was armed with a Sten gun, and issued with a specific number of rounds of ammunition. Lee Enfield .303 rifles were available in the guard hut as backup, and side arms were also available. At night, each man carried a torch.

The instructions were simple. Any disturbance or suspicious noise was to be challenged. The protocol dictated that the guard was to stand up behind the sandbag wall, shine his torch in the direction of the noise, and voice a loud challenge in three languages, 'HALT', 'STAMATA', 'DUR'. Allowing for human reaction, if this protocol had been followed to the letter, the challenger would almost certainly have lost a significant proportion of his cranium by the time he reached 'STA'. Of course, the majority of noises during the night were not created by intending assassins or saboteurs, but by wandering domestic or feral animals. As in these instances, if the challenge received no response, and suspicion remained, the duty guard was at liberty to open fire. Over time, more than a few dead goats and donkeys were revealed by the morning light.

The protocol that directed the issue of ammunition was very strict. Twenty rounds issued, twenty rounds must be returned, or evidence and justification of use must be presented. This would require a body. An animal cadaver would provide acceptable explanation that there had been sufficient suspicious noise in the darkness to justify a spent round. However, should the morning light reveal a human corpse, justification required more comprehensive evidence of the requirement to open fire. Unofficial advice made clear the simple need to place an object into the hand of the victim, thus providing support to the stated belief that the victim had been about to throw a grenade or other explosive device.

To the novice, the newly arrived, or the simply terrified, these were anxious occasions, and no-one ever embarked upon night guard duty or patrol without some degree of apprehension. Training had brought familiarity with the anatomy of a machine gun, chipping chunks from a distant rock with a Bren gun had afforded abundant evidence of its lethal capacity, but pulling the trigger on an unseen noise in the dark? Here was a situation for which neither training nor practice could bring adequate preparation. But suppose that the scenario had been played out in reverse! Having heard the unseen noise, you were part way through your three-language challenge. Perhaps a finger on another trigger was about to terminate your utterance at 'STA'. Hesitate, or direct twenty rounds into the darkness? Perhaps it had simply been a goat, or as daylight revealed an empty road, perhaps a figment of an over-active imagination.

While night guard duty sharpened the awareness and the senses, perimeter patrol at night subjected them to the tender caress of a wire brush. The perimeter wire, though fairly unassailable, required constant armed patrol, a task that befell each in turn, and in pairs. In darkness, more than one pair in pursuit of this task would impose the real and severe hazard of an own goal, and to counter this, the patrolling pair reported regularly to each of the guard posts. At very regular intervals inside the perimeter wire, powerful sodium lamps directed a pale yellow glare outward and deep into the bundu beyond. The standing directive instructed that patrols were to make each steady circumnavigation between the lights and the wire. Thus exposed, patrols would become ludicrously easy targets for any prospective assassins on the outside. Patrolling in the deep shadow, however, just a few paces behind the lights, provided excellent visibility as far as the bundu thicket would permit, and relative invisibility to the defenders of the faith. The directive was incomprehensible, extremely hazardous, and universally ignored.

The more quiet, remote and dark corners of the perimeter wire induced the greatest trepidation, as the patrol meandered between the sodium glare and the intense shadows of the dark scrubby bundu that remained within the wire. I became destined to share many of my night patrols with a timorous, uncommunicative, and highly nervous individual who seemed to pose a greater threat to my safety that any lurking Eoka desperado. With loaded Sten guns at the ready, we stumbled off into the night. On his insistence, and he would have it no other way, we never walked side by side, but always in line astern, he to the rear. He was fearful of the capacity of the human voice to be carried on the breeze so we never spoke, but as he walked behind I was always conscious of the clicking of his weapon at almost every step. Some comfort perhaps, as this indicated that his weapon was not cocked and ready to fire, but I suspected that he was clutching the cocking handle, and that the motion of his body at every step drew back the bolt and the firing pin and then released it to rest once more against the breech.

In addition to being highly inaccurate, the Sten gun was a rudimentary piece of weaponry that employed equally rudimentary safety devices, and was sometimes referred to as a blow lamp. It was without a breech lock, and the bolt was retained in the 'closed' position only by the pressure of the firing spring. When in the closed position, it was well known that any sharp knock or jerk could cause the bolt to withdraw far enough against the pressure of the spring, and on return to scoop a round from the magazine, insert it into the chamber and begin the firing sequence, single shot or automatic. I feared a serious stumble as we made passage across the rocky and uneven ground, which would surely distribute twenty rounds in rapid and liberal fashion in every direction, and with undeniable probability, substantially in mine.

Perhaps the character of the Sten gun was most admirably summed up in a short poem by S.N.Teed, and entitled 'Ode to a Sten Gun'.

You wicked piece of vicious tin,
Call you a gun? Don't make me grin!
You're just a bloated piece of pipe,
You couldn't hit a hunk of tripe.
But when you're with me in the night,
I'll tell you pal, you're just alright.

So it was! But the clicking continued.

Armed also with torches, night patrols were charged with a few additional duties, involving the inspection of buildings or installations vacated for the night, the vital electricity generating units, parked vehicles and machinery, and the radar and radio transmitting installations. The latter were well lit, were situated close to the permanently manned operational units, and were thus afforded the protection of twenty four hour activity.

At the opposite side of the technical compound, the MT section also required the protective scrutiny of the night patrol. Sinister by day, tucked away in the bundu and without light, it was even more forbidding by night. However, the MT section was also a place of nocturnal opportunity, and lifestyle 280 demanded that opportunity was never to be overlooked or missed. Sleeping on guard duty was a very serious offence, and would inevitably attract equally serious punishment. However, for those weary and chilled souls padding the perimeter, the comfortable and relatively cosy cabs of the parked three ton trucks offered refuge for a few moments of rest and repose, or even a modicum of slumber for any individual whose internal alarm clock permitted cat-nap. Failure to make rendezvous at the appointed guard hut at the appointed hour would surely raise a hue and cry. On a chill night however, these unlocked cabs were an asset of considerable benefit for a few moments of repose and a smoke, and found nightly use for these purposes.

The MT mechanics, gruff and unwelcoming by day, were characteristically untidy in their workshop habits. Perhaps in the belief that their kingdom was sacrosanct and thus inviolate, their daytime equipment was randomly abandoned at the close of each working day, no doubt in ready preparation for the day and the task to follow. All manner of good and useful items carelessly littered their workbenches, and somehow became spirited to another place and another purpose. In spite of ready temptation, rapacity would have been folly, but liberation item by item, in a steady undetected sequence, allowed subtle relocation for many a small tool or device. Indeed, I believe that just a few such borrowed items remain in my tool box to this day.

The curious case of the optical maggot became manifest during one night perimeter patrol. One of a duo of patrolling guards complained of pain in one eye. On flashlight inspection, a small quantity of pus seemed present in the extreme corner. This was removed and the patrol continued. The discomfort persisted, and on further inspection, the offending material was observed to be mobile, and indeed turned out to be one of a small bundle of unidentifiable larvae of the fly variety. Hasty despatch to the MO ensured that these were removed before permanent harm ensued. At some stage, it was presumed that a tiny fly had laid a small clutch of eggs in or close to the eye, which had hatched and had now been observed galloping across the offended cornea. The species of fly may never have been positively identified, but it was speculated that any delay in treatment and removal could have resulted in permanent damage to the eye, or could even have been life threatening.

Patrol duties became manifest in many and varied guises. Deep in the bundu beyond the eastern end of the main Akrotiri runway, and approximately equidistant from the Cape Gata perimeter wire a small hut stood in solitary abandonment. It was a guard hut, though just what it was guarding was less evident, presumably any infiltration to the more remote end of the runway. Because of its close proximity to 280, and its much greater distance from the Akrotiri hub, guard duty had been delegated to Cape Gata's fighting force. It was to be occupied by a Sten gun wielding pair only during daylight hours, and normally only during periods of busy airfield activity. Normally a boring and uneventful commission, the two defenders of security were to be shocked from their reverie on one sunny morning.

The hut was of the metal, rondavel type, and these were unbearably hot when the climate dictated. On this occasion, while seated outside we were abruptly aware of a rapidly approaching noise akin to a major forest landslide. As we looked in horror towards the tumult we observed the very rapid approach of an aircraft. To considerable relief, the tumult, and the aircraft came to halt just a few yards from the hut. Two foolish guards peered upward toward the cockpit of the aircraft and into the gaze of the equally foolish pilot, who was looking sheepishly at the guards. On coming in to land, a Gloster Javelin Aircraft had suffered the loss of power from one engine, resulting in systems failure and the loss of hydraulic power. Thus the pilot had been unable to lower his landing gear, which also left him with no capacity for braking except to rely upon friction. Thus, the pilot had become obliged to make use of the bundu as his only braking system. The 280 guard duo was quickly withdrawn, and replaced by one of a more professional nature until the damaged aircraft could be retrieved.

There were very few occasions when 280 personnel were required to mount off-camp guard, escort, or patrol in public places. However this did happen from time to time. Often referred to as 'jollies,' these of course, were occasions that imposed far greater hazard than any routine duty, but were welcomed by many as a means to ease the tedium of daily camp life. Indeed these duties could be actively sought through volunteering, and just occasionally a finger would be pointed, a name would be called, and one 'volunteer' embarked upon a 'jolly' with anticipation and apprehension in equal measure.

The regular movement of equipment provided such opportunities, as indeed did an almost daily run up to Troodos and Mount Olympus. Later, and in more peaceful times, the Troodos runs could be utilised as a bus service, and short periods of leave, or skiving, could be enjoyed in the more agreeable mountain climate, finding residence at the requisitioned 'Pingo's Hotel' or at the nearby rest camp. Delivery runs that involved passage through more urban areas were almost always far less comfortable with the attendant risk of coming under fire from aspiring rooftop assassins, or from a variety of projectiles directed from ground level.

Patrols to other parts of the island, or to more remote units were few, but those that were obliged to find passage through Nicosia, were always accompanied by considerable apprehension. The main thoroughfare, Ledra Street, commonly referred to as 'Murder Mile', was the scene of many killings and ambushes, and in such a narrow and sinuous part of the old city, such incidents were easy to conduct, be they missiles from ground level or firearms from window or rooftop.

Three armed escorts were the normal required accompaniment for a three ton truck, two occupying the rear of the vehicle, and the third as turret man. This latter occupied a position standing on the engine cowling inside the cab, with head, the upper part of his torso, and his trusty Sten gun protruding through a hole in the cab roof. He was the most vulnerable member of the crew, not just from possible sniper fire, but also from the installation of piano wire, strategically tensioned at throat height, between trees at opposite sides of the road. Decapitation was the intended outcome. To counter this threat, vehicles used in vulnerable areas were fitted with a steel frame in the shape on an inverted 'V' that protruded ahead and above the front of the vehicle. This was welded firmly to the chassis of the vehicle, and was designed to break and sweep aside any lethal wire.

More commonplace perhaps were high explosive devices set into road surfaces and pressure or vibration detonated by a passing vehicle, or remotely from a short distance. One regular, and very necessary run from Cape Gata transported accumulated rubbish to the nearby station at Episkopi for processing and disposal. Three trucks formed the convoy, escorts fore and aft, with the cargo vehicle between. As one such convoy proceeded, not too far from Akrotiri village, the lead truck detonated a device and slewed to a halt in the side of the road. The following trucks stopped safely, and all of the crew members dismounted and took refuge behind or beneath. A number of randomly directed rounds were discharged, but there was no returning fire, and one load of rubbish failed to find its intended destination.

In spite of its close proximity to the principle encampment, convoy and vehicle harassment in the vicinity of Akrotiri village persisted. In one incident, the rear of a passing truck was in receipt of a thrown grenade. The missile rolled around for a few moments until one of the crew seized it and safely ejected it into the road, where it exploded. In response, a contingent of RAF Regiment and RAF Police, sought retribution, and though the miscreant was never apprehended, a 'heavy gang' of Rockapes and Snowdrops can inflict considerable damage when the blind eye is turned.

The first half of 1959 bore witness to the ponderous process of truce, though for many months hard-line Eoka groups continued with their programme of harassment and attack. However, the tide was turning, and the military authorities took the decision that married personnel may once more be reunited with their families. Accommodation was available close to Limassol in a compounded area that was fenced and afforded closely guarded protection by the military police. Living-out personnel, as they were known, were to be afforded escort to and from their appointed units. This task clearly enjoyed the potential of a very good skive, and as a welcome substitute for strobes and azicators, it soon became somewhat overcrowded with volunteers.

Not quite so comfortable was the daily requirement of school and compound inspection. A small nearby primary school served the educational purposes of the children of these families. The school was secured within a compound but vacated at night, and the protection of the building and its contents was limited to passing exterior inspection by the patrol making its rounds of the perimeter of the living-out area. Eoka had become masters of the small and superficially innocent booby trap, and the simple task each day involved moving everything inside the building that could be moved. Desk lids and toilet seats were to be lifted; doors and windows to be opened and closed; books, teaching equipment, and all of the furniture was to be moved. Any electrical equipment was to be switched on, including all of the lights. Among their many other nasty little anti-personnel devices, the septic inventiveness of the bomb makers art had devised the means to detach the glass globe from a light bulb, or drill a tiny hole into it, to insinuate a small quantity of petrol, and to reconnect globe and bulb to the circuit. The unwitting flick of a switch, and the air became filled with tiny shards of high velocity flying glass. Teaching staff were instructed to secure small items, the pens, containers, markers and especially any tubular items of daily use, in a locked cupboard. Any such items out of place were to be afforded a temporary wide berth, until bomb disposal took the appropriate and expert action.

On one such early morning occasion, as I walked towards the school, I passed an elderly lady, dressed in traditional black and sitting on her step. I raised a hand in friendly greeting, and bade her a cheery good morning in English and my best Greek. She spat at my feet. I was shocked and dismayed at such a despising gesture.

Toward the middle of 1959, a more peaceable climate was creeping over the landscape of Cyprus. A small number of extremists insisted upon the continuation of a personal war of attrition, in spite of the clear indication that the powers of the day were about to close the shutters on a conflict that had cost more than 400 British and allied lives over a period of almost five years. For those military personnel still in pursuit of their tours of duty, this heralded the beginning of a period of liberation. Liberation from incarceration, liberation from constant fear and apprehension, liberation from the loathsome and mostly undeserved feeling of alienation?

Well almost!!!

Cautiously at first, release into the outside world was permitted in organised excursions, and later in slightly more casual groups, but all still under arms. Visits were restricted only to prescribed areas of townships, and in compliance with the hours of limited curfew, to shops, bars, and places of iniquity and carnal worship. This was not without hazard, and to ensure that the imposition of hazard was sustained at a minimum level, patrols were mounted during all of the permitted hours, and later if roll call revealed a missing miscreant. In the euphoria of liberation, the failure of roll call was inevitable, and not infrequent.

The increasingly imposed task of maintaining an adequate urban patrol service quickly became more than the RAF police were able to sustain, and opportunity became revealed for those who would find preference for off-camp duty to volunteer to fill the dwindling ranks. Patrol details were numbered four to six strong, all armed with Sten gun, side arms, or both. Sounds formidable, but these were not search, engage, and disarm exercises to winkle out lurking insurgents, more authoritative tours of various dens of excess and iniquity. Their purpose was to caution excess, to rescue the afflicted from further injury, to find safe passage in a following truck for those who were beyond ready advice or assistance, and to curb further excesses among those who may have reopened hostilities with the local population.

While a watching brief was usually the only requirement on the street, the bars and the brothels could be guaranteed to provide a far greater selection of tales of the unexpected. In these establishments, any volunteer members of the patrol merely made up the numbers, while any required action was handled by the professionals. By mid to late evening most of the more disreputable bars would be awash with spilt beer and vomit, and possibly with one or two disconsolate and totally bemused individuals sitting in it. The incapacitated would be removed to safety, and provided that there was no violence, the remainder would be permitted to continue along the road to oblivion.

The brothels, often the same establishments in all but name, were a slightly more unknown quantity as activities therein were conducted under a more covert cloak. Here, the service providers and those seeking the service, often shared a common bond. Both were broke! The girls, frequently working as dancers in sleazy bars and clubs as they waited in vain hope for the call to show-time fame, invariably earned insufficient to survive. Many were very attractive girls, the sorry victims of unscrupulous employers, whose sole aspiration was the exploitation of their bodies, one way or another. Thus necessity dictated the need to resort to a more altruistic mode of enterprise to ensure that there was marmalade for breakfast.

Their clientele, confined as they had been for weeks or even months, were eager, if not desperate to ensure continued functionality. However, and alas for carnal aspiration, many had earlier squandered the facility for purposeful performance, that having become sacrificed to yet one more brandy sour. They continued to feel the need, even if the urge and facility had lost its purpose. Thus they lingered in the hope that returning libido would find accommodation and that their turn would become fruitful.

Thus this sweaty boudoir industry became the provider of a shared commodity. The desperate endeavouring to satisfy the requirements of the needy, with each of the component parts satisfying the description of the other. These were sometimes somewhat crowded places in which the requirement for seclusion and privacy had been abandoned. Some waiting, some hoping, some doing, and some having it done. It brought marmalade to the breakfast table.

Many of the rooms, of course, provided temporary and noisy habitation for the occasional overweight Greek who had pleaded the home requirement in order to obtain of a pack of cigarettes and a glass of Ouzo. Presently bearing explosively down upon the slender frame of the utterly bored victualler of his libidinous requirements, whose simple consoling reverie was that simple pot of marmalade. As he substantially absorbed her slender frame among his ample abdominal folds, the patrol would make its exit with as little polite disturbance as could be achieved in the simple click of a closing door.

For the patrols, the task in hand required a blind eye, a solemn word of caution, a voiced reminder of curfew, or a step further up the corridor. Unless of course there was indication of distress among the participants, fisticuffs in the queue, or any one of the many and diverse outcomes of earlier excesses.

As curfew tolled the bell of passing night, the upright were ushered into the truck, those for whom the street no longer enjoyed identity or location were herded like sheep in the general direction of the truck, those whose final brandy sour had rendered them immobile were carried to the truck, and those whose carnal excesses remained incomplete, endured flagrante interruptus and were pointed in the direction of the truck. Those waiting, hoping, or having it done, simply had to gather the personal effects that they were able locate, and hope that the queue on the next occasion would be more accommodating.

We working lads? Well our turn would come.

Chapter 6. Skiving - The noble art of being unobtrusively obvious.

... "Little Francis home from school." ...

*

*One of the highlights of the working week
is the opportunity to report sick with some spurious malaise,
or in the wake of some deliberately committed misdemeanour,
to enjoy the diversity of a free 'jankers' holiday.*

*Normal duties range from the irresistibly soporific
to the questionably attractive bullet in the head.*

*Volunteering for anything and everything, though not normally considered advisable,
enjoys the facility, through careful management, that the 'willing volunteer'
is never employed to do anything and that his whereabouts are ever obscure.*

*Care in management planning can even permit
a modest supplementary income from unseen occupation.*

*

A few short weeks before I was due to embark upon my personal journey of mystery and imagination, a great friend of my father's placed an arm around my shoulders, and made to deliver a short speech.

"My boy," he said, "As you embark upon this adventure, and as an ex-serviceman, I am about to give you the best piece of wisdom and advice that you will ever receive during your period of service."

"Thank you Tony. I will be pleased to receive it."

"Never," he said solemnly, "Never ever volunteer for anything."

Tony! Tony! How could you have been so naive or ill-directed?

As I made my tentative and apprehensive early progress into this new and very different world, my shy, retiring, and inexperienced persona faced the prospect of social competition with others who were clearly far more worldly wise than I. Theirs the sometimes harsh classroom of the streets and alleys of London, Birmingham or Glasgow, which had taught them many of the facts of life as it is lived in their urban environment. My antithesis was polar in its dissimilarity. A totally anonymous tiny rural community, without church, shop, pub, or meeting place, where a passing tractor, one of my mother's goats up a tree, or the broad beans coming into blossom, constituted an event. The social contrasts could hardly have been greater.

However, does street wisdom harbour an arrogance that restricts the view ahead, and insists upon the head butt where greater vision would be more edifying?

Does the social limitation of rural residence evolve a less belligerent attitude to imposed social change, and a more reasoned disposition towards personal adjustment, harmony, and mutual benefit?

I believe that my disposition directed me towards the latter course of action. Lacking the self-assurance or the disdain of street wisdom, I elected to keep my head below the parapet, to tread carefully on the path of obedience, and to learn from the wisdom of co-operation. Though our internment may have sometimes seemed akin to an open prison, better to learn its ways and to use them to best advantage, than to take up arms against an apparent or contrived sea of troubles. Thus, square bashing and occupational training passed without personal mishap or discord, while some of the more worldly-wise continued with their pedantic and unprofitable war of attrition. However, whatever mayhap individual persuasion or inclination, whether pedant or pugilist, pacifist or profiteer, stately passage through the pearly portals of 280 introduced a change of pace so profound that the mighty once more joined the meek to jostle for position under starters orders.

As already observed, the daily demand of duty and work did little to fire the interests of those whose tenure of the uniform that they wore would be of limited duration, and whose shortly predicted metamorphosis would redirect them once more, on to a more familiar road. During those first few introductory weeks, each new arrival became obliged to embrace a succession of steep learning curves that would segregate and separate this reluctant body of students. For some, graduation earned an additional sleeve insignia and capitulation to a foreseeable future dominated by the tedium of daily routine. For others, perhaps of a more acquisitive, enterprising, or opportunist character, the same sleeve adornment, but in addition, the evolution of the need to seek and find a measure of diversity soon became evident.

While routine may impose discipline, the regularity by which it is directed leaves it vulnerable to attack. Its soft underbelly is perforated with chinks that can be readily exploited with a little subtlety and camouflage. No single routine directs the entire machine, and each of the many overlapping rituals that combine in its industrial endeavour, is equally possessed of chinks of vulnerability. Subtle combination of these points of weakness, provides a cautious springboard for exploitation, and the means to take advantage of the routine of the very system that provides and imposes the daily direction.

There must be a science that associates with vulnerability. Misbehavioural brinkmanship will suffice. One of the keys to the likely successful exploitation of misbehavioural brinkmanship is the keen observation of the chinks as they become manifest, and the retention in memory of their evident weaknesses. Regular routine is a powerful influence, and will impose adherence to its order upon those who readily become resigned to its caress. For others, a carefully orchestrated equivalent order can permit deviation into an alternative routine that will allow the luxury and satisfaction of a seriously enhanced and diversified manner of living. All of this while apparently maintaining allegiance to the status quo.

Of course, taking unfair advantage of the dominating system can be achieved by utilising a fair way or a foul way. Fair or foul? In a small, overcrowded, close knit, totally confined community like 280, the foul way could only be achieved to the detriment of the community of fellow inmates, and especially to those who also aspired to exploit their own calculated style of misbehavioural brinkmanship. The fair way, on the other hand, seeks only to exploit the system, to the detriment of no-one.

The secret of success was the application of misbehavioural brinkmanship in a manner of subtlety sufficient to ensure the bamboozlement of those whose duty and responsibility was its prevention. In a routine and system of monotonous regularity, authoritarian complacency can be a powerful, if unreliable ally. It is not, however to be taken for granted, can mutate without warning and on the inconstancy of a mood swing or a hangover, and will not tolerate the transparency of repeated use or abuse. Are these the treacherous quick-sands upon which to construct an enterprise in vocational skiving?

For many weeks after my arrival at 280, Tony's words of wisdom and advice remained locked into my memory. Shortly, however, they became replaced and reversed as my observations began to appreciate the potential of volunteering. After much pondering, a simple viewpoint had come to dominate my conjecture. If, I mused, I were to volunteer my services to every situation, to every available task, to every single undertaking that required a modicum of manpower but which was not enshrined in the daily routine, and if I made public proclamation of this selfless gesture, there was a chance that no-one would know where I was or what I was doing, for most of the time.

The facility to put this theory into practice appeared from a slightly obscure and unexpected direction. In a community where 24-hour function is obligatory, where a state of military emergency imposes confinement, and where living conditions are close to the abominable, the imposition of discipline is lax, and accepted misdemeanour is frequent. That is not to suggest that discipline is absent, and in order to maintain order and authority, it is necessary to set the occasional example. As misdemeanour was totally endemic, a miscreant could readily be identified at almost any time. For example, a slovenly individual is making his way to the technical site to undertake his period of daily duty, clad only in underpants and wellington boots. He is challenged by authority and tenders the excuse that it was hot, he had just come from the ablutions and was dressing en route. This is not misbehavioural brinkmanship, but blatant abuse of a relaxed system. He would become the victim of his own folly. He would be charged with disorderly conduct, and ordered to present himself at the administration cabins on the following morning, where his charge would be read and where he would receive his punishment.

The commanding officer of 280 Signals Unit was a generous judge, and offences of a minor nature were most frequently dismissed with an admonishment, or with the imposition of work detail on a less than pleasant task. More serious offences, damage to property, fighting, excessive drunkenness, deliberate demonstration of disrespect to flag and service, were justifiably afforded more severe reprimand. Loss of privileges, a step up from admonishment, could be applied at most locations, but as there were no privileges at 280, this application became invalid. Instead, the miscreant would become obliged to spend a couple of nights in the guardroom cells at Akrotiri. Here the sunrise obligation was the feeding of a pack of killer canines, trained specifically to tear the throat from any unworthy, at the command of the Snowdrop handler. For the remainder of each punishment day, the offender merely lounged about the guardroom, playing cards or socialising with those on duty. Collectively, these measures of retribution were known as 'jankers'.

I digress! 280 Signals Unit was defensively surrounded by extended coils of barbed wire, stacked two upon two, and retained by wires strained between anchored steel posts. The perimeter was of substantial length, the substrate was naked limestone, and the entire structure was inherently insecure. As a result, there was a constant requirement for repair and replacement, and it was to this highly unpopular task that those on 'jankers' were frequently banished.

The task was a simple one that required little or no practical skill, and the minimum of training to facilitate the use of a very noisy machine. The entire perimeter structure was under permanent and damaging bombardment from the elements. The wind, the rain, the Mediterranean sea air and galloping rust. Thus, every part required periodic replacement, and the nature of the structure dictated that every part of every part be replaced when this was attempted. The modus operandi was fairly undemanding, requiring only a strong back and a pair of gloves. The decaying wire coils were released, collapsed and dumped. The retaining wires were cut and discarded. The posts were left in situ and replaced. To facilitate replacement, a compressor and pneumatic drill were utilised for the drilling of holes into the limestone, into which were driven new posts, with the addition of a little cement for greater security. New coils of barbed wire were extended and located between the posts, and the installation of retaining wires completed the job.

By anyone's standards, a doddle! However, many of these locations were remote from the occupied portions of the unit, and were therefore vulnerable to ambush or attack. To compensate, and to reduce the element of risk, each working party would be eight in number, all armed with Sten guns or side arms, and working on a hourly change rota of four working and four guarding. The only imposed condition dictated that each section of the fence to be replaced was completed and the camp made secure within any single working day. Consequently, a single section only would be the daily detail and requirement. While the work was physically demanding, each section could be completed in three to four hours, half of the time was spent in lounging mode while guarding, and half of most working days was spent in unseen idleness. Not a job for high summer when the daytime temperatures were dangerously high. Nor a task for periods of inclement winter weather that would impose mechanical hazard and extreme discomfort. Thus, the task was limited to days of favourable climate during the winter, spring and autumn.

I made my first encounter with this potential sinecure during an early period of admonishment, and quickly began to appreciate its potential. Though it was indeed a doddle, it was also a most despised pursuit, especially among those of a more sedentary nature. As a result, it was never to become the object of willing volunteering. However, for a country boy, more familiar with a milking parlour than a radar receiver, and with trees growing out of his ears, here was opportunity indeed.

Skiving is a time-honoured pursuit, and providing that it is undertaken without detriment to others, and only at the nominal expense of authority, it may be considered an honourable pursuit. However, success in this endeavour is dependent upon the strict application of procedure and rule. Failure to comply will inevitably result in exposure, in failure, and in the rapidly descending wrath of the offended body politic.

It is absolute folly to apply the same ruse repeatedly or too frequently. This error of judgement will quickly become revealed, will equally quickly become exposed, and however clever, will be lost forever.

Never be blatant about any aspect of skiving. No need to touch the proverbial forelock, but if making an approach to underhand volunteering, always be superficially sincere. While there is no requirement to cringe, avoid the 'I'm doing this for the good of mankind' attitude.

Avoid expressing over enthusiasm about an unpleasant or unrewarding task. This will always arouse suspicion, the implication will persist through subsequent false gestures of philanthropy, and will severely cramp the style of others in pursuit of similar dubious strategies.

Volunteer with ostensible sincerity. Never, ever boast about your strategies or your successes. Someone with a grudge, who is consumed by moral righteousness, or is simply pissed off because he failed to devise the scheme himself, will be sure to blow the gaff, and your enterprise will endure a terminal fate.

Thus, the scene became set, and my association with the felons on the wire became inaugurated. While a few brief, and completely unjustified occasions, imposed a few days of punitive chastisement on 'jankers' parade, my volunteering for the freedom of the bundu was approached with caution. A team of eight was obligatory, and volunteers were sought when a 'jankers' party failed to reach this number. I kept my ears to the ground, and when an opportunity seemed imminent, I made a point of being in the vicinity.

"OK Sarge! I'll do it!" My tone of offertory reluctance never failed, and thus relieved of the soporific and endless revolution of the wearisome strobe, I enjoyed many happy hours, shaking, rattling and rolling with the dancing drill, and taking my ease in the bundu sunshine.

To describe 280 as casual would be to deliver an understatement of monolithic proportions. In fairness, it was a hot and dusty place during the summer months, and one of mud, mire, and muck during the wet periods of winter. Thus, boot shine was never a realistic expectation, and provided that a reasonable degree of tidiness graced our uniform while on duty, sharp creases and shiny brass buttons were never in evidence.

However, there was a set of rules that dictated adherence to the expected dress code, and many were they who fell foul of its guidelines. Scruffiness was endemic, and though the tolerance levels were extraordinarily generous, there were occasions, there were individuals, perhaps there were times for all of us, when attitude degenerated into denial.

"Sod it! I can't be bothered."

Mostly such misdemeanours were of a trivial nature, requiring no more than a bellowed instruction from the sergeant of the watch, or a mild admonishment from the officer of the day. Socks slumped around the ankles, bootlaces trailing in the dust, shirt tails flapping in the breeze, a day's growth of facial stubble, hands in pockets, cigarette dangling, all of these were of complete inconsequence, were corrected when apprehension dictated, and were promptly ignored.

Tolerance was far less generous when the misdemeanour involved any permanently physical adjustment to the uniform. Strictly against the rules, practices such as these were considered disrespectful to the uniform and to the service, and at the very least, were greeted with a formal charge. Under the threat of such penalties, motive for these practices was a little difficult to comprehend. Perhaps there is a little ostentation in us all. This was pride, braggadocio, vanity, seeking to demonstrate the cool dude. In other circumstances it may be to attract the attention of others, notably of the fair sex. Why then, at scruffy 280 SU, where members of the fair sex had never set dainty foot, would the cool dude find even the most fleeting consequence?

The most abundantly adjusted piece of daily apparel was the headgear, and mostly this could be achieved without attracting too much critical attention. The crowning item of dress uniform, best blue in common parlance, was a cap. The rigidity of its flat top was maintained by a stiffening wire around the interior rim, and it sat atop the wearer's head like a cranial dinner plate. This was not the headgear of a cool dude. Adjustment to a slightly more raffish mode could readily be achieved by bending the stiffening wire, fore and aft, at four points, until either side adopted a modest downward inclination, a much more appropriate adornment for a strolling dude.

Even the humble daily beret did not escape a small measure of vainglorious attention. Indeed, it is eminently possible that the beret has become the most abused garment in military history. The new and unadulterated beret perched as uncomfortably as an upturned saucer upon the head of the wearer. When adjusted to the left in the approved manner, the upper fabric of the beret projected horizontally, somewhat more in the fashion of an aerofoil than an item of acceptably fashionable headgear. For the airman-about-town this was unacceptable, and required urgent modification. The offending beret became the victim of a period of systematic abuse. It was slept on, slept in, soaked, washed, boiled, battered, crumpled and starched until the desired flexibility permitted the wearer to manipulate it more closely to the shape of his cranium. To further enhance the effect, a series of small cuts were insinuated into the rim, and the desired effect became complete. The beret, now paler in hue than the original air force blue, adhered to the wearer's skull like a surgical implant. The projecting aerofoil was now pointing directly toward his shoulder, and the front right portion had become raised to a roguish angle around the cap badge. As a means to ensure that this mould should be retained for all time, and would resist any potentially misaligning influence, the beret was afforded one final soaking and starching. This done, and while still saturated, it was placed upon the head of the wearer, and permitted to dry in situ. There are no recorded instances of cranial shrinkage resulting from this practice.

The tropical substitute for the beret was a khaki cap, perhaps somewhat inappropriately, of the Afrika Corps genre, that folded laterally behind its small peak. Manufactured of fairly flimsy material, in its original form, it embraced the wearer's skull like a knotted handkerchief. Hardly alluring, this item was treated with great care to induce greater rigidity, and thus to perch more theatrically, if somewhat less securely, at the preferred angle of rakishness. The repeated application of starch achieved this desired effect, and rendered the cap almost as rigid and unyielding as the hull of a model ship.

Badges of rank and achievement were awarded as and when appropriate, and generally worn with pride on the sleeve. They came in shapes appropriate to the insignia, and were to be stitched on to the appropriate location on the sleeve. The recently promoted Senior Aircraftman proudly proclaimed his rank on each upper sleeve of his uniform. His three bladed propeller insignia was presented on a rectangular background of air force blue, which announced that he had now become SAC Joe Bloggs.

For SAC Tillotson, this proved the catalyst to downfall. Just like all of the other young blades, I aspired to assert my youthful self-confidence and indicate my panache, and I quickly formed the view that the rectangular badge of office was, in the parlance of the day, 'square'. How much cooler it would be, I mused, if the badge were to be trimmed and attached to the sleeve as an inverted triangle. This much might have escaped notice or been ignored had I not become stricken with a bout of chronic idleness. I simply could not be bothered to take the trouble to stitch them to my sleeves, and figured that a much more expedient way would be to use an adhesive. Perchance, I had in my possession a tube of the fluid variety of that reliable but messy gunk, Copydex. The application of a generous quantity to the reverse of each badge allowed instant attachment to sleeve left and sleeve right, and the job was done in seconds. I congratulated myself on my ingenuity and returned the uniform to its place in the hanging locker.

Alas for my misguided and misdirected confidence, I had overlooked the time required for the Copydex to dry and set, and its capacity to dribble if suspended in the vertical plane. The error of my ways had quickly become clear when next I opened the door of my locker. Each of my proud triangular badges of rank had become circumscribed by a narrow translucent halo. Worse than this, each halo had extended in a festive streamer for several inches down the length of each sleeve. Copydex is not an easy substance to remove, and after several days would probably require a solvent sufficiently caustic to dissolve the entire sleeve. No antidote to Copydex invasion was at my disposal, and although I made my best attempts by making use of detergents, and caustic soda scrounged from the mess, it was to no avail. The stains of my guilt remained indelible and apparently permanent.

I faced the disciplinary firing squad, and received instruction to subject my uniform to the immediate mercies of professional cleaning. They did a fairly tidy job. However it was a 'jankers' offence, and my considerable consolation was a banishment to a few more days rocking and rolling in the bundu.

One of the most despised of all regular duties were the parades. These were not daily or even frequent events, but they were despised because, they were always early morning obligations, and endemic scruffiness became supplanted by the rude imposition of best blues and tidy apparel. Unlike the daily practice on most stations, parades at 280 occurred at around monthly intervals on a regular basis, interspersed by impromptu last-minute events designed to make captive the habitual dodgers. Their purpose was to serve reminder of camp discipline, of military standards, of our part and purpose in a fighting force, and that we were on active service where vigilance was a requirement at all times. The parades took place on the area of open ground adjacent to the administration cabins, and where a languid flag fluttered atop a somewhat makeshift flagpole.

The normal practice involved several loose ranks being brought to order by the duty sergeant.

"Maaaaark to the right!"
"AAAAAtten... wait for it, wait for it... Attention!"
"Shoulder AAAAArms!"
"Left turn... Quiiiick March."

The squad shamble-marched to the perimeter of the square.

"Squaaaad Halt!"

There was a measure of ill-timed and inconsistent boot thudding on to the baked earth.

"Abouuut Turn. Quiiiick March."

The shambling parade proceeded to the opposite perimeter, passing flag as they did so where the Commanding Officer or his Adjutant took the salute. A repeat performance returned the squad to the flag.

"Squaaaad Halt! Riiiight Turn! Sllooooope Arms! Staaaand easy! At ease!"

There would then follow a brief address by the saluting officer in which he reminded us of the huge value of our service to the defence of the nation. He repeated the caution that terrorists were everywhere, that we were to maintain vigilance at all times. He prompted us that the equipment and information that we were handling was sensitive, hugely confidential, and would be of immense value to the enemy. Thus, he warned, we were to exercise extreme caution in action, communication, and in any social interaction. The walls have ears, and the enemy is everywhere. The address followed a similar pattern on each occasion, though I guess that different faces populated his small unkempt audience on each occasion, comprising, as it did, almost exclusively, of those who had failed to fabricate an excuse not to be there.

In conclusion, he returned the event to the direction of the sergeant. "Squaaaaaaaad disssmissss." At which point the assemblage shambled off in the direction whence they had come, and returned to their respective endeavours or to dedicated idleness.

Though the parades were obligatory for all those not currently on duty or those just signing off night duty, such was the level of contempt for these events that the excuses and reasons for not being in attendance far outnumbered those being brought to attention at 07.00. The pretexts offered were many and varied. "On watch!", "Just off night watch!", "Jankers!", "Escort duty!", "Touch of the runs!", "Volunteering!", "Sick Parade!", "Sports training!". Of course, each of these feeble justifications could readily be checked, but so great were the numbers of presented pretexts that such a time-consuming and futile task could not be justified. Thus, the status quo simply found acceptance.

Of course, it remained imperative to continue to observe the rules of skiving. In any context, repeated absence would be noted, checked, and punished accordingly. Thus, the rules of engagement made clear the need to speak to the duty sergeant on each attending occasion, thus confirming dutiful attendance. Equally so, the use of blatant or regularly used excuses would quickly become subject to scrutiny and investigation. If on quaking ground, supportive backup in the form of an equally dishonest trusty, or practical evidence in justification always afforded promise of disregard.

One of my favourites was the sick run. 280 had no medical centre, no clinic of any kind, and no resident practitioner. Sick parades were held daily in the sick bay at Akrotiri, and an irregular shuttle truck transported the halt and the lame each morning. Operated correctly, the sick run was infallible, as the miscreant always returned with the evidence of his 'affliction'. While medication provided some practical corroboration to the claim, the all-important sick note was the vital catalyst to sick-skiving success. Signed and dated, this simple piece of paper was immune from challenge. However, any attempt to fabricate a sick run, or to counterfeit a sick note, would inevitably meet with failure, retribution, and severe reproach from fellow sick-skivers.

I made use of the sick run on a number of occasions, usually to avoid the morning duty watch. Take the morning sick parade truck at around 08.00. Attend the sick parade to present the affliction of the day. Spend a lazy morning at Akrotiri to return to 280, and to report back for duty just as the morning watch was concluding, and to the explosive rage of a furious sergeant.

"Where the bloody hell have you been?"
"Sick parade Sarge!"
"Sick parade? You don't look bloody sick to me!"
"What is the matter with you anyway?"
"Dandruff Sarge!"
"Daaaanbloodydruff'!"

At this point the sick note is proffered together with the little bottle of yellow tincture, and while the sergeant recovers from his apoplexy, I quietly rejoin the closing few moments of the morning duty period.

Aching limbs, twisted knee at rugby practice, nocturnal nose bleed, recurrent headaches, ear wax, stiff neck, athlete's foot, bad back, nightmares, any one of a dozen afflictions of the alimentary system could provide fabricated justification for the morning run to the sick parade. I am unaware of anyone attempting to use period pains as a ruse, but who knows, perhaps a sleepy and unquestioning nursing orderly might have afforded his signature to the all-important piece of paper, and supplied a bottle of aspirin. The golden rule was imperative. Never, ever return from a bogus sick parade without the sick note passport.

The workplace provided one facility for the avoidance of work without contrived absenteeism from duty. The function of each working watch was directed by a rota. This simple device ensured that each operational position was manned for a limited period, and that no-one became stuck on the same task for an entire six or eight-hour period. The rota included regular break periods to allow for refreshment or the necessary execution of bodily functions.

A large marquee on the technical site provided services for those taking their break from duty. Here could be obtained tea, coffee, cold drinks, crisps, biscuits, chocolate bars and the like. At the start of each watch, the call for one volunteer to take up the duty of canteen manager, usually met with very little response. For reasons unclear, this was not a popular job, perhaps because the task included washing up, cleaning the canteen area, restocking, and accounting at the end of each watch. I considered this opportunity as providential in the extreme, relieving me as it did, of the burden of strobes, tubes, and cabin claustrophobia. My volunteering for this task became increasingly frequent, and as it never faced challenge from a rival, my role as canteen manager became a semi-permanent sinecure.

For a short period my relatively innocent volunteering for this distasteful task was no more than yet another skive, albeit one that found 'official' approbation. That is, until its potential gradually became evident. At the termination of each watch, it was the task of the canteen operator to undertake a stock check, to count and record his cash takings, and to reconcile the two. Every item carried a stated price, was sold and purchased at that tariff, and was accounted for at the end of watch stock take. The one exception to this regulation was the coffee, which was sold by the cup. Coffee was supplied in small size tins of Nescafe, prepared in the mugs, normally with the addition of evaporated milk, and sugar if required.

The imposed rules of engagement were simple. The canteen management was instructed that each tin of Nescafe must be apportioned to provide twenty mugs of coffee. Sold at five mils per mug, the mathematics is simple, one tin would place one hundred mils into the till. Using mathematics no more complex, it is clear that if the number of mugs of coffee from each tin could be increased, a small profit margin would be created. It might seem extravagant and perhaps even somewhat perilous to extend the apportionment to forty mugs of coffee, but if this could be achieved, one hundred mils became surplus to the required book keeping, and no-one had become in any way disadvantaged in the process.

Success in this little delusion, and care in its execution were paramount. My preferred system functioned on a contrived illusion of customer satisfaction at all times of customer awareness. Our four watch system ensured that every period of twenty-four hours was afforded full radar coverage. Though aircraft came and went throughout this period, the night watch was generally very quiet, and focussed mainly upon incoming arms smuggling, illegal landing activity on the remote coastline, and unauthorised activity of any kind. Night watch was dull to soporific and coffee was often an essential stimulant. While the afternoon and evening watches could be fairly quiet, morning aerial exercises often extended into these periods, imposing equivalent busyness upon the canteen. During most mornings, however, the locally based aircraft were airborne and were engaged in practice combat, interception, bombing practice and the rehearsal of all of the activities that would be required during periods of warfare. All of these aircraft were under ground control and direction, and all had to be directed safely from take-off to landing. These periods were often busy in the extreme.

My system, strategy and practice engaged seamlessly with the contrast between busy and soporific. During quiet periods, when stand down was more abundant than stand by, coffee was served at regulation strength, each tin providing carefully measured twenty mugs (never less to avoid profit bruising). During very busy periods, everyone on watch was dutifully engaged, free time was limited to essential bodily functions and high speed coffee. Rest periods were unknown. Here, the art of coffee making achieved its most sparse endeavour. Water was boiled in a large urn, and always maintained at boiling point or close to it. Mugs at the ready, just below the counter level, to ensure speedy, but unseen delivery.

"Quick coffee!"

To a mug three parts filled with boiling water was added a generous dash of evaporated milk. This grisly substance was guaranteed to grossly disfigure any flavour, and at the same time provide the illusion of taste. A damp spoon was dipped into the coffee tin, dashed off against its side, and plunged into the insipid dilute evaporated milk, just sufficiently to afford it a faint pale khaki hue. A copious quantity of additional sugar (not rationed or accountable) added the final disguise. The beverage was inevitably too hot to drink anyway, even if haste had permitted, and the customer generally left after a quick and noisy slurp.

The exceptions were the officers of the watch, who generally ordered coffee to be taken to them in the operations cabin. Theirs of course, was of regulation strength.

At the termination of each morning watch, stocktaking recorded the number of tins of Nescafe that had been used by the ever-grateful members of the hard working crew, the takings were counted and the books were reconciled. I was frequently very surprised to note just how many mugs of my insipid infusion could be manufactured from the contents of a single can of Nescafe.

As my virtuous deceit continued through the months, I began to realise that just a few members of the other watches too had adopted the mantle of semi-permanent canteen manager, and for the same remunerative purposes. Another of the principle rules of engagement must apply. Never show your hand! So, not a word to Nellie in the hope that Nellie would apply the same rule. Alas, this did not happen, and at some stage, Nellie became appraised of the situation. A careless word, a small boast considered confidential, a momentary lapse in personal security, whatever had been the leak, the reaction was rapid. The Special Investigation Branch (SIB), were summoned, and conducted a series of lightning and unannounced random search forays upon canteen and living spaces.

SIB were specially trained Snowdrops. RAF police personnel with a dedicated penchant for seeking and finding the truth or evidence thereof. Their unsupervised approach combined methods that might have evolved at the hands of the KGB, of the Gestapo, of Interpol, of the IRA or of the Mafia. They were ruthless, meticulous and rapid, and as personal search areas were exceedingly limited, there was nowhere to conceal anything except in a hole in the ground. Canteen operatives were clearly in the front line of suspects, and the first in line for investigation. My turn was accompanied by smiling innocence, and after most of my personal effects had been strew liberally around the tent, the Snowdrops departed empty-handed, and hopefully satisfied. Most of my ill- gotten gains had changed hands yet again, mostly over the counter in the NAAFI.

Not so for one unfortunate soul, who had been sufficiently foolish to keep a book of his illicit activities, and who even had the evidence of his most recent extortion in small stacks of coins in his locker drawer. He was pilloried, and a permanent veil was drawn over one of the best little bandwagons of the day.

Chapter 7. A more honest approach? - but skiving none the less.

… "There lived beneath the city wall, a student who was strong and tall," …

*

*In addition to providing landscapes of unparalleled beauty,
our guests enjoy distant views of the misty blue mountains of mysterious Troodos,
elegantly and picturesquely snow capped during the winter months.*

*Although a more contemporary scene occupies the foreground,
the majestic curve of Limassol Bay
directs the view toward the quaint and ancient town
wherein may be found and obtained facilities and services
that will bring ready satisfaction to each and every bodily function, craving or desire.*

*Closer to home, the Cape that is your personal haven of tranquillity,
boasts a truly wondrous coastline of undisturbed bays,
of secret hidden coves, of magnificent cliffs and of irresistible turquoise water,
as clear as crystal and as inviting as a smile.*

Our location is steeped in history.

*Ample evidence informs that earlier mankind also
found peace, tranquillity and a pastoral livelihood on Cape Gata.*

*Untrammelled by more conventional tourist traffic,
all this is yours to enjoy.*

*

Of course, there were other, much more legitimate tactics that could be employed in the avoidance of strobophobia or chronic cabin weariness. At the very commencement of National Service, each individual had been awarded an annual leave allowance of two weeks. In recognition of overseas service this became increased to three weeks, and further enhanced in recognition of the state of emergency, which had precluded any opportunity to take leave on the island. The enhancement permitted and provided complimentary flights on commercial airlines to any one of the nearby Levantine nations. This did not include Turkey, but could allow for travel to Jordan, Lebanon, Syria or Israel, but clearly never, ever to Jordan or Lebanon or Syria, AND Israel.

Application to take leave of absence, to make visit to one of the approved countries, and to take advantage of the assisted passage, all required application and completion of the prescribed proformae. These forms were not unduly complex though some of the information they carried seemed to bear little relevance to the request and served only to impose a little confusion, often a valuable asset when rule-bending was planned. They did however, require signatures of approval in a sequence from an admin orderly, across the desks of the administration department, and ultimately to the commanding officer.

Time and experience would indicate, among the confusion of forms passing through the various departments, that perhaps here too, there may be some facility for a little manipulation. Some elected to reduce leave taking to a minimum during their first year, to carry the maximum over into a second year, and to make use of it for a prolonged home visit, perhaps to take their marriage vows or to attend a major family event. During my early months, local leave was only possible if residence was arranged at another base or approved rest camp. This was only really practical at RAF Episkopi or at the leave camp on Troodos. Later, when the reduction of hostilities permitted residence by families in protected compounds, it became accepted practice to be signed out to a residential address.

I elected to make use of the Troodos encampment on a number of occasions, or to reside at the RAF barracks at Pingo's Hotel. The mountains provided considerable relief from the soaring summer temperatures on the coastal plain and on the cape. However, these short-term forays imposed severe erosion on a limited leave allowance, and if pursued, would seriously impact upon intentions to travel further afield.

Twin leave forms working in very careful and cautious tandem might expand flexibility, and even permit a little duplication. A spare leave form could readily be obtained, and an early attempt to make use of duplication functioned without redress or apparent suspicion. However, I recognised that this was swampy ground, and one slip could mean serious sinking into the mire. I had considered making use of one form for local leave, and the other for more distant application, but concluded that this was too obvious. More secure perhaps, simply alternating leave applications on duplicate forms, but the threat of the mire still loomed large in this strategy, and it too was shelved to the rear of my consideration.

My observation, and a little inside information, had indicated that the required successive endorsing authorisation signatures followed the first with no more than the most cursory glance. It followed then, that if the first signature could be that of a trusted fellow, in pursuit of his trade in the administration department, the rest would probably follow without further inquisition. This strategy could be further enhanced if that same trusted fellow was prepared to delay onward passage and to allow forms to accumulate into a substantial and potentially annoying bundle. Collusion secured, a couple of trial runs indicated that collected forms did indeed pass before the eyes of co-signatories without so much as a moment's scrutiny.

With due consideration, I devised an alternative strategy that had the potential of significant improvement on the dodgy duplicate system. The key to the potential of this strategy was controlled document abuse. Crumple the leave form, soak it and dry it a couple of times until the ink has run and smudged, drop it into a muddy hollow and wipe it clean, impose a small tear or a damaged edge, generally abuse the document until it has clearly arrived at the end of its useful purpose. Then once and only once, and at a time close to the middle point of service or leave taking, present it as an application for a brief period of local leave.

"What the hell have you done with this?"

"Sorry Sarge, it went through the laundry."

"Well! It is no bloody good in that condition. Hang on, I will issue another one."

So all evidence of the first substantial period of continental leave becomes lost in the dustbin. Re-application is made on the new form for the short period of local leave, and in a brief wave of the magician's wand, the scene is set for the next substantial application for travel to a more distant place.

A similar fiddle involved the manipulation of the watch system. Three working days were always followed by two free days Add to this a 48-hour pass, which equated to the next period of three working days, again followed by two free days. To this was added two days from the annual leave allowance. The annual permitted absence allowed 21 days of leave and twelve 48-hour passes. By dividing annual leave into two-day periods, and adding the manipulated periods of permitted absence it was theoretically possible to enjoy 101 free days each year, to which can be added an additional 132 days that was inherent in the watch system. In practice, all of this somewhat complicated manoeuvring and manipulation only permitted local leave of absence, or on camp freedom from work. This did little to satisfy my leave taking aspirations, so I did not venture in that direction.

For any in pursuit of this line of manoeuvring and who had become unhappily rumbled, perhaps the line of defence most likely to find success would be to submit an initial 'guilty' plea. This to be followed in mitigation by a full and detailed explanation of the entire inscrutable scheme. With luck, boredom and incomprehension would attract summary dismissal or at worst an admonishment.

My first period of substantial leave required the acquisition of one more document. I had never owned a passport, and this seemed a most appropriate time to obtain one. In due course, document number 643585, new, blue, hard backed, and proudly embossed with the Royal Standard, which informed the world that I was to be allowed to pass freely without hindrance, and to be afforded such assistance and protection as may be necessary, in the name of Her Britannic Majesty, arrived in the 280 post-bag.

The period of leave for which the passport was required was to be taken in Israel. With two buddies, the intention was to fly to Tel Aviv, find our way by bus northward to Galilee and to offer our voluntary services in support of the state, at Kibbutz Ammi'ad, which is located close to the northern shore of the Sea of Galilee. A visa would be required to permit entry to Israel, and document 643585 was duly despatched to the Israeli Consulate in Nicosia, returning shortly with the very first entry in my very first passport, a full-page indication of welcome to Israel. Exciting prospects for a rural lad from a northern rural fastness.

A short time before leaving, information from another 280 resident who had visited Tel Aviv somewhat earlier, suggested that bottles of whisky, available in the NAAFI at rock bottom prices, might prove lucrative items, if concealed among my baggage undergarments.

"You'll make a huge profit, and a guaranteed sale at any bar."

Though this kind of wheeling-dealing was somewhat beyond my sphere of experience, I accepted the word of my informant, and packed away a couple of bottles in my case. We lingered in Tel Aviv for two or three touristic days during which I peddled my wares up and down the length of Dizengoff Street, from bar to bar, cafe to cafe, but failed to find a single proprietor or bartender who was in the least interested in my cheap scotch. None was wasted or lost. We cut our losses and simply took it with us. It provided a late-night noggin in places where none was readily available.

From Tel Aviv we travelled north by bus to Tiberias, and from there to Kibbutz Ammi'ad, our haven of rest and very hard work for the following ten days or so. Our first few days were informative, enlightening, and inspiring. We were afforded a small house in which to live, our formal hosts were a British family, a couple with two young daughters, and the freedom of the kibbutz to familiarise with the surroundings and its citizens. Much later, I was to encounter that same family once more, in the unprepossessing surroundings of a cinema car park in Swindon. By chance we had both come to see the very first film of the James Bond genre. They had become disillusioned by the questionable future of kibbutz life and had returned to seek a future guided by the more familiar experience of the past. Away from its founding context, our rekindled relationship endured for a few months.

Initially, we became enthused and inspired by the collective ideology. We posed for photographs beside their monuments. We expressed our admiration for kibbutzniks, for their willingness to abandon an established way of life, to work collectively for the common good, and to seek little but subsistence in return. Theirs was a philosophy that was truly socialist, a doctrine of collective practice that demanded only dedication and hard work, which took satisfaction from mutual benefit, and which made no demand for personal advantage or commodity. Human nature surely could afford no guarantee of success.

Kibbutzniks were not paid. Every daily requirement from canteen to tobacco was provided. The food was wholesome, plentiful, but lacking in any gourmet variety. The provided cigarettes, 'Odem' by name, could well have been manufacture from shredded ragwort and camel dung. Life expectancy for the heavy smoker must surely have been perilously limited. Any additional requirements, clothing, new shoes, household goods, and cash for personal purchases, would be subject to application.

Theirs was a society of equality, with few divisions for gender, experience or ability. The first was merely a matter of biology, the others could be readily resolved by learning or experience. We welcomed our temporary membership of this youthful utopia, and joined the army of 'sabras' in their daily endeavours.

Their working philosophy was simple. Everyone made their equal contribution to every aspect of daily industry and social endeavour. There were, of course, exceptions. Only a few were trained and equipped to operate heavy machinery, drive the tractors, or to prepare the daily food, but these specific skills apart, work was directed by seasonal variation and by the weekly rota. Work was hard. The morning reveille for work in the fields came rudely at 03.00 for coffee and to commence work at 04.00. It concluded by around 11.00 before exposure to the rising temperature became unbearable. Huge numbers of chicken were raised in vast sheds, running free for meat production, or in cages where the end product was hundreds of eggs. Work in these buildings commenced a little later in the morning, but was a sweltering task in chokingly dusty and malodorous conditions. Working with other livestock was slightly less punishing to the senses, as it largely enjoyed the freedom of the open air. On a more domestic note, the kitchen and dining room provided daily for several hundred people, and while it was mostly self-service, the inevitable by-product was washing up and cleaning at industrial dimension.

The collective effort was not restricted to daily life, but applied equally to daily recreation. The not-so-rough and tumble of mixed team football was something of a novelty for three lads more familiar with the cut, thrust, and gravel of sporting endeavours at 280.

We worked, but we also walked the dry Galilean hills and valleys, sometimes together, sometimes alone, sometimes in the company of a fair young sabra. Sometimes we became lost in the labyrinth of stream-less valleys, and with only innate sense of direction to provide navigational aid, the glistering waters of Galilee's lake became a welcome beacon. Sometimes we encountered others of a different culture. Nomadic herdsmen and their families, whose sheep and goats required constant shifting in search of adequate fodder among the sparse vegetation. We always exchanged a friendly greeting. They always invited us into the shade of their canopy, and true to their tradition of hospitality, they never failed to offer us tea. Muslin and Jew living cheek by jowl, and far too preoccupied with the business of living to lock horns over little understood political or ecclesiastical differences.

Ammi'ad lies under the Golan Heights, perhaps uncomfortably close to the hugely sensitive border with Syria, and its residents were not unfamiliar with cross-border skirmish or the occasional incursion. Within walking distance was the Sea of Galilee, and lakeside banana plantations that claimed the world's highest productivity of the fruit. One day, we ventured to the ruins of Kefar Nahum (biblical Capernaum), unaware that the site actually straddled the border. The afternoon heat was oppressive, and cooling off in the lake seemed a good idea. We were without swimming togs, but there was no-one in the vicinity to offend, so we simply stripped off to seek skinny-dipping cooling relief. It was a long hobble across the shallow rocky shore until we encountered water sufficiently deep for immersion.

Refreshed, we began our return hobble, to observe a small group of young nomadic girls driving their herd of goats along the shoreline. Observing our clear discomfiture they stopped, sat down, and giggled. Then and very cheekily, they lifted our bundles of clothes, and placed them a short distance further from the shore. We had no alternative but to await the recovery of their composure, the cessation of their giggles, and the need for them to catch up with their wandering herd of goats. While our only disturbance was this source of considerable amusement, we were to learn later that the wife of a visiting diplomat had been shot dead while swimming at that same location only a few weeks earlier. Had we made our intentions known, we would have been advised not to visit this sensitive and hazardous location.

One evening, in the company of a group of Kibbutzniks we travelled to the hilltop town of Zefat, a short distance to the north. Here we were to listen to an open-air oration by David Ben Gurion, the Prime Minister. Although we understood not a word, except for a whispered summary, it was presence, and gesture, and charisma that conveyed the passion and the fervour of that evening and of his address. David Ben Gurion was small of stature and stocky of appearance. However, what he may have lacked in stature, he compensated in his huge and splendid shock of pure white hair. Not only did this enhance his eminence, he made excellent use of it as a means to emphasise a point, with equally gesticulating arms. He left his silent and awestruck audience in no doubt about the sincerity of his message.

Perhaps as a small gesture of gratitude, or perhaps simply because we were asked, we agreed to make a donation of blood to a visiting donation unit. The procedure was no less clinically sterile, and sensitively performed than earlier encounters in Britain, and procedurally far superior to experiences at Bridgnorth and elsewhere. However, despite our declared willingness, and several attempts by the team to locate a vessel willing to yield, not a single drop could be urged from either of our respective arms.

Time to leave Ammi'ad, and to explore a little more of the country before returning to the warm bosom of 280 SU. The public transport system was adequate for our requirements, and it ferried us to Nazareth, to Acre, and to Nahariyya before dropping us in the pleasing city and port of Haifa, where we found lodging in Karmel. For two or three days, we visited its places of interest and history, shrines and temples, and met a few of its cafe society citizens, of generation equivalent to our own.

Perchance, one of my buddies, perhaps in a moment of temporary sensory distraction, enquired if one of the young ladies of our recent acquaintance would care to accompany him in a visit to the pictures. In the common parlance of the day, this related to the cinema, not to some questionable exhibition of lurid art or images. She accepted and the date was fixed. The occasion was seemingly enjoyed by both parties, nothing of questionable morality or of cultural offence occurred, and in response to the courtesy of his escort, she invited him to meet some of her family. Alas for the innocence of youth and cultural enlightenment. Escorting, holding hands, meeting family, these simple gestures equated to an early proposal of marriage and engagement to this end.

On the following day, mercifully our final day in Haifa, we planned to take lunch at a restaurant that we had favoured, before heading for Tel Aviv. We had convened at the appointed place for a pre-lunch noggin, when a message was received from the family of yesterday's companion. The marriage was to be arranged promptly. Honour must be respected. Any failure to accommodate this would be met with severe retribution. The message left no doubt of the possible outcome of failure to comply, and by whom the retribution would be carried. Points to ponder over lunch, and before heading promptly for the bus to Tel Aviv.

Lunch in the sunshine of the day proceeded agreeably, outdoors but beneath the protective shade of a huge awning. While thus gastronomically engaged, and with startling abruptness, Karmel became engulfed by a fiercely dramatic and totally unseasonal thunderstorm. Amidst the celestial electricity, and the roar of its noisy cousin, the deluge was truly biblical. Our table was located centrally and directly beneath the rapidly increasing inverted rotunda that was the awning. In response to their observation of the inevitable, the staff were ushering customers from their tables, transporting their food into the interior of the restaurant, and relocating to tables within. Alas, their haste would fail to relocate the entire customer complement in time, and they urgently signalled that we should move. The stiff upper lip prevailed. A nudge. A glance. "We're British chaps." "Toujours la politesse." "Wait until everyone else is relocated before making our stately way to shelter." Finally, we signalled for our plates to be relocated. As we walked from beneath the awning, it split with a crack like a rifle shot.

Hundreds of gallons of water shifted tables and chairs as it hit the floor and surged in every direction. Our faces were pictures of smug superiority.

However, we left on the afternoon bus, and before the matrimony-seeking brothers descended demanding a dowry, a matrimonial commitment, or perhaps a human sacrifice. Our charabanc sped us away from unwitting commitment and unintending donation.

After overnight transit in Tel Aviv, an early train brought us to our final destination, and a brief visit to the more recently established portion of the city of Jerusalem. Politically divided cites are always places of lament and sorrow. Many urban locations are divided into cultural quarters in which religious rites, cultural events, dietary requirements, and traditional practices can be conducted in harmony. A politically divided city permits none of these things across the gulf of its sterile fracture. Walls, barbed wire, a broad avenue of demolition, a hideous no-man's-land of rubble, and a resentful, frustrated, unhappy human population on either side. Most of the old city, and the greater proportion of the historic and religious edifices and artefacts were located across that great divide, and were therefore inaccessible to us. Our opportunities were limited to the ascent of a few towers and steeples, to gaze across this dreadful and contrived wasteland to another place beyond, and to reflect on the folly of our species.

Even within the bounds of this more modern city, there were quarters where casual visitors wandered innocently, but at their peril if dressed for comfort and not on the direction of orthodoxy. The Mea She'arim district welcomes none but the compliant devotee, and rewards those considered improper with stones or water, even though innocence or accident had brought them into the range of undeserved hostility.

It had all been a journey of interest, intrigue, and enlightenment, but our time was out, 280 beckoned, and we were obliged to hasten back to 'Hell on the Hill' where the familiarity of daily life awaited.

It was the late winter of 1959 / 60. My association with the Royal Air Force was drawing to a close. Following repatriation in a few months, I would re-adopt the mantle of studentship, and relegate my intimate relationship with Cape Gata to the status of a memory. However, my honest manipulation (scam is such a vulgar word) of leave allowances, application forms, facilitated passage and the like, had apparently worked without question or hindrance, in spite of which, or perhaps because of, it appeared that a substantial portion of my leave allowance remained intact and unused.

Time, I mused, for a final journey of discovery. In the wake of my earlier visit to Israel and to Jerusalem, I harboured a considerable urge to visit Jordan, to find access to the old city, and to visit locations and features sacred to many religions. Equally, I was also very keen to make a final visit to Kibbutz Ammi'ad to bid farewell to the many friends that I had made on that campus a few months earlier. Therein lay the problem. I was aware that the scheme permitted travel to a nominated country, but equally aware that travel between countries was not permitted, and in any case would not be countenanced into Israel from any of its neighbours. Was I stymied? Was my grand plan to be abandoned before reaching the first hurdle? Well, maybe not.

I made application for a period of leave on a previously unused and unmarked leave form, and thus for a period that was modestly in excess of my remaining allowance. No questions were raised and the application was afforded the necessary seal of approval. That was the easy step. I then prepared two separate applications for assisted travel. The first was for an outward journey from Nicosia to Amman, Jordan, but via Beirut. To my surprise, this one found uncontested and unchallenged approval. With the ticket securely tucked away, I made a second application, this one for a return flight to Nicosia, from Tel Aviv. This too found approval, and with travel plans thus accommodated, I became faced with the task of resolving the greatest conundrum. How the hell was I going to make this work?

Just how these bogus applications had passed before the scrutiny of critical administration remained a mystery. It was a conundrum that I found no reason to question, and unless some eagle-eyed administrative zealot should perchance to espy the deception, all I had to do was to evaluate the likely success of my naive attempt to violate an international boundary that was steeped in on-going conflict.

I had created a shit or bust situation, a fanciful image in which I figured naively that I had nothing to lose. Dishonourable discharge? Seemed a bit extreme! Loss of privileges? Few and far between at 280! Extended jankers? OK! A spell in the guardhouse? Not likely to extend beyond my discharge date! Arrest and imprisonment for attempting the unregulated and unannounced crossing of a conflicted international boundary? Um! Cross that bridge when we come to it. Of course none of these dread impositions would apply if I managed my crackpot scheme successfully, and no-one became the wiser.

As my grand plan evolved, it became increasingly evident that my chances of success without major impediment were diminishing by the day. Entry into Lebanon, Jordan, and Israel would require the appropriate documents. As my passport contained an Israeli entry visa, I would be unable to use it to make entry into Lebanon or Jordan, or indeed to reveal it to the authorities while in those countries. As a serviceman, my RAF identity card, the invaluable 1250, was an acceptable substitute for a passport, and this I would use to obtain entry to my first two ports of call.

So this was my simple, and hugely improbable plan. Enjoy just a few days in and around Beirut, perhaps with a brief foray into the mountains, before proceeding to Amman. Make my way from there to Jerusalem and secure a base in that city, from which location, day tours by public transport would permit inexpensive visits to reasonably close locations of interest. On the appointed day, make my way to the point of departure, present my exit credentials, leave the country, head for the Israeli entry point, present my passport and visa, and... Job done!

The advanced planning process had, however, revealed a huge flaw, a loophole into which I would surely fall unless I could find the means to circumvent its deadly entrapment. The city of Jerusalem was not simply a divided city, but two quite separate conurbations partitioned by a zone of rubble and demolition some quarter of a mile wide. I had viewed this from an elevated position during my last visit, and should have realised that passing from one nation to the other required more than a document at a turnstile. The only crossing point was the Mandelbaum Gate, guarded against incursion, night and day, by the respective national militia and police. Crossing was only ever undertaken by diplomatic persons, only ever under driven and armed escort by UN militia, and only ever in pursuit of mediation or official business. Such crossings were intermittent, irregular, and subject to application at high level. What chance a lost wanderer?

It was clear that no amount of head scratching would ease the burden of this dilemma, and resolution, or a Jordanian jail, would have to await my arrival on the scene.

I booked my seat on the daily Pembroke to Nicosia, with a night in hand before heading for departure, and my few days in Beirut. 'The Jewel of the Eastern Mediterranean' was the manner in which this small country and its capital city were described in those days. That was until incomprehensible ideology blew it all to pieces. A popular tourist destination before tourism became a major industry, little Lebanon could offer beach sunbathing after breakfast, and top-class skiing after lunch in the mountains that dominate the horizon to the east. In my springtime visit, I did neither, but simply enjoyed a couple of days in a most relaxing city, and a single excursion to higher altitude among the cedars.

Time to move on and to head for Amman. But first to Damascus and a pause for reasons unexplained before re-boarding and increasing the passenger complement. Ours was an aircraft of modest proportions, seating for fifty or sixty people, and I was allocated an aisle seat. Adjacent and at the other side of the aisle was a gentleman who was clearly ill at ease. As we headed for take-off, he fidgeted and squirmed, was sweating profusely and muttering a succession of incomprehensible mantras, and seemed on the verge of some kind of panic attack. As we reached cruising altitude, he seemed to relax a little until we encountered a brief period of atmospheric turbulence. His panic erupted. He left his seat, ran back and forth along the central aisle, screaming and vomiting, and threatening major disruption. The cabin staff failed to subdue him, and it took several of us to pin him to the floor and hold him there pending a decision from the captain. A return to Damascus was decreed, and the unfortunate individual was 'escorted' from the aircraft.

He was followed by the rest of the passenger complement. A couple of hours passed, before the announcement that the intended flight to Amman would be delayed until the following morning. Some other, unidentified problem had occurred, and passengers were to be found accommodation for the night in Damascus. Morning brought the news that the 'problem' had not found resolution, and that Air Jordan were sending another aircraft enable the journey to Amman to proceed. Departure was not expected until the afternoon, thus providing the opportunity for a few hours of familiarisation in Damascus.

We were finally heading south in the early afternoon, and in an aircraft of dimensions similar to those of yesterday's failed vessel. I enquired of one of the cabin crew if it might be possible to take the small detour that might allow us to qualify for membership to one of the world's most exclusive clubs. The 'Below Sea Level Flying Club' was an Air Jordan initiative, and involved a qualifying manoeuvre that was permitted only by that company. In the interests of safety, aircraft size, and thus manoeuvrability, this was restricted to those of only modest proportions. Eligibility for membership requires a sustained period of flight at an altitude of at least one thousand feet below sea level. This can only be achieved over the Dead Sea, which lies at thirteen hundred feet below. Those were the days! The detour was requested, to which the captain readily agreed. At three hundred feet, the shimmering waters of the Dead Sea were in splendid late afternoon view.

Late arrival in Amman demanded lodging for the night before heading for Jerusalem the next day. A few spare hours in the morning permitted the flavour of central Amman, before an afternoon bus transported me westward, across the valley of the River Jordan just to the north of the Dead Sea shore, and into old Jerusalem in the early evening. The speedy discovery of relatively inexpensive accommodation was a relief, and as it turned out the slightly down-at-heel, but cheap and cheerful Jerusalem Hotel, was to provide a convenient base for my entire residence in the city. Located just outside the city wall, and only a few paces from the Damascus Gate, access to all points in the old city could not have been easier.

It had been reputed that a strong, tall, hugely monorchid student lived nearby, but I could find no mention or trace of him in the vicinity. Enquiry too of a reputable lady by the name of Kathusalem drew only the blank gaze of incomprehension. Most likely now in retirement from her life's endeavours, I thought perhaps to locate successors in feature, form and function. None were forthcoming.

The Jerusalem Hotel was owned by the family Ibrahim, and the son of the house, Tewfik, was a young man not much older than myself. He was a snappy- dressing young man about town, and he drove a white Volkswagen Beetle. I figured, with the establishment of a mutually agreeable arrangement, that Tewfik, and his carriage could possibly render me a valuable service in the days to follow.

I was keen to make best use of the few days that were at my disposal, and to this end, I became obliged to abandon any aspirations to make long and time-consuming journeys to the south of the country. Instead, I would make the Jerusalem Hotel my base, from which location I would use public transport to make single or part day visits to relatively close places of interest. Thus, I journeyed north to Nablus to commune with a good Samaritan or two on Mount Gerizim, to make communion with Jacob at his well, and to indulge in that splendid legacy of the Ottomans, the Turkish bath.

I wandered south to Hebron, there to bring greetings to Abraham and to Joseph. Once the oldest Jewish community in the world, now reduced to a few hundred in the city community, together with seven thousand or so in the adjacent township of Kiryat Arba. By comparison, the Sunni Muslim population numbers around 170,000. I made the short journey to Bethlehem, did my touristic thing at the Church of the Holy Nativity, and grimaced at the artificiality of the scene that becomes an annual portrayal in shop windows across the world in advance of the contrived season of irreverent over indulgence.

In Tewfik's little white beetle I travelled to Jericho where Joshua fought a battle and the walls came tumbling down. From there to indulge in salt assisted defiance of gravity in Dead Sea water that redefines the meaning of salinity. The satisfaction of a long held pipe-dream perhaps, though no great shakes for an aspirant snorkeler. The salty atmosphere followed as we proceeded a further few miles southward along this arid and encrusted coastline to Qumran and the caves that revealed many of the origins of Judaism, and perhaps the precursors of Christianity.

My remaining few days were dedicated to a personal exploration of the old city. On entering through the Damascus gate, I immediately entered the gloomy labyrinth that is the maze of interconnecting alleys, passages, arcades, and tunnels that entwine in a sinuous and mesmerising convolution that is the suq. Here is everyman's market place. A cornucopia of commodity for every purpose. A sensory bombardment that denies perception, confuses intellect, and thrusts consciousness into overdrive. Each street an avenue of alcoves, and within each alcove, a vendor, a tradesman, an artisan, a craftsman, or just someone minding the shop.

Many of the streets were dedicated to a specific art, craft, or profession - silversmiths, tailors, spice merchants, vessel makers, basket weavers, coppersmiths, and butchers. Others were an intimate mix of the providers of every other human requirement, bakers, coffee vendors, hookah hirers, dentists, shoe sellers, mystics, fortune tellers, pharmacists, herbalists and medicine pedlars, pilgrims, priests and self-flagellating ascetics. Most welcomed attention and were eager to demonstrate their craft, permit a photograph, or exchange a greeting, no doubt in the hope of a sale. Others were more reticent, and the butchers were openly aggressive. Theirs was an ill-lit charnel house of stench, blood, entrails, hacked-off limbs and heads, and dead, staring eyes. They resented my intrusion, and resented even more my attempts to record their practice on film. A cleaver raised threateningly in a bloodstained hand was sufficient deterrent, and I fled.

To add to the considerable charisma, donkeys roamed these narrow alleys, sheep were driven through to market or to slaughter, and goats were often mischief bound to disrupt the cacophonous harmony. The suq was a place of intrigue, a place of daily trade and banter, a place where all of the life of old Jerusalem was enacted on a daily basis, and for me, a place in which I was content to spend many hours. My pedestrian voyage of discovery into these dusty caverns enjoyed considerable additional enhancement because I was alone in my quest. Not for me the anonymous isolation of group visitation, nor the imperative monologue and urgency of a guide, but simply the untrammelled and uninterrupted delight of sharing with those who were sharing with me. My hours of simple communication without a common bond of language, were as many as I was able to accommodate in the time available to me, but inevitably, too few.

No less imperative were the many other sites and sights of this ancient city. Jerusalem has been, and remains the central hub around which the many sects and denominations of Christianity, Judaism and Islam revolve. It is the home and the temple of Christ, of God, of Jehovah, and of Allah. Nowhere else on earth are these four deities worshipped in the same backyard. I chose to visit them all. On the Temple Mount, I joined the wailers at the Wall, clad in borrowed robes of appropriate modesty, joined the shufflers in the Al Aqsa Mosque under the gleaming Dome of the Rock. I clocked off the fourteen Stations of the Cross along the Via Dolorosa, and paid my small homage at the Holy Sepulchre.

Close to station one on the Via Dolorosa, I encountered a deranged man who was apparently broadcasting his devotions to his Gods and to the passing public. In a small garden, atop a wall some ten feet above the thoroughfare, he raved, shouted and gesticulated wildly for several minutes before falling silent. He then stooped, picked up a bottle from his feet, and drank the contents. What was contained I was never to learn, but it must have been corrosive, caustic, or fearfully toxic. His death throes were hideous to hear, and though others at the same elevation rushed to provide aid or comfort, he had uttered his final homage long before he could receive the attentions of a priest to administer absolution or medic ease his fearful suffering.

Beyond the Golden Gate and the City of David, and across the valley of Kidron, the Mount of Olives provided a garden of peaceful delight. Here, many who have also arrived at their respective pearly gates have left their mortal remains at rest. The Blessed Virgin at Gethsemane, ancient followers of Judah in the Old Jewish Cemetery, all celebrated in the harmonious peace of Gregorian music at the Russian Orthodox Church.

What more appropriate place to conclude my celebratory tour of ecclesiastical harmony, than the Church of All Nations among the trees at Gethsemane. Having paid homage and respect to each and equally, how depressing thereafter to emerge into the sunlight, and to the rubble strewn spectre of man's inability to pay heed to the identical messages from his respective deities.

As I made my reflective, meandering way back through the city towards the Damascus Gate, I pondered my next necessary move. The time was fast approaching when I must make my bid for freedom and approach the task of broaching two international and insurrectional borders. Indeed, my enquiry of Mr. Ibrahim of the magnitude of my hotel bill made it clear that the time to flee was now. While the hotel bill was not excessive, I had seriously underestimated or overlooked the magnitude of my debt for my day of chauffeured luxury in Tewfik's beetle.

My brief intending residence in Israel would be inexpensive, little more than a couple of bus journeys to and from the kibbutz. However, I would need a little more than loose change, and continued residence at the Jerusalem Hotel would bring my financial resources critically close to the negative.

I packed my bag, settled my debts and made my farewells to the Ibrahim family early the following morning. My plan involved a stroll to the relatively close Mandelbaum crossing point, the presentation of my credentials to the Jordanian authorities, to be afforded a warm handshake and good wishes, and to pass on my way unmolested across the road to Israel. So much for best laid plans, like those of mice and men, this one was to quickly gang a-gley.

The road to the frontier gate ascended a modest incline, at the summit of which was located a guard building and a barrier, This short section of road was closed to vehicle and pedestrian alike, and access was prevented by an armed member of the militia. My approach was brisk, meaningful, and entirely incongruous. I was halted by the guard, to whom I showed my identity card, and my indication that I wished to continue. The fact that he spoke no English was of no relevance, as he simply thrust his rifle into my chest and indicated that I should return whence I came. Protestation was to no avail, and to avoid an international incident, or being shot, I retreated.

Time to reconsider. With very limited means of support, I could not remain in Jordan. Equally, and without the facility to leave the country in a more conventional manner, finding passage by some means had become a fairly urgent requirement. I lingered in the vicinity until I considered it likely that guard duty would have changed. This time, I walked up to the foot of the incline, elevated one hand to indicate my identity card and simply kept on walking. This time, the rifle muzzle was thrust firmly into the small of my back.

I turned and smiled apologetically, and while attempting to explain my identity card and my intended purpose, my captor remained unimpressed and impassive. No English again. During our confrontation, the muzzle of his rifle was pointing directly at, and was uncomfortably close to, a portion of my anatomy that had not yet, in my view, satisfied its entire life's purpose. We were at loggerheads, he pointing one way and insisting that I leave, and me pointing the other and indicating that I wished to speak with the duty officer.

I could not afford to lose this war of attrition, so I stood my ground, and indicated on his sleeve and my own that I wished to speak to the man in authority. At length he relented, and though he could not leave his post, he walked part way up the hill with me to indicate the appropriate entrance to the guard building. A small, if somewhat tremulous, victory.

To my relief, the officer of the day spoke a little English, and listened patiently while I spilled out my tale of woe - or at least most of it. He did not ask for any other form of identity, perhaps because his only course of action was inevitable. He explained what I already knew, and anticipated. There was no way that he could permit me to pass into no man's land, this could only be done with the blessing and the escort of United Nations Authority. Such passage was undertaken on an approximately weekly basis, and the last crossing was only two days earlier. I must return and attempt to seek the authority to cross.

Back in the city, I pondered my dilemma. I needed assistance, and with considerable urgency. None was likely to be forthcoming by sitting on the street, so I adopted the only course of action that I was able to bring to mind. I headed back to the Jerusalem Hotel, requested the use of their telephone, and made a pleading call to the British High Commission. After listening patiently to my sorry story, a sympathetic gentleman instructed that I remain where I was, that an envoy would collect me in a few minutes, and we would talk through the problem.

It was lunchtime, and on arrival my potential saviour kindly offered to take me to lunch. The lunch was memorable if only because it was the first time that I had eaten an entire roasted sheep's brain. He listened once more to my weary tale, and was absolutely candid in his response. He could probably pull sufficient strings to have my name added to the roster for the next UN escorted crossing. However that was likely to be several days distant. He was quite unable to take any steps that would guarantee a crossing today, tomorrow, or at any other time. However, he could go so far as to prepare a note on High Commission headed notepaper, affirming that I was a British citizen, that I was a Royal Air Force officer currently serving in Cyprus, and that I urgently required to cross into Israel before returning to my unit. He conceded that this was not very plausible, but perhaps it may assist.

We headed for the High Commission to prepare the paper, and after thanking him, I returned, somewhat timorously, to the Mandelbaum Gate. I met the same guard, and the same testicle threatening rifle. My identity card and the additional letter was sufficient passport for him allow me to approach the guard post. Once inside, same officer, same look of barely tolerant frustration, same gesture that indicated the clear message, "It won't make any difference".

He scrutinized my note, glanced once more at my identity card, and then at me. He simply shook his head. I sensed another oncoming rejection, and chose to circumvent it by playing a final card. It was a spontaneous decision on my part, and one that might induce a positive outcome, or possibly a death sentence. I handed him my hitherto concealed passport. Though neither anticipated outcome had been the immediate expectation, a kind of slow burning reaction prefaced a small explosion. His scrutiny of my passport was of somewhat longer duration than that of the High Commission note, and his reaction was an incomprehensible bi-lingual tirade. Only two entries graced the pages of my passport, the visa to enter Israel, and the visa, entry and exit stamps that clearly indicated an earlier visit.

Though apoplexy was averted, his bilingualism was well demonstrated in the outburst that followed. Part English, part Arabic, no doubt significantly profane, and a fusillade of words far too rapid for my comprehension, though I seemed to detect "my country" and "you will leave" somewhere in the mix. Somewhat taken aback at the apparent vitriol, I made no attempt to respond, but remained open mouthed and silent until the verbal barrage had subsided. After a few moments of calm he directed me to the door, where he barked an order to the current guardian of the barrier. The guardian duly raised the Jordanian frontier, and the officer pointed a finger silently toward the space.

I required a few moments of confused comprehension before I concluded that I had just been kicked out of Jordan, and I was being instructed to leave. I picked up my bag and walked into no man's land.

I didn't look back, but as I headed into the unknown, my confused emotions became subject to a rapid evolution. I had desired nothing more than peaceful and friendly passage across an international border. Instead, I had unwittingly become an enemy of the state and I had been booted unceremoniously into limbo. Any change of heart and return would not be entertained. I had not the faintest idea what the ensuing fifteen minutes or so would bring. I was stateless.

As I walked up the continuing shallow incline, I felt no victory or success. Initially, I felt hurt at being so unjustifiably wronged, but as the enormity of the situation in which I found myself became clear, and as the fog of confusion and uncertainty became ever more dominant, resentment was quickly replaced by apprehension, which in turn evolved into terror.

On either side rubble, and ahead the rising road, but with no destination in view. After a few hundred yards, and at the apex of the incline, the road turned fairly abruptly to the left, and through almost ninety degrees. For a few moments, at the apex of the bend I was no longer in view of my Jordanian oppressors, nor yet of my urgently aspired friends in

Israel. At that point of invisibility, and while surrounded by a wasteland of inhumanity, I sat down on a concrete pedestal and considered my situation and prospects. In a few moments, the Israeli guards would witness a small, lone figure, carrying a small brown valise heading from the enemy encampment and in their direction. It is likely that they will never before have encountered such a situation. I could only speculate upon their interpretation of this circumstance, and indeed their reaction. Will I find a welcome, or will I be shot as an out of hand precaution? Should I wave a white handkerchief to indicate the arrival of a dove and not a hawk? No responses to these urgent questions came out of the ether, and my somewhat parlous situation became clear. Once more, shit or bust!

Without a single alternative to consider, I picked up my little case, continued around the corner, and with resolution commenced the few hundred yards toward the Israeli post. No warning shots pinged off the road, no dramatic instructions to halt and raise my arms, no apprehension and instant arrest, indeed nothing dramatic happened at all. As I approached, half a dozen guards emerged from their post and leaned on the gate. A little closer and I could hear their comments and laughter, and it was only then that I began to appreciate the utter incongruity of my situation. Not a bustling land rover full of important people to be respected and saluted, but a solitary, slightly down at heel, somewhat dishevelled individual, carrying a small bruised suitcase, looking utterly forlorn and confused, and perhaps even seeking a friendly face.

On arrival at the gate, I was greeted, afforded a cup of tea, given time to provide an explanation sufficiently credible to find plausible entry into their daily log, and welcomed to Israel. At that moment, relief was a very large word indeed.

It was late in the afternoon, too late to find a bus to distant Tiberias, so accommodation for the night would be a requirement. Easiest would be the YMCA, but alas there was no room at the inn. There was no available stable in evidence, but thankfully, and if a little out of order, the YWCA around the corner were pleased enough to provide refuge. My presence in the morning did pose a few questions, a raised eyebrow or two, and even a few giggles at breakfast, but I did not intend to linger for long.

An early bus whisked me to Tiberias and to Ammi'ad, and quickly back into the routine of hard work and most tortured hours. However, my few days here were inexpensive and relaxing, in familiar surroundings and with equally familiar company. I was pleased to have made the effort, and run the gauntlet, and I was thus able to enjoy a final re-acquaintance before retracing my steps to the familiarity of the 280 routines.

However, this was not to be, at least not yet. After those few days of relief, of pleasure, and of the security of familiarity, another brief, unplanned and unexpected adventure awaited. It had been my plan to spend my two final nights in Tel Aviv, with no particular aspiration or plan, merely a final city stop before returning to the warm bosom of 280.

Accordingly, I made my farewells at Ammi'ad, and took an eastbound bus to the coast. A late morning arrival demanded a fortifying coffee while I pondered the question of accommodation. Resolution came from an unexpected direction. I fell into conversation with a friendly fellow in the coffee shop. We were from quite different backgrounds and life histories we each had a tale to tell the other, and thus, conversation extended into the afternoon.

During the late 1940's many followers of Judah had made illegal entry into Palestine on vessels of various kinds, most of which had sailed from ports on the Mediterranean coast of Europe and simply beached on the Palestinian coast. He was an American Jew who had served in the US navy, and had apparently captained one of these vessels from Marseille. He had run his ship aground somewhere to the south of Haifa. He now lived in Tel Aviv as a member of a commune, and I would be welcome to reside there during my stay in the city. I welcomed this gesture and opportunity, and happily accepted.

Unknown to me at that moment was the status and orientation of his commune, and it later transpired that it was party to a wider gay community in the city. Of course, at that time, homosexuality was illegal in Britain, probably equally so throughout Europe, and in all probability no less so in the State of Israel. This was of no concern to me. At no time during my brief stay did any of the members pose threat or expectation, and I lodged in their house simply as a guest.

My single intending day in Tel Aviv was without express purpose or aspiration. A day with nothing in particular to do, and all day in which to do it. That suited me well. At least, that suited me well for a while. I was enjoying the ambience of a morning coffee shop, with a few of my housemates, when we were joined by a hugely attractive, and astonishingly vivacious lady. She was clearly familiar with my companions, and after introduction, our morning conversation enjoyed the considerable enhancement of her irrepressible effervescence. I related to her a little of my travels, and of the Mandelbaum incident, which induced something of a chuckle. This, I explained was the final stop on my return journey to the RAF in Cyprus and to my unit.

"Ah!" she said, "My husband is an officer in the Israeli army."

"But," she went on, "you cannot spend your final day in the stuffy city. It will be very hot this afternoon. We will go for a drive. We will enjoy some fresh air, and you will see a little more of our country. I will pick you up at three o'clock."

And then she was gone.

Though I was more than a little nonplussed by the events of the morning, I was delighted to be invited to join this utterly charming, somewhat larger-than-life lady. I ensured my prompt arrival at the coffee shop. True to her word, she arrived at three o'clock, complete with car and driver. I joined her in the rear seat and off we went.

She was an amazing raconteur, and while I shared my earlier and present life with her, and indeed some of my aspirations for the future, her delightful conversation proceeded almost without interruption. That is not to say that it was, at any point, any less than fascinating, as she shared her life with me. She was British by birth, had been a model, was an actress, had enjoyed minor roles in a few screen presentations, and was presently understudying for the film 'Exodus'. She had been the first wife of Roger Moore, and had now settled permanently in Israel. I sat back and listened with a combination of fascination and amazement.

We headed northward up the coast to Netanya, where we paused to enjoy the sea air and an afternoon tea. She decided then that a tour of the hinterland would be a pleasant way to spend the evening. To this day I have no idea where we went, but our journey became a whistle-stop peregrination of villages and townships in most of which we found a bar and paused for a drink. There was neither space nor time in the back of the car for either hanky or panky, just her wonderful chatter and the passage of the countryside around us, at least until darkness approached

During each of our stops for refreshment, our driver sat dutifully in the car and awaited our return. I have no idea who he was, who owned the car, if it was a hired car or if it was a taxi, it really didn't seem to matter. Her company was an absolute delight, and while the onset of darkness curtailed our sightseeing, in no way did it suppress her enthusiasm.

"We will go to a nightclub," she announced.

My ineffectual protestations were as feeble as their intent. "My flight to Nicosia leaves very early in the morning, and perhaps we should not be too late making our return to Tel Aviv."

"You worry too much. We will be back in good time."

As we trundled on through the darkness, purposeful navigation adopted an increasing air of uncertainty.

"I know there is a nightclub around here somewhere."

Our impassive and long-suffering driver simply turned when he was told to turn, and came to a halt when thus instructed. Eventually we located a place that was buzzing, whether the intended one or not, and this became our destination. I was never great shakes on the dance floor, but after a couple more drinks, sufficient consciousness returned to shuffle for a while until imminent closure became apparent.

By now it was somewhere in the early hours, and the prospect of purposeful sleep before my necessary airport call, seemed somewhat remote. We were heading back towards the city, when she called abruptly to the driver.

"Stop! Stop here!" Our driver dutifully pulled up in front of a large well-lit building that bore the title 'Sheba Medical Centre'.

"Let's have a bit of fun."

With a few deft moves, and a couple of spare garments, my lovely companion transformed herself into a heavily pregnant lady, and taking me by the hand, demonstrated her theatrical art and competence. Though I must have been fifteen years her junior, I assumed the role of concerned father-to-be. Though our ruse did not last long, her portrayal of imminent motherhood was sufficiently convincing to motivate sleepy night-shift staff into action and preparedness for our happy event. It was all fairly good humoured, and happily, the staff all appreciated the jest. Perhaps it was just what they needed at a fairly dead hour of a very quiet night. They allowed us a cup of coffee before we sped off into the night.

Though we headed speedily toward the city, it was clearly too late to enjoy any restorative sleep. Instead, we headed for the community house, I collected my bag and left a note of thanks, and we continued to the airport.

"Thank you for your splendid company, and for a memorable day."
"Another time perhaps."

Alas, that was never likely to happen. And it didn't!

I checked in and dozed until my flight to Nicosia was called. At the top of the aircraft steps the greeting air hostess took my boarding card, and smiled.

"Thank you sir! Follow me please."

While the rest of the passenger complement were finding their seats, my hostess beckoned me to the front of the aircraft and into the first class cabin. I didn't understand, but I made no protest. I was travelling with Olympic Airways, and my assisted passage had permitted no more than the aerial equivalent of steerage. I sat tight in my stately home and lorded over the settling in of my fellow passengers.

As I did so, I became aware of boarding card colour differences. While every other passenger was clutching a green card, mine inexplicably, was a shocking shade of pink. I drew the conclusion that this had been a simple administrative error, committed during the sleepy confusion of very early morning check-in.

I was sufficiently content not to demand a return to my proper place in life. Mine was the exclusive use of the first class cabin, I enjoyed a positively sumptuous breakfast, stewardship service that did everything except powder my nose, and a complementary glass of champagne before arrival in Nicosia. Thank you Olympic!

Plenty of time to reserve passage on the afternoon Pembroke to Akrotiri, and then to find a truck heading for pastures more familiar.

"Did you miss me 280?"

It was my sincere hope that this had not been the case.

Chapter 8. Those well-earned moments of rest and repose.

... "Always playing on the village green." ...

*

To enjoy the ultimate in tranquil relaxation
or to seek a few undisturbed personal moments of quiet contemplation or inspiration,
we recommend a stroll through the colourful and extravagant
flora and fauna of our exotic gardens.

No effort, expense or endeavour is spared in the creation of these floricultural masterpieces
prepared as they are, to fill the evening air with nectarious perfume.

A little later in the year, gloriously coloured fruits appear among the blaze of flowers,
and provide for the needy, a source of valuable additional vitamins.

*

One of our most perilous subliminal adversaries at Cape Gata was boredom. Its undetected invasion into each individual psyche could, and did erode the rules of behaviour that governed and directed normal and acceptable human conduct, demeanour, and reaction. For some, the conflict within was insurmountable, and intense depression, to the point of suicide, demanded and required professional help, and posting to a less perilous location. For others, some even of a superficially mild temperament, aggression would erupt from the most insignificant of moments. Yet more became driven by psychosis to the verge of delusional insanity. Boredom lurked in the dark corners of the mind. It snarled at joke and gesture. It tormented when moments were tense, and it struck from behind at any misinterpretation of a jest. It was insidious, omnipresent, unpredictable, and psychologically destructive. It was with us all.

We, its victims, were young men. We had been deprived of creature comforts and the normal means to satisfy the urges of early manhood. We were engaged in a ceaseless war of attrition, with an unknown, unseen, and undetectable adversary. We had no priest to cast out our demons, no shaman to communicate with an alternative world, no trees to hug, and no nurse to sooth our fevered brow. In those early days of 1958 and 1959 we were simply imprisoned. The barbed wire barrier marked the edge of our daily world. Our sparse facility was that which lay within, the view beyond mostly out of reach.

How imperative, therefore, that we, the incarcerated, make best and maximum use of our individual and collective ingenuity. Thus, to combine, our skills, our abilities, and our inventive genius, to thwart the dark forces of boredom, to create an alternative world within our compound, and to ensure our continued sanity. This is precisely what most of us did.

The provision for our social well-being was limited. We had a cinema, which was well supported and used. We had a Navy, Army and Air Force Institute, (NAAFI to the drinking classes), and as the only social provision available to us, it was extremely well supported. In addition, each residential tent enjoyed the provision of a simple radio receiver. This provided us with audio contact with the outside world, and as our only regular source on information, it was in constant use. The BBC World Service, London Calling, and the local Forces Network, together with the contents of the occasional post bag provided our only source of information from beyond the perimeter wire. Apart from these, and to fill the long hours of idleness, programmed or contrived, we had only the products of our own creative invention, and the 'surplus' that came our way in its support.

Ours was a peninsular existence. Projecting in a southerly direction from the south coast of the island, the twin promontories of Cape Gata and Cape Zevgari, intrude into the blue waters of the Eastern Mediterranean. The slender Cape Gata was ours, and thus we were surrounded on three sides by our principle playground. Our particular patch of ocean was very close, though access to the cool caresses of Lady Med did require the safe descent of a crumbling, near-vertical cliff. Given a youthful excess of agility and energy, this imposed no greater obstacle than would have been encountered by an Alpine Ibex. We ran up, we ran down, we traversed its spiky ledges just for the hell of it, and we explored its many nooks, crannies, coves and caverns.

At the foot of the cliff, a perfect rectangular pool awaited each alpinist. Of several acres in surface area, partially enclosed to protect floaters, swimmers and divers alike from any troublesome swells from the open ocean, it enjoyed easy entry for the timorous and diving depth for the more venturesome. It supported a colourful miscellany of fish, molluscs, crustaceans and hydroids, anemones, polychaetes, various marine creepy-crawlies, and the occasional small octopus, all to entertain the more biologically minded. It was the kind of idyllic lido that leisure seekers of today might travel half the world to locate. Except of course, it had no beach, it had no ice cream parlours, it had no restaurants, it had no amusement arcades, it had no beach bars, it had no sun loungers, it had no barbeque pits, it had no lifeguards, it had no flower-bedecked maidens. It had an abundance of beach bums, but no bathing beauties - well, not many.

This exclusive maritime paradise was appropriately entitled '280 Pool' Not very original perhaps, but there had never been a best caption competition, and the local tourist industry was not particularly robust. Adjacent to the pool, an extensive, smooth, flat, rock platform provided a perfect arena for those who preferred to lounge in the sun. What more could we possibly have desired - perhaps just the occasional image of one of those illusory flower-bedecked maidens.

280 Pool, together with its attendant rocky platform was a magnet, a Mecca, a maritime honeypot that was an immensely powerful attractant, and which dispensed its unique order of hydrotherapy. It was a peaceful place, an oasis in a sometimes desert of frustration and discontent. It was invisible to the rest of the world, a place of sometimes peaceful mayhem or noisy solitude. It was an escape, a welcome bolt hole only yards from the invisible tedium of daily routine. Its provisions were as simple as you preferred, or as complex as you cared to make them.

It would seem likely, season and weather permitting, that almost everyone on the unit would have made regular, irregular or occasional use of this exceptionally fine swimming pool. By day, the rocky sun lounge was always littered with bodies. Night watch sleepers often preferred a rocky mattress to the sweltering microwave that the summer time tent had become. Off-duty days would frequently be frittered away in their entirety, with a book, a towel, a regular cooling dip, or a snorkel assisted scrutiny of the ocean floor. Evening or even the hours of darkness often witnessed an impromptu party, the ritual guzzling of a few bottles of Keo, or a bunch of beach bums serenading the moon.

For those of a more investigative nature, snorkelling somewhat further offshore would bring the rewards of larger denizens of the deep. Large groupers, moray eels, octopus, or even the occasional small shark, induced later tales of epic encounters with giants of the deep, and the occasional creature unknown to science or imagination. Just a few took to the use of vulgar and unpleasant harpoon devices, and sought the momentary accolade of trophy triumph, however small and pathetic. Some of these were added to the daily diet, which garnered some justification to the slaughter. A wonderful place to waste a little time, and equally so for those with an abundance of spare time on their hands. This of course, applied to most of us!

The geology of the cape is extremely porous, and another flat rocky platform, at the opposite side of the pool, carried features that attracted the inquisitive. This platform, which was permanently submerged to a depth of twelve or fifteen inches, revealed two or three vertical caverns that disappeared into the darkness. They were of sufficient width to permit access by a swimmer. Early tentative dives induced panic and rapid return to the surface. But then, emboldened by the foolish influence of curiosity, they were plunged to their nadir, and to relief, no lurking Kraken was encountered. From the sandy floor of the marine pit, it became evident that light was entering the cavern from a different source, and this was revealed as a horizontal extension to the cave that emerged some many yards into the distant open ocean. More air and a substantial infusion of additional courage or foolishness were required in preparation for the traverse of the flooded chamber, but every gurgling moment of progress through the tunnel brought rewards of enormous beauty. The roof of the chamber was deeply pitted and eroded, and every chink and depression glistered like mercury, reflecting light from a million trapped bubbles of air. The tunnel exited many yards off shore where the base of the cliff met the sandy ocean floor.

The pool was not without its dedicated industry. Materials that had become 'surplus' to daily requirement, or were just about to do so, were readily available, and could be recycled, re-designated or simply purloined. The necessary tools of industry enjoyed similar re-assignment. Timber could be sawn, shaped, formed and secured to create a frame or a shell. Tent canvas is a most versatile material, and can be stretched, secured, and painted or varnished, and when stretched over the earlier fabricated frame, a hull has been created. Mast or oars, the choice was yours, but while the good residents of 280 would never have claimed to have created a navy, a flotilla was well within their entitlement.

While seaworthiness was never a term that could be applied to these craft, they did float, though rapid capsize usually followed quickly on the heels of any attempt to climb aboard. For those aspirant sailors who aspired to utilize the wind, the lack of any form of weighted keel usually proved their undoing. Wind propelled rafts enjoyed rather more buoyancy success, but were completely lacking in any directional facility, and thus rarely left the confines of the pool. More successful by far were those vessels that could be loosely described as kayaks or canoes. Paddle power enjoyed a clear and distinct advantage over any other form of marine locomotion, and provided that the oft-encountered leak did not scupper voyage aspirations these vessels could, and did, venture further into the marine environment.

Alas the character and fragility of a naked canvas hull does impose flaw and weakness that will be exploited by the unforgiving ocean. The weight of the human frame imposes considerable stress upon the cockleshell skin, and any weakness is further exacerbated by the vibration of passage through the water. Any small hole or abrasion will suffer abrupt extension into a major breach, leaving the aspirant voyager still sitting in his stricken vessel, but with gunwales and the ocean surface now in perfect synchrony.

Though these shipbuilding ventures were usually the outcomes of personal ingenuity and endeavour, their use was not jealously guarded, and much in line with the shared character of most of the facilities on the station, fairly free use was made of them by other marine explorers. Thus it was, on one idle day, that I was joined by a companion, and together we commandeered two of these fine vessels, and headed out of the haven of the pool and on to a fairly benign ocean. Our intended voyage was to take us in a southerly direction along the coast, as far as the rocky extension beyond the lighthouse that is the promontory of Cape Gata, and to return, replete with the memory of a voyage no less adventurous than those of any latter-day Captain Cook.

That southerly extension of the coastline is heavily indented by a series of narrow, rocky inlets and coves, mostly not suitable for landing, and just a single, more generous bay and beach known as Sharks Cove. We paddled lustily for a mile or so, to a point just to seaward of the lighthouse, a short distance from the rocky point of the cape, and with the Nile Delta the next landfall to the south. At this point we made the decision to return. At a little more than a third of the distance to our destination, and with the potential havens of Sharks Cove and the narrow defile of Fisherman's Cove well behind us, we found ourselves at the mercy of a sudden, unexpected, and extremely vigorous squall. A strong wind quickly whipped the surface of the sea into choppy mayhem, and increasingly large incoming swells were clearly far in excess of the structural or navigational capacity of our flimsy craft. Capsize, swamping, or structural failure at this location would have been terminally hazardous, and as all three seemed well within the bounds of probability, we required a rapid alternative strategy.

We made the decision to seek shelter in one of the narrow nameless inlets until the squall had passed and the sea surface had returned to a more navigable condition. One such cove was within ready reach, and seemed to be a small harbour of more placid condition. We paddled in that direction. On arrival it quickly became clear that it was no less affected by the incoming swells, and if we had become trapped inside the narrow inlet, our vessels would surely be dashed to pieces against the rocky walls.

Our salvation, and now our inevitable destiny, was borne forward in the swells themselves. Each of the alarming walls of water, rose above and flooded a rocky platform, and drained it to exposure once more at each backwash. I proposed that we each choose a swell, ride it on to the platform, and make fast somehow to avoid being taken by the backwash. We could safely stow the boats beyond the platform. I manoeuvred my craft to a position that was broadside to my chosen incoming swell, reasoning hopefully that the broadside would lift the boat bodily and not simply capsize it. I was afforded an exhilarating lift, a thump as I hit the rock, and a clear threat of backwash into the water. Happily, my swell had not been too powerful and I contrived successfully to seize the rock and to secure my precarious position.

Having shifted my canoe to a position beyond the water, I signalled for my pal to follow and to adopt the same procedure. This he did, and with initial success. However and alas, his chosen swell harboured far greater malevolent energy than had mine, we were quite unable to secure his canoe and he was swept back into the wash. The volume of water that had landed on the rocky platform had been huge, and so great was the power of the backwash, that it created a monstrous gulf twixt rock and water. Into this pit was swept both canoe and its occupant, and for a few terrifying moments I was gazing into the watery abyss, with him sitting helplessly between a vertical wall of water on one side and one of rock on the other.

This was no less a moment than the biblical parting of the Red Sea, though I suspect that Moses may have enjoyed greater confidence than I about the outcome. I fully expected that the water would simply close the gap and engulf the hapless and unfortunate occupant. Not so however, the craft remained upright, and he popped to the surface like a rising cork as the next incoming swell filled the gulf. This more modest incomer deposited him securely beside me on the platform. We hauled our vessels to a secure location, and as the squall showed no sign of abating, we took a more diplomatic terrestrial route to the relative security of the unit.

A short distance along the coast in the opposite direction, but just around the corner from 280 Pool, a huge sea cave had resulted from millennia of relentless erosion of a geological fault. The process had created a cavern of intimidating proportions and terrifying demeanour. When the ocean was in benign mood, gentle swells would roll in through the mouth of the cavern, and a profound and angry boom would roar out in response. When whipped up by climatic tempest, the sea would hurl huge waves into the maw, and the roar that emerged would have struck terror into the heart of St. George. Here, in its depths, for sure the Kraken did live.

Only a short swim around the rocky corner from the pool, I had often approached when the sea was gentle, and the noise from within was akin to a snore, and comfortingly suggestive that the Kraken was sleeping. Until much later, when I had plucked up sufficient courage to enter the monster's domain, the depth and dimension of the cavern remained unknown, only its voice gave hint of caverns measureless to man. On that flat calm day when curiosity had vanquished foolish trepidation, I swam cautiously through its yawning portal, and into the dragon's lair. Even the gentle swells of the day induced a low rumbling from within, and induced a rippling shudder. On into the darkness, urgently dispelling the irrational fear that at any second, some tender part of my anatomy would be seized and would become a tasty morsel. Within, the walls of the cave converged, and the roof sloped steeply towards the surface of the water.

A relatively small rocky aperture marked the entrance to an inner cavern. The irrational once more crept into my consciousness.

"Oh my God", I thought. "I hope the bugger is asleep."

Once through the entrance, I sought the support of the cave wall until my vision had adjusted to the gloom. The inner cave was substantial though not huge, perhaps even smaller than the Kraken's angry roar would indicate. As the limited reflected light slowly permitted me to discern detail, the dimensions of the dragon's lair became apparent. I had entered a rocky dome perhaps ten feet from apex to water surface and somewhat more than that in diameter. I began to comprehend the dragon's roar when the sea was angry. As the swells made entry to the outer cave, their latent energy became increased as the body of water was thrust towards the inner entrance. Restricted entrance would induce the roar, as the chamber rapidly filled and the air within was forcibly excluded. Once capacity had been reached, and now under pressure, the water would exit once more, this time in explosive manner as energy became dissipated and dispersed, and the Kraken's rumbling dyspepsia burped forth.

Some months earlier, and not too long after arrival, two of us had wandered along the cliff from the pool to the rock ledge that formed the outer lip of the roof of the big cave. From that point to the surface of the water is a drop of around thirty feet. We looked down at the clear water below, and then to each other.

"I dare you," I said.
"I will if you will."
"OK! You go first."
"Maybe not! You can go first."

This pointless dialogue continued until stalemate.

"OK'. I said. 'Let's go together."

Neither of us had any idea of the depth of the water. Equally we had no idea of the nature of the sea bed at this point. Sandy or rock? It looked clear and smooth, but through an unknown depth of water, it could have been either.

There was a moment of hesitation as we removed our shoes and outer clothing and left them for later collection.

"Geronimooooooo!!!!!!"

We left the rock together, and entered the water with equal simultaneity.

On entry, I flexed my wrists to present my palms to the water thus slowing my descent and ensuring a shallow dive. Not so my fellow diver who continued his plunge until he hit the bottom. Happily, he ended his descent in the yielding softness of a sandy sea bed, and he surfaced, smiling broadly, shortly after me.

Diving from these rocks and even from the rim of 280 pool did not always enjoy the same satisfactory conclusion. One recent arrival, overwhelmed perhaps by the euphoria of it all, took a plunge into the pool without first checking depth and submerged hazards. The top of his head made heavy duty contact with a rock, and at an angle that stripped away a substantial proportion of his scalp. With copious quantities of leaking blood, and with a towel in place in an attempt to keep his detached scalp where it should have been, he was assisted to the top of the cliff and to medical help. He, and his scalp, recovered and returned to dive another day.

To my knowledge, only one individual endured a comprehensive fall from the cliff path. He was making the ascent when he slipped or stumbled, failed to recover his equilibrium, and fell to the rocks at the head of the pool. Though seriously injured, and requiring helicopter rescue, he survived, his fractured bones healed, and he too rejoined the party, though somewhat later.

Given the sometimes copious consumption of Keo, especially at evening poolside parties, it was perhaps somewhat astonishing that a greater number of hapless souls did not endure similar mishap. One contrasting event introduced hazard of a very different character. One individual had been making it known how unhappy he was at 280, how much he hated the place, and how much he desperately wanted to find posting elsewhere. In the darkness of one nocturnal poolside shindig, he was once more bending every ear with his relentless lament. As usual, no-one was taking any notice. Suddenly, he was missing, and clearly no longer with the poolside party. Amid the speculation that he may have returned to the unit, and quietly gone to bed, a splash was detected just beyond the sea entrance to the pool.

He was hailed from the closest terrestrial point.

"What the hell are you doing?"
"I hate this chuffing place. I'm leaving,"

"Where are you going?"
"I'm going to swim to chuffing Egypt."
"Egypt is 200 miles away."
"Don't give a shit, that's where I'm going."
"You'll never be able to swim that far."
"Yes I bloody will."
"You are heading in the wrong direction. Egypt is the other way. Turn around."
"Bollocks."

He was clearly not to be deterred or to be dissuaded from his foolish and potentially catastrophic escape plan. There seemed little choice but to attempt to head him off, and to persuade him to turn back. Three or four of the strongest, and least intoxicated swimmers took to the ocean, and fairly quickly overhauled him. At this point, the marine equivalent of the slightly earlier dialogue was repeated, with the continued stubborn refusal to abandon his Egyptian odyssey. At length, perhaps the cold was beginning to induce sobriety, or perhaps he had become finally convinced that the Egyptian coastline was in fact only a few hundred yards distant in the opposite direction he relented, and was escorted back to landfall.

One further hazard awaited the unwary, and one that was afforded official recognition and alert. Every new arrival was made aware of the power the sun and of the hazard and probable effect of prolonged or unwary exposure. Indeed, careless or foolishly contrived sunburn of severity that required medical attention was a chargeable offence. Thus, it could never be used as a clinical skive. One unfortunate individual, recently drafted in from a home base, and resident on the unit for only a few days, found a quiet cliff top location to engage in a little afternoon sunbathing, and to begin to dispel the inevitable 'moonie' stigma that haunted every new arrival. Face down on his towel, he unfortunately fell into a deep sleep. This was high summer, and when he awoke, in considerable agony, his back had become partially cooked. In a remarkably brief period, he had become so severely burned, that most of the skin on his back had become raised in a single huge blister. He was in deep medical trouble, and his recovery subsequently required prolonged hospital treatment.

The entire Akrotiri Peninsula, embracing Cape Gata and Cape Zevgari, though neither entirely nor securely enclosed, was designated sovereign territory. While much of the hinterland comprised dense, spiky, snake infested bundu, and thus did only rarely feature in our daily perambulations, it was not without its archaeological interest. Fairly extensive ruins of an early monastic establishment provided location for prospective scratching among the dust and rubble, though the discovery of human remains, evidence of forbidden ritual, rare jewellery, or an enormous hoard of monk-purloined coins of enormous value were never reported. Most of what remained was confined to gloomy subterranean chambers, the considered habitat for the peninsula's venomous viper, and were thus entered only by the bold and with some trepidation. The cliffs, the coves, the cape, the sea, and the pool remained our principal daytime playgrounds.

The hours of darkness found provision for a no less popular, and equally well attended venue.

On my arrival in 1958, the NAAFI provision was housed in an old marquee, and its management entrusted to an equally ancient gentleman of Egyptian nationality. Known affectionately, but probably inaccurately, as Mustapha, it seemed that he had been in service with the British military for many years in his native Egypt. In 1955, when the British withdrew from the Canal Zone, it appeared that Mustapha had simply accompanied them to Cyprus, as part of their baggage, and there he had remained. Sadly for him, civilian employed staff had become implicated in a number of attacks on military bases and on personnel, resulting in the banishment of all non-British civilians from British installations. Mustapha had to go. He was inconsolable and he made his departure to the accompaniment of much lamenting on both sides. We could only speculate upon what became of him.

Without a manager, it would have been necessary to impose closure upon this invaluable facility and resource. Protestation about this lamentable situation, brought about an agreement that the NAAFI could remain open, for agreed and limited hours, if daily management was undertaken responsibly by volunteer airmen. In their own time of course, thus avoiding any prospect of an additional avenue for illicit skiving. This interim arrangement would operate pending the appointment of a British civilian as permanent factotum, and terminate immediately thereafter. It was conducted on an agreed free-time 'shift' basis, and not only did it work well, it opened up tiny opportunistic windows, and modest 'perks' for those who had selflessly offered to dedicate their time to the service and well-being of the wider community. This may also have been the birthplace of a more enterprising endeavour and the inauguration of lucrative sidelines that fall into the deserving ambit of the willing volunteer.

At around this time, we were eagerly awaiting the completion of a permanent building, which had been under construction alongside the marquee for some time. This was to be our brand new, sparkling NAAFI, and a welcome replacement for the dusty and grubby marquee. When finally inaugurated, late in 1958, it was indeed a vast improvement, and in many respects, it brought transformation to our very limited social lives. Our working watch system allowed freedom from duty for around one third of the station complement on every day of the week, and no evening would pass without the foregathering of a NAAFI crowd. In our purpose built tavern copious quantities of Keo beer were washed down by more copious quantities of Keo beer, all to a noisy but cheerful accompaniment.

Given any gathering of human kind, of complement akin to that of 280 SU, it will surely represent a complete and comprehensive cross-section of human society. Cape Gata enjoyed the benefit of a huge range of profession, skill, ability, interest, passion, and every aspect of human character from the absurd to the academic, from the timorous to the ostentatious, from the gregarious to the aloof. This diversity of character and this multiformity of humankind, were essential elements that contributed much to our retained sanity. Our daily assemblies in the NAAFI bar brought out the best and the worst of these attributes and individual idiosyncrasies, and frequently, aided and abetted by the courage of Keo, these would be broadcast to the assembled throng, and anyone unfortunate enough to be within hailing distance.

The 280 community of souls could boast a small number who were tolerably skilled musicians. With the available miscellany of instruments, guitar, clarinet, saxophone, trumpet, a bongo bucket, and the imperative one string tea chest double base, they could bang out a recognisable tune. There were also those who sang. Very few could, just a few thought that they could and did so despite the relentless barracking, and an additional small number of aspirant participants definitely could not. This latter group normally only took to the stage when both they and the audience had reached fairly advanced stages of inebriation, by which time it mattered very little whether they were able to sing or not. Individual performances at this stage of the evening proceedings were generally quite brief.

The intending entertainer would arrive at the microphone and fail to remember why he had taken these few steps towards a howl of derision. Equally, he may arrive there and would simply forget the opening line, or indeed the title of his intended song. During delivery ill-advised attempts to emulate some Elvis-like gyration frequently resulted in entanglement with an item of furniture or the microphone cables and perform instead a noisy descent to the floor. The orchestra might strike up with the requested tune, and the aspirant singer would eventually join in with another one. Having risen to his unsteady feet, and lurched as far as the microphone our bleary-eyed Perry Como might abruptly realise his urgent need to be elsewhere. Late evenings in the NAAFI bar were rarely edifying but never dull.

The rules and regulations that guided drinking at the NAAFI bar were not writ hard and fast upon a tablet of stone. Hours of opening were flexible partly to accommodate the all-hours watch system, and partly because strictly designated hours would have simply been ignored. However, the merry bunch of boozers were obliged to afford respect to the civilian manager, whose solitary station behind the bar demanded long and tolerant hours, and when he gave usually generous notice of intending closure, his word was accepted as the law.

However, this did not necessarily impose termination upon the Keo-sodden activities. Bottles were purchased up to the maximum level of portability, transported to a selected tent, and the party continued. Such tent-based choral orgies were frequent, could occur at any time between nightfall and insensibility, and were always fearfully noisy. Tents that accommodated three sleeping residents, and which were uncomfortably crowded when everyone was at home, became the venue for thirty or more inebriants, all at various stages of becoming more so. At each and every one of these shindigs, the entire repertoire of songs and ditties of indescribable vulgarity was bellowed into the night air. While 'Little Angeline' must have been familiar to the good citizens across the bay in Limassol, equally so, the entire residential complement of Akrotiri must have been aware of the extraordinary proclivities of 'The Lady of the Manor'.

Those more honest souls within the encampment and vainly endeavouring to find much needed slumber, were treated on these occasions to a discordant cornucopia of astonishingly insomniac lullabies. Melodies of seashore dogs and rooftop cats; of remarkably disproportionate anatomical anomalies; of a civic gentleman with an uncommonly hirsute daughter; of a tardy ecclesiastical campanologist; and of the lovely Tallulah Johnston Black. The Keo minstrels resonated with songs of circus life and extraordinary animals; of camels, of hedgehogs, of crocodiles, of oomigoolie birds, and of lost pygmy tribes. The nocturnal glee club sang songs of lament, of Mr. Banglestein who kept us waiting in Mobile while his sister Lily was moved to consider that it was all such a bleeding shame.

Far into the night, the strains of these lovely old traditional refrains regularly filled the air, and echoed twixt the tents and down the lines. Remarkably perhaps, not an officer, nor an NCO ever ventured into this discordant choral arena to put a stop to it all and to allow the more worthy to get some sleep. Perhaps the cacophonous cantillation of the night was sufficiently screened by the centrally located buildings, to ensure that their snug residences were somewhat less prone to disturbance by the horrors of anal strictures and the occasional prolapsed womb.

Ah! The pure joy of 280!

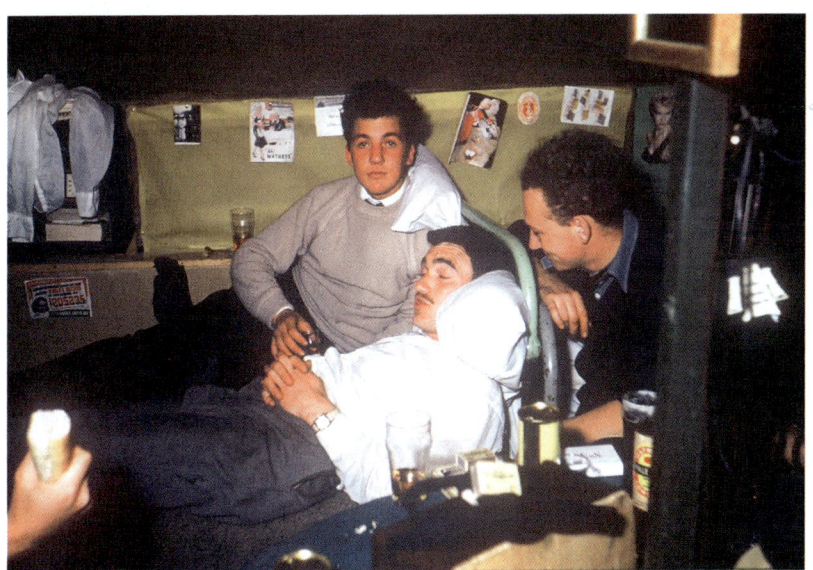

Of course, our life of leisure was not simply one prolonged and uncontrolled Keofest. Other pursuits included the regular exchange of books, which embraced a wide range of subject matter as well as a huge selection of fiction. The unit did not enjoy the services of a library facility, but there was a book depository in the cinema that was available to all. I guess that some of the guys probably read more during their time at 280 than they did during the remainder of their lives. No-one hoarded books, which freely, readily and frequently changed hands. For a time, I formed an attachment for the dark and sinister writings of Dennis Wheatley, and the ghastly and ghostly peregrinations of Gregory Sallust, Simon Aron and the Duc de Richlieu. These volumes may have promoted the germination of a distraction that was to follow.

Some, myself included, were destined to return to further education or professional study following demobilisation, and for many, studies were not neglected. I could not, in honesty, claim that I dedicated too much time to my future professional enlightenment, but a little vocational reading helped to keep the brain cells alert. One small and select group convened irregularly, ostensibly to discuss, to debate, and to think great thoughts for the benefit of all mankind. They afforded themselves the title of 'The Bowery', though the designation remained obscure. Historically an area of Manhattan dominated by saloons, dens of iniquity, petty criminals, and derelicts, where anti-Catholic and anti-Irish prejudice became manifest, or even more historically a derivation of the Dutch word for a farmstead. As neither of these applied, it was assumed that the principle subject of debate were the merits of Keo, relative to every other available tipple.

The cinema was an extremely important recreational facility, and the only official entertainment provision. The building had been constructed for the purpose with stage, projection room, and facility for the sale of limited refreshments. This latter was run along very similar lines to the technical site canteen, and it is alleged that it too was a 'nice little earner'.

Films for our screening made somewhat irregular arrival at 280, and thus no regular and predictable programme was in publication. This was of little consequence, a buzz would quickly circulate the unit when a screening was due, and to accommodate the watch system, this would be repeated several times before the film was relinquished. Screening almost always followed the same pattern. A couple of short films, frequently cartoons, and perhaps a current news feature, would precede the showing of a feature film. Feature films were many and varied to suit all tastes and preferences, comedy, adventure, crime, musicals, westerns, a little swashbuckling, and even the occasional swoony romance. Inevitably, this latter category was usually accompanied by ribald remarks about what to do with various articles of feminine attire at critical moments of heavy breathing - never included in films of the fifties of course.

The most popular cartoon features were those involving the antics of Tom and Jerry, frustrated tomcat versus wily mouse. These film were of American origin, the production of which was credited to a man with a slightly unfortunate name. The plaudits always appeared in advance of the story line, and in full screen for the acclaim of the producer.

PRODUCED BY
FRED QUIMBY

The howl from the crowd was inevitable and immediate.

"Wey-Hey Fred." "Good old Quimby." "How's your quim Fred?"

Thus the banter and genitalesque hullaballoo continued until the reel was changed and the opening sequences of the feature film flickered on to the screen.

I clearly recall one such occasion when Fred had faded from the screen, and the pre-title, pre-credit sequence had commenced. The feature of the day was the Hammer Films production of Bram Stoker's 'Dracula'. This was the first of the genre, and for aficionados, probably still the best. To the accompaniment of Hammer's most melodramatic, blood chilling, ghoulish, cymbal clashing overture, the opening sequence featured a coffin with great gobbets of blood splashing on to the lid. During these first few minutes, the cinema was shrouded in a cloak of total silence, and nothing interrupted this uncanny and unfamiliar stillness until a heaving, bodice-clad bosom reignited the mood and the levity.

For a time, and for the interest in so doing, I volunteered my services as an assistant projectionist, but it was also to find access to a considerable store of archival material that was tucked away in the projection room. To describe it as pornographic would be inaccurate in the conventional and usually accepted sense of the term. It was mostly footage that had been taken during the conflict of the Second World War, and it was clearly not for public viewing. Graphic in the extreme, it was a stark reminder of something called inhumanity for which people like me had been wearing its regalia for centuries. Most shocking were the scenes of brutal execution, illustrating the power of ideology, however misguided, that would direct someone like me to pull the trigger, to thrust the bayonet, or to wield the decapitating samurai blade on someone else, also just like me.

In this age of escalating ideological tension, of increasing extremes of sectarian violence, of religious and ethnic bigotry, of an increasingly over populous and unsettled world, should images such as these become obligatory viewing or should they be removed permanently from the public domain? Better not to go there perhaps.

We locked them in the cupboard and left them there.

Though it was an enormously valuable recreational asset, our cinema compared most unfavourably with the up-market and much more sophisticated 'Astra' at Akrotiri. Our single projector whirred manfully, but reel changes imposed tedious breaks in transmission, and our lens projected an image of limited proportions. The news that we were to be delivered of a new lens was welcome indeed, but even more so was the information that it enjoyed far greater projecting versatility, and we would thus be able to enjoy screenings in 'Cinemascope'.

The lens arrived and was lovingly fitted to the projector. The house was full to capacity to experience this innovative piece of technology, and to enjoy full screen capacity. Perchance, the first film to be shown was a classic western. The lights were dimmed, Quimby was despatched, and our first, eagerly awaited screening in 'Cinemascope' flickered into life.

But hang on! What? Heads turned from left to right to left in stunned incredulity. The scope in 'Cinemascope' had far exceeded our aspirations, or indeed the capacity of the cinema. Not only did the image fill the screen completely, such was the scope and the imagery of the lens that the picture extended far beyond the limits and the dimensions of the screen. Indeed, it occupied about one third of each of the adjacent walls. OK! The walls were conveniently painted white, and if a visit to the cinema included a gratis workout for the neck muscles, could this be considered a bonus.

Well! Maybe, but for one small detail. The upper walls of the cinema had been fabricated from corrugated metal sheets. On this first occasion we watched in patient amusement as our hero and his cohorts undulated on horseback across the serpentine corrugations. What could we expect in the future? Severe motion sickness during high speed motor pursuit. Villains concealing themselves from the pursuing police behind a corrugation. Battle scenes in which weapons do shoot around corners, passion scenes in which coitus interruptus adopted an entirely new and novel meaning.

A distant, but more sedate relative of cinematography perhaps, still photography had been a passing interest while I had been at school, mainly using an ancient Brownie Box camera, and an equally elderly folding bellows Kodak. At 280, an earlier generation had constructed a small building and had fitted it out as a very functional darkroom. I made purchase of a small single-lens reflex camera, a Dacora Dignette if memory serves, and made early attempts to hone my limited photographic skills and to learn the techniques of photo development. Initially this provided a valuable additional interest, but with the benefit of increasing familiarity, I began to view the possibility of a small business venture. All of the film and darkroom materials that I would require were readily available at the Akrotiri pharmacy, and these included a range of professional photographic tints.

From a cliff-top location on the cape, I had taken a single picture of a sunset. As a black and white print, this produced a passable image. However, I discovered that by making eight successive single-stop adjustments to the enlarger, the process allowed me to produce eight pictures of the same image, in a sequence of gradually increasing darkness, and to pass this off as the progression of a genuine sunset. Colour film was unavailable or difficult and expensive to obtain at this time, but by making use of the photographic tints, I could produce a very passable eight stage colour sequence of 'Sunset at Cape Gata'. I am no artist, and it took time and practice to perfect this small spoof, but once I had perfected my brush strokes, I could knock off a series of eight in a couple of hours.

A limited market, but they sold like hot cakes for a while.

The internal forces radio broadcasting service was attractive to some who would aspire to serve behind the microphone or as broadcast compilers. Indeed, in celebration of

Christmas, all units were invited to enter a competition to sponsor a chosen radio programme, and to become involved in its production and broadcast. To its considerable credit the contribution presented by 280 SU in support of the 'Wireless for the Blind' initiative, won the accolade for the best radio presentation in the Christmas 1960 competition. It presented an hour-long programme in a successful bid to raise £2000.

To a young man of the greenwood, the burden and the urgency of carnal endeavour can find some relief in alternative forms of biological undertaking. Modest horticulture is well known for its capacity to soothe the savage breast and to calm the turgid gonad.

The small area of open ground between the interconnecting concrete path and the front of each tent measured some twelve feet by around six or seven. This was bisected by the short concrete path leading to the door, which left two areas of dusty soil, each about six feet square, and which could be extended, without trespass, to the limit of the guy ropes. It would require a very fertile imagination indeed to create even a bonsai image of these two little patches of earth as rolling wooded hills or verdant pastures, but with a little horticultural determination, perhaps something green could be coaxed into life. 'Out of the strong came forth sweetness', as the saying has it. Perhaps conversion to 'Out of the dust there came forth greenness' could be considered an appropriate substitute.

It was clear that a garden of this magnitude and magnificence was hardly going to require a complex management plan. Equally, it took no more than a casual glance at the two patches of grubby and apparently lifeless dust to appreciate that a few additional facilities would be required before the Hanging Gardens of Paradise Lost would come into being, and Nebuchadnezzar would be bringing Amylis to tea to seek advice for his own pendulous endeavour. Tools of the horticultural trade were unknown at 280, but this omission could readily be rectified by the liberation of sundry items from the cookhouse. The total lack of seeds or any other form of ready propagation would require a little investigation. Water would be required in fairly copious quantities, but this could be carried from the bowser, or in second-hand form from the ablutions. Organic enrichment however did pose a bit of a teaser. The natural soils of Cape Gata are thin, and overlie porous limestone. In the natural world they support sparse grass, and dense spiky bundu, both of which are tolerant of long periods of drought. When this is stripped away, the environment is left with my unpromising garden substrate - dust.

As cultivation on Cape Gata was unknown, available compost or any other form of organic enrichment occupied a similar rarity niche as teeth in a chicken. To obtain decomposing organic material from the only local source available to me would be to commit an offence so heinous that I would probably find myself heading whence it came. To make my own would have been the obvious solution, but without the basic raw material, where to start posed a serious dilemma. The hard, waxy, xerophytic leaves of the bundu scrub would require an entire season to rot down, would require tons to make ounces, and would make lousy compost anyway. The solution was closer to home. Kitchen waste included an abundance of cooked and uncooked fruit and vegetable, ideal composting material, if only there was available and acceptable space in which to pursue this honest undertaking. Alas, ready availability was lacking!

My solution was simple in the extreme. I merely excavated a surface layer of soil from my two patches of ground, set this to one side until I had filled the holes with a colourful melange of cabbage, banana, onion, potato, beans, carrot, tea leaves, porridge, custard, the occasional discarded dog turd sausage, and much besides. As it seemed likely that this would attract some unwelcome and critical attention, it was completed only under cover of darkness. The soil was returned, and apart from two low mounds, the first steps in my horticultural undertaking remained unseen. Water was added, and, hey presto, nature could do the rest.

Improvisation and a little pilfering equipped me with all of the tools that I would require. Most urgent were a couple of buckets and these, and a large liberated spoon were all obtained from the culinary department. Fresh tomatoes and cucumber provided a ready, if somewhat uninspiring source of seed, and a more diverse selection of seeds and cuttings found easy liberation from some of the proudly tended floristic presentations in the Akrotiri married quarters.

Thus equipped, I sowed, planted, watered, and waited. Not for long! Despite my unpromising location, green shoots soon heralded my horticultural masterpiece. My verdant floriculture grew quickly, and in addition to the prospect of succulent tomato and cucumber, tall sunflowers nodded in the breeze, hollyhock provided a haven for nectar seekers, and geranium adorned the dusty plot in a riotous blanket of many hues.

Alas, this worthy endeavour was not appreciated equally and by all, and the balance tipped unfavourably on the day of an inspection by the CO. He lingered for a few moments among my spectral viridescence, and after a brief complimentary word, a casual remark made the suggestion that it would be splendid if all of the tent lines could be thus adorned. While no such order was ever posted, those junior officers who wished to curry early favour took it upon themselves to 'encourage' a gardening ethos.

Rebellion ensued, and mutinous rumbling was audible deep in the 280 inner bowel. Alas for the Hanging Gardens of Paradise Lost, this green arbour became the template and the target for the collective frustration and wrath of a party in opposition. Despite this upsurge of resentment, no latter day Wat Tyler raised cudgels and set about a rebellious path of destruction. In the wake of the complimentary remarks from the Commanding Officer, this would have been too transparent. With far greater subtlety, there began a more insidious war of attrition. An accidental encounter felled a path-side tomato.

Nocturnal sabotage uprooted a handful of geraniums and blamed a passing wild animal. Most subtle of all were the bringers of impending doom. At dead of night a hand wielding a sharp blade would skilfully incise a stem but leave it standing until the morning breeze brought down hollyhock or sunflower leaving its botanical splendour spread-eagled on the path to suffer the undeserved indignity of a passing boot.

A reasonably polite notice made request to the countryside despoilers to leave the bloody garden alone. The life span of this small and well-meaning placard was remarkably brief, and heralded a continued wave of clandestine destruction. I persisted. Unwelcome assault by those who lived in fear of imposed and compulsory floriculture slowly subsided, and the war of attrition became transformed into an uneasy truce. The perceived fear of the dreadful imposition of 'gardens for all' faded, and not another single green shoot ever infested the frontage of another tent.

For those whose brass neck attitude inspired a little elevated enterprise, more uplifting opportunity could become available. Middle East Communications Squadron at Akrotiri was the home base of a number of aircraft that were used by qualified pilots to maintain their required record of flying hours. It was rumoured that empty seat occupancy could be realised if a polite and diplomatic approach were to be made to one who may be sympathetic to such a request. While such activity was probably against the rules, perhaps yet another blind eye was turned in the direction of these practices, in recognition of the many other deprivations of the day.

I followed the recommended approach, and made my way one morning to the squadron apron. An officer in flying suit approached, a Flying Officer by rank, and probably not much older than I was.

I stopped him and made the most simple request.

"Any chance of a flight sir?"

He stopped and silently looked me up and down for a moment. Then he smiled.

"OK! Why not? Let's go and get you togged up and looking the part."

He found me a flying suit bearing the same rank as his own, and we walked back to the compound.

The aircraft of choice for this continuity flying was the Gloster Meteor, a twin-engine jet fighter, at that time coming to the end of its active service.

We climbed aboard, someone of my lowly rank secured and checked my parachute, and as we taxied to the end of the runway, my pilot friend explained the controls. Flying the thing seemed to be an extraordinarily simple business. One item of furniture he was at pains to point out was a large red knob.

"Do not," he said, "for any reason, press that knob. That is the ejector seat control, and activation will find us sitting on a cloud."

This was my first experience of jet propulsion, and acceleration and take-off were at far greater velocity than I had known previously. Very quickly we were aloft, and I was smiling broadly as I gazed down upon Akrotiri and the rather forlorn tent lines of 280. We flew for around an hour or so, northward to Nicosia, over the Troodos Mountains, and at low level along the coast. I found it exhilarating even before he decided to put the aircraft through its paces. Perhaps he was testing his own mettle, or perhaps mine, but I determined to bottle any twinges of terror that I may have felt. Happily, I did not vomit, I did not pass out, and I did not panic. Indeed, I believe that I enjoyed every single exhilarating moment. Sensibly, he warned me before each manoeuvre. Then we looped and we rolled, we dived and we climbed, and for a time, in the mountain pass between Limassol and Nicosia, we were in inverted mode and looking up at the ground. My most eye-popping moment was a vertical power dive over the sea, when tiny ripples abruptly became major swells, as we hurtled towards them. As the G-forces welded me to my seat, and just as noisy submersion seemed imminent, he transformed the dive into a climb, and I soared, somewhat open-mouthed into the blue.

For me, this had been a most exhilarating and exciting hour, and before returning to base, he permitted me the feel of the controls, and the basics of flying. I felt as high as a kite, or perhaps as a Meteor. After we had landed, I asked him if there was any chance of a repeat.

"Oh," he said, "I should think so."

And we did!

On these occasions, and as we walked across the airfield, we spoke of our respective life and times, of our hopes and aspirations, and of our very different lives within the service. In many other ways we were contemporaries, and in spite of our different current stations, a slightly unlikely friendship evolved, he a serving officer, and me a very time limited national serviceman. Memory forbids my recall of how many times we flew together, for him a routine and regular exercise, for me an opportunity unlikely ever to be repeated. He was happy, on these occasions, for me to take the controls, and I suppose that I learned to fly a meteor, though never to land or to take off. Forgive the pun, but that would have flown in the face of the regulations.

Indeed, it was the rigid imposition of the regulations in the wake of two tragedies that brought this adventure to a close. The Canberra bomber was sufficiently accommodating to allow the occasional passenger. Shortly after take-off during one such 'joyriding' event from Akrotiri, the aircraft plunged into the sea with the loss of all on board. Whatever the cause of the crash, so far as I am aware, this remained locked in files marked 'confidential'. Of course, speculation was rife, and one theory suggested that the passenger had panicked during the high speed and possibly bumpy takeoff, and had disrupted the control of the aircraft at a low altitude, critical moment. A second occasion also involved a Canberra aircraft with joy-riding passengers on board. It had been a simple training flight to Aden and return, and it too fell out of the sky on take-off from Aden killing all on board. Once more, the cause of the tragedy remained unknown or undisclosed.

Years later, I did it all again, but this time, and most recently in a Tiger Moth. It commanded somewhat less velocity than the Meteor, but the exhilaration of a loop, of a roll, of a dive, or of a climb to stall and flutter, had not diminished.

Middle East Communications Squadron provided a home station for another facility that was freely available to all who wished to make use of it. A twin-engined, twelve seat, 'Pembroke' aircraft provided a daily or regular shuttle service between Akrotiri and Nicosia. Intended mainly for officers in pursuit of essential business at both locations, any unfilled seats on any flight were available for use by anyone who cared to occupy them. Indeed, not infrequently, a solo pilot would call for a volunteer to fill the co-pilot's seat, in order to satisfy the regulations. This service was ideal for an individual seeking a temporary change of scene, and a two or three day period of freedom from duty.

While the change of scene was no more than a station to station excursion, billet could readily be obtained in the Nicosia transit camp, the food in the mess was a refreshing alternative to the 280 gastro-fare, and the NAAFI provided a change of scene if not of tipple. It was one such long weekend trip that brought me perilously close to my own demise, and to a scene of total and horrifying carnage.

In Nicosia, I had hopefully booked a seat on the morning return 'Pembroke', and had decided that a clear waking head was preferable to a debilitating hangover or the risk of missing the flight. In consequence, I had elected to leave the hugely noisy farewell party that was dominating every clamorous moment in the NAAFI. A final Keo brandy for the short walk to my billet, and I bade farewell to my companions at the bar.

I had taken no more than a few paces from the entrance when a huge concussion struck me from behind. Dazed and sitting on the dusty path, for a few seconds I remained totally confused and disoriented. Gradually increasing awareness revealed that though the NAAFI door and small porch had been almost totally destroyed, remarkably perhaps, there remained some illumination inside the building, from which was issuing a steady pall of smoke and dust.

In spite of intense trepidation, but perhaps driven by an innate desire to bring aid, to help those who were in need of help, or perhaps in response to some of the lessons of those distant training days at Bridgnorth, I made a cautious return to the shattered doorway. Where there had been a vibrant and noisy party a few short moments earlier, there was now only a blue grey haze of suspended silence, broken only by a cough, a shuffle or the scrape of a piece of moved furniture. It was clear that there were injuries or worse, but in those first few moments as the more conscious and least injured victims began to recover sufficiently to disrupt the deathliness of the moment, I remained immobile, open mouthed, and without useful purpose.

My indecision was abruptly interrupted by the arrival of the emergency services, a team of medical orderlies and the military police, and to my somewhat relief I became absolved of the requirement to make any further decision.

What followed was an efficient restoration of order and necessary evacuation. Those who were unscathed, those with only minor injuries, and the otherwise walking wounded were ushered or helped from the bar, and escorted to an adjacent building to await a physical or medical examination. The remainder were treated in situ, as their injuries demanded, before also being evacuated to an appropriate medical centre. As I appeared to be completely unscathed, I was dismissed out of hand, and instructed to continue with my intended purpose, subject to a precautionary visit to my own medical centre for check-up. Accordingly, I boarded the morning 'Pembroke' as intended.

Investigation of the incident revealed that a powerful, timed explosive device had been concealed in a three-seat settee, and had been set to explode during a predictably busy period of the evening. At the moment of the explosion, three servicemen had been occupying the settee, one of whom died shortly afterwards. It was considered that the culprits had been members of a team of electrical contractors who had undertaken some routine maintenance earlier on the same day. I have no idea if they were ever apprehended and brought to justice, but in the circumstances this would have seemed unlikely.

The young man who died had been one of a small group of army personnel who had just completed a full tour of duty and were on their way to repatriation the following day. This had been their farewell party.

Another 'Pembroke' moment while returning with an almost empty aircraft from Nicosia was creative of a temporary white knuckle or two. While making a landing approach, the pilot realised that he had lost all of his hydraulic capacity. Thus he would enjoy no braking facility on touch-down, perhaps not a potentially terminal prospect for an aircraft of that size, if we were able to trundle into a sturdy head wind. More importantly, he would be unable to lower and engage his undercarriage. Salvation was at hand. These elderly, heavier-than-air, flying machines had not entirely dispensed with the more manual crank, and at a few turns of a handle, the port and starboard wheel assemblies obligingly clicked into the locking position. However, we remained dependent upon the strength and durability of the mechanism, and a bevy of fire engines and ambulances, each competing for our touch-down speed, was a sobering sight.

Just occasionally, diversionary recreation could project participants far beyond the realm or the range of mere aircraft, indeed into the ethereal world of ectoplasm, psychomancy, clairvoyance and theosophy. Perhaps those occultic novels of Dennis Wheatley had not been without legacy, but whatever the influence, it had injected the tiny germ of an idea. What a jape!

To engage convincingly with the wispy and indistinct dwellers of the spirit kingdom, the practitioner requires facility, equipment, and expertise, none of which were readily available, but all of which could be obtained. Secrecy in preparation would be vital, and this would not be easy in a place as public as 280. A team of two would hatch the plot, undertake the preparations and the practice, and hopefully bamboozle a breathless audience. An appropriate and atmospheric stage would be set, and a seance event would endeavour to commune with the astral.

Our initial step required the manufacture of a stage. With very little free space in a tent, this must take the form of a centrally located table. With standing room only, the table must be at an elevation ideal for the manipulation of the mystic equipment. Our earlier installed pedestal had been a somewhat rickety affair, and it had suffered use and abuse during many months of service. It had clearly become unsuitable for our intended and somewhat elevated purpose. Once again, construction material was fairly readily available, nails and tools were pilfered, and in a remarkably brief period, a superior table had materialized. However, even this fairly rough-hewn pedestal would require a measure of refinement before the tools of the occult trade would slide effortlessly across its surface. A tent was requisitioned, dismembered and quickly reassigned. A large square of its fabric was deftly excised, was stretched tightly across the wooden table boards, and was tacked securely into place. The stage was almost set, though still somewhat distant from final preparedness.

Installation however, would require the further modification of a portion of the firmament, and a skilled and deft exchange of tables beneath the earlier dismembered central tent pole. To ensure a flawless performance, we had considered that the new table should exceed the height of its predecessor by a margin of around three inches, and thus an adjustment of similar proportion would be required to the tent pole. To collective relief, these adjustments proceeded without hitch or hindrance. While manual support prevented the collapse of the entire structure, the old table was removed. With remarkable continuity, a further three inch length of pole was detached, and the new table was shifted swiftly into place. A little adjustment to ensure symmetry, and the stage was ready to receive its properties and adornment.

In the interests of security we must first replace the tattered rag that had concealed our contraband and tent abuse these many months. Our defensive curtain presently bore the stains of sundry spillages, of food items that had failed to reach their intended destination, and of the all-embracing dust that clung to them all. Perchance, a recent night patrol had discovered a quantity of far superior fabric in a storage building close to the MT compound. Greater in quantity than our requirement, the appropriate length was simply removed, and the original returned whence it had come.

While the canvas table covering was satisfyingly taut, it bore none of the essential characteristics of a curling rink. The MT section provided the remedial ingredients. A large tin of varnish, white spirit, and some brushes, and these, in combination with many days of tolerant patience were creative of the surface we required. Each day, and for many days, another thin coat of varnish was added to the table top. A heavy application at any time would risk surface wrinkling as the varnish dried and set. As coat succeeded coat, and day succeeded day, constant vigilance was the urgent requirement to avoid any contact with the surface. Extreme caution was an equal requirement when entering or leaving the tent to ensure a minimum swirl of atmospheric dust. Such disciplined vigilance was difficult, required as it was at every waking moment to ensure that unwary contact did not blemish the accreting glaze.

At last, and after many days of defensive vigilance to ensure that no falling object had blemished our gleaming diligence, a sheen to rival a dragon's eye and a lustre to challenge a star. Thus the stage was indeed set for our occultic communion, leaving only the essential assemblage of a few necessary tools of the occult trade.

A short electrical extension was required to conduct power from the central light socket to an extended socket to be suspended less than twelve inches above the table surface. This lower socket was to carry a small red bulb, and this would provide the only illumination. On test, it proved highly effective. The bulb was of the kind used to indicate the location of an artefact, and not to provide a source of purposeful illumination. In our suspended scenario, it cast a low level of red light on to the glistening surface of the table, and this became reflected upward and into the void of the tent, a most satisfactory illusion.

Only two action points remained before readiness would permit the cautious distribution of a little publicity. The first requirements were the tools of delusion and rehearsal. If we were to achieve and enjoy maximum effect, our little pantomime had to be flawless, anything short of that would reveal its hollow pretension. We required only a single item of stage property, but one that must be selected with care. Weight and balance would be essential capacities of our sliding glass. A pint glass was simply too large, and far too readily tripped by any small raised blemish in our table surface. A whisky tumbler the opposite, too small to navigate effectively and too squat, and while it skimmed the blemishes, smooth simultaneous control by three or four fingers was difficult. After careful and diligent search and trial, we selected our ideal vessel. Just a nondescript tumbler, broad of upturned rim for the avoidance of capsize, weight sufficient to provide stability without loss of manoeuvrability, and of sufficient size to admit ready manipulation by four gently placed single fingers.

Testing on our shiny table surface revealed just too many tiny raised blemishes. The many coats of varnish had fallen slightly short of the plate glass sheen that would be the requirement. Furniture polish? 280 was truly a desert zone in this department. However, we did have boot polish, and a vigorously polished micron thin film of dark tan added that extra satin silkiness. However, the final revelation arrived by accident, and one that we had been assiduously avoiding during these weeks of preparation. A spillage on the hallowed surface. The disaster that flashed before our eyes was quickly dispelled and replaced by an abrupt enlightenment. Our elixir of the ultimate slither was Keo. Our table had become a horizontal glissade that would put a smile on the face of a penguin.

Easy to move. Easy to stop. Two finger control to perfection. However the intended drama required additional assistance, and the recruitment of two utterly trustworthy collaborators was imperative. Two such were duly inducted into the dark world of the pseudo-occult, and final four finger training honed the sinister art into perfect seamless sleight.

Publicity? Not a good idea! This would inevitably attract the attention of authority, and an abrupt termination of our weeks of preparation. Word of mouth would be all of the broadcast that we would require. Date and time selected, the whisper was abroad. After weeks of practice, and remarkable success, a more public attempt would be made to make further contact with 'the other side'. Anyone wishing to attempt to establish contact would be welcome. A12, 'Paradise Lost' would be the venue.

Our final requirement! Deliberately left until the closing hours, we sought the cooperation of two or three additional 'trusties'. Not difficult to recruit, they were to take their places in the audience, to lead into questions, and to provide convenient affirmation when responses were spelled out on the table. We needed them to dominate throughout, to occupy maximum time, and thus to parry questions for which we had no possible opportunity for rehearsal, nor could conjure a creditable or plausible response. These were inevitable and we had practiced our rhetoric in order to provide meaningless but convincing responses that would eventually lead us down a blind alley.

Our melodrama of mystery, intrigue and nonsense was prepared, and we awaited a posse of persons who may wish to make contact with Auntie Flo. Perchance we had selected a particularly gloomy night, one perhaps when nature's more sombre atmosphere might presage a more sinister aura among the unlit tent lines. To this effect we had deliberately delayed our cabbala until 22.00 hours.

The low red glow reflected from the glistening table top was truly eerie, and when reflected from a couple of dozen pale staring faces it would have brought credit to a voodoo ceremony. The tent quickly filled to more than capacity, with perhaps thirty people standing at various elevations around the table. For the benefit of that portion of the audience standing outside in the 'Garden of Delights', and trampling the geraniums into oblivion, we rolled up the tent flaps fore and aft, rendering their hollow faces spotted red through the mosquito netting as if suffering the terminal stages of rubella.

Our charade began quietly enough, with absolutely no response to our choruses of "Is anybody there? Can anyone hear me?" Time to pep it up and to start communicating with a spirit or two. At length the glass twitched and stopped a couple of times, and then identified a series of unintelligible letters and numbers. It stopped again, and then steadfastly refused to make further movement, clearly (we hoped) while awaiting a tangible question. This was a prompt to one of our trusties, who claimed recently to have lost an uncle. We called upon Uncle Fred, and while Uncle Fred made no direct response, an indeterminate message was received and our 'trustie' indicated that this did indeed appear to be Uncle Fred.

However, Uncle Fred then returned to his well-earned celestial rest, and we required another, perhaps more experienced spirit. Long-gone grandparents seemed promising subjects, and a trusted query echoed from the red haze, rendered positively ghastly by the accumulating cigarette smoke. This became much more animated. Questions were asked and responses were forthcoming, including facts that could not otherwise possibly have been known. First Granny who expressed a love of spring flowers, and then Grandpa who had loved playing bowls until the day before his death.

Then came the first unrehearsed question, and one that must be parried convincingly. We had rehearsed this dilemma, and the trusties induced a low sibilant murmur by whispering to neighbouring heads and seeking response. This disturbed the spirits who retreated to their subliminal haven of peace. Rhetoric was an equally efficient tool when responding to questions far beyond the range of our wildest realms of imagination. A last resort, and a very efficient one, was agitation and the rapid and erratic journeying of the glass to a series of letters and numbers that indicated simply an unhappy or restive spirit.

The seance continued in a ghostly red silence until a signal from one of the trusties indicated a degree of audience agitation. Time for finale! An obscure question that touched upon the dark side of spiritualism, induced a violent spasm of activity from the glass. The Keo-smeared table top was superb, offering neither resistance nor trip to the guiding fingers. The excitation continued with unintelligible gibberish interspersed by exclamations of obscenity, vileness, defilement, utter vulgarity, and threat. Then it stopped abruptly in the middle of the table.

Guiding and controlling the glass had been hard work, and this pause provided a few moments of respite for weary arms and fingers. However, the guiding digits remained in situ, and did not break the contact or connection. The tent was filled with the huge weight of a heavy red silence. No-one made a sound. Even breathing seemed to be subdued.

Slowly, the glass resumed its movements. Initially without apparent direction or definition, more a languid tour of the table. Equally abruptly, it paused once more before beginning a series of lightning strikes, each one approaching a letter, pausing momentarily, and then returning to the middle of the table. Each pause permitted precise location of the next intended digit. To another letter, and then another, the glass hurtled across the table in violent and uncontrolled lexicology. A message unfolded.

"T-H-I-S I-S E-V-I-L." It shrieked.

"Y-O-U A-R-E E-V-I-L."

"M-Y N-A-M-E I-S N-O-R-A S-A-D-N-E-Y."

"I P-L-A-C-E A C-U-R-S-E U-P-O-N Y-O-U A-L-L."

"A H-E-L-L-F-I-R-E E-T-E-R-N-I-T-Y A-W-A-I-T-S Y-O-U A-L-L"

"I-N T-H-E P-I-T O-F H-A-D-E-S."

This was as much as the aching fingers could accommodate, and it was time to bring the charade to a halt. During the course of Nora's malevolent malediction, one of our carefully positioned trusties had moved slightly, and by so doing had created a contrived space in the throng. As Nora delivered her final obscene salvo, the glass hurtled from the table, was projected through the gap in the crowd and smashed noisily on the concrete floor beside the door pillar.

It delivered the shock of a rifle shot. The tent became filled with pale-faced, red-hued, open-mouthed silence. There was no protest, no cries of derision, no accusations of travesty, no denunciation, no impeachment, only sepulchral silence. For several minutes, that silence hung on the glowing air until the first shuffling towards the door heralded exodus. Treading carefully around the shattered glass shards, the crowd slowly made its exit, and fragmented into the night.

Or so we thought! It was later revealed that some of those present had sustained such shock to their senses and sensibilities that they braved the guards on gate duty, ignored the risk of ambush on the dark couple of miles to Akrotiri, and went in search of a priest and some measure of personal exorcism. They survived the exodus, and hopefully felt better for the purge.

As word of this fearful event later emerged and circulated, Station Standing Orders issued the clear instruction that henceforth any activities relating to the supernatural, to the paranormal or to pseudo-psychology are strictly forbidden, and will not be practiced on this station.

While just a hint of evasion and duplicity, perfidy and the paranormal, brought welcome diversity to the 280 routine, as 1959 progressed into its second half, hostilities began to abate, and as they did so, opportunities became apparent that would introduce a little welcome glitter into our daily lives. We were to be permitted to take a more relaxed peek into the world beyond the wire. While extreme caution must remain our guiding bywords, an occasional visit to Limassol or Nicosia could be anticipated. A walk down the street, friendly intercourse with local people, shopping, visits to places of interest, just a few of the daily pursuits that are part of everyday function in any 'normal' society.

However, and as we were frequently reminded, this was not a 'normal' society. Hostilities were of very recent history, with active pockets of more extremist resentment still smouldering in cities, in villages, and in the countryside. Huge areas remained out of bounds, only villages of declared neutrality could be entered, and large precincts of cities and towns were strictly forbidden. Any journey into the civilian world was subject to an absolute set of regulations, and strict curfew would be applied to every visit.

At first, small groups were transported as passengers on trucks that were engaged in other specific duties. They were dropped in a 'safe' location with clear instructions about the time and place for later collection. Each group would number no less than four, and all of the members of the group were to be armed. Before leaving camp, each individual would be issued with a weapon and a set number of rounds of ammunition. The instruction was to return them intact, or to provide an extremely plausible explanation why that was not the case. Sten guns were the normal weapon of issue, though side arms did begin to substitute later, though only to one or two members of each perambulating group.

Walking the street thus clad was intimidating, embarrassing, and unnerving. Attempting to exchange any kind of friendly greeting while brandishing a light machine gun was welcomed with suspicion at best, and hostility more frequently. What else could we expect? Any purchase from shop or market stall was the necessary subject of strict procedure. Two members of the group, each with a Sten gun must take up station at each side of the road. The purchaser must enter the shop with his remaining companion, both armed of course, make the required purchase as quickly and expediently as possible, return to the street, and regroup. The duration of a visit to any shop, and thus the division of the group, must be held to an absolute minimum.

These strict procedures were to become relaxed quite quickly, and though we were to remain armed for some time, weapons became shouldered or holstered, and not held in readiness to defend or to react to the ping of unfriendly fire. Incidents did happen, though they were few, and mercifully reducing in frequency. All of these opportunities may have seemed exciting while back in the confines of 280, but in reality they were alarming, phobic, menacing for all concerned and simply unpleasant. For most, the experience of two or three such outings was sufficient, and they became content to await the inevitable coming of more peaceable undertakings. They did not have too long to wait.

One of the early indications that 'peace in our time' was enjoying considerably increased stability, came to us in the form of an organised excursion. How this was organised and by whom has long been lost to memory, but a charabanc would be summoned to take a bus load of 280 inmates on an excursion to Nicosia. 'First come, first served' would be the simple maxim that would allocate seats in the bus. Well versed and alert in matters pertaining to early warning, and with the benefit of volunteering experience (thanks Tony), I quickly made to ensure that my name was high on the roster of aspirant travellers.

The list had been over-subscribed and the bus was full to capacity as we headed for our first relatively free visit to the city. For once, we were not armed, but were under the protection of an accompanying posse of military police who were. Our instructions were clear. We would be restricted to an area in the centre of the city, trouble of any kind and in any quarter would not be tolerated, and we must report back to the bus for the return journey at 22.00. To our surprise, Ledra Street, the infamous former 'Murder Mile' was in bounds, as was the maze of adjacent streets and squares.

Our arrival in the late morning permitted a long day to do as we pleased, for once unencumbered by heavy armament, but for safety reasons better to remain in small groups. I guess that we did little during the day except enjoy the sense of freedom, the facility to communicate without threat, and the joy of mingling without suspicion. We roamed the squares and the byways, took coffee in the sunshine, visited places of interest within the ancient city walls, made purchase of the occasional souvenir, and for the first time we relaxed into an ambience that exuded a long-denied aura of friendship.

In the evening, and inevitably, we gravitated towards one or more of the bars, where alcohol was consumed copiously if somewhat unwisely. Elated by our new-found freedom, we no longer confined our quaffing and our tipple to the familiar Keo, but expanded our libation to include every eau-de-vie, grog, firewater and hooch that was on offer, or that could be concocted. By middle evening, not a sober breath was being drawn.

I found my haven of delights in a small bar, just below street level, close to Salomos Square, and with the comfortingly familiar name of the Castle Inn. The bar service was in the provision of a delightful young lady whose name was Nikki. Thus, the final couple of hours of my day in the city became totally dedicated to serenading this vision of beauty, with whom I had fallen instantly and deeply in love. I have little doubt that my serenade was not a particularly pretty thing to behold, or indeed to listen to as I slumped ever more precariously, at the bar.

My song of endearment was one that was currently popular on the air waves of the day, and which was sung by the equally popular and hugely energetic Little Richard. My seductive rendition made no attempt to emulate any of the energetic or indeed, the vocal attributes of the worthy Little Richard.

Baaaby Face.
You got the cutest little baaaby face.
There's not another who could take your place.
Baaaby Face.
You got my poor heart jumpin.
You sure have stated somethin.
Baaaby Face.
I'm up in heaven when I'm in your warm embrace.
I didn't need a shove.
I just fell in love.
With your pretty little baaaby face.

While my drooling serenade lacked the athleticism of Little Richard, and while its endless repetition may have failed to convince the lovely Nikki of the sincerity of my wooing, the constant and increasingly discordant reiteration is likely to have either amused or infuriated anyone in the bar who had called for a quiet drink or an equally romantic interlude.

Time perhaps to adopt a more predatory approach to my amorous serenade.

"BAAAAABY FACE!!!" I growled menacingly.

Nikki simply continued with her work, while the customers continued with their social discourse, and I continued to slump ever further across the bar.

The heavy macho approach had failed to whisk Nikki from behind the bar and into the warm embrace of the night, so perhaps a seductively crooning Perry Como serenade might enjoy a little more success. Precisely what it was that I was attempting to achieve remained unclear to me, or to anyone else. Thus making use of the silkiest, most alluring tone that my cognac fuelled larynx could manufacture, I whispered across the bar.

"Baaaaaaybeeee Face"
"You got the cutest..."

Thus my tedious serenade continued until a burly member of our escorting military police who was rounding up the bar room wreckage announced that it was time to go, and bundled us all into the street. My meandering progress toward the waiting bus was arm in arm with someone, but to my wailing lament, it was not Nikki.

"Baaabeee Face" had become a soft elegy.

On a recent visit to Cyprus, I returned to Salomos Square. The Castle Inn is still there, just a few steps below the street. Alas, Nikki was not, and a repeated serenade to the bloke behind the bar seemed less than appropriate, and very likely to induce an unintended impression.

The return journey to Cape Gata was truly the stuff of nightmares. In those distant days, the road between Nicosia and Limassol was not the fine highway of today. It was torturous throughout, narrow and slow at many locations, and it passed through a number of villages where freely expressed friendships had yet to be declared. Hostilities were not far behind us, and ambush remained a real threat, especially at night. So before we made our departure from Nicosia, the driver made it clear that he would be unwilling stop at any point on the journey.

He had inherited, and had become nominally responsible for a bus load of drunks, and in a very short time it had become clear that many would be quite unable to contain themselves throughout the entire journey. The driver was understandably anxious to complete the journey as quickly as safety would permit, so he made speed when he could, and sometimes when it seemed somewhat ill-advised.

As the bus swayed and bumped through corners and pot holes, the first calls for comfort / toilet / vomit stops rang out. True to his word, the driver refused. There were, he said, only two or three locations along this route where he considered that it was sufficiently safe to make a pause of adequate duration to accommodate the evident requirement. He could not afford to risk someone disappearing into the night and thus initiate the call out or muster of a search party. Containment until arrival at a safe haven was the requirement. It was clear that this requirement would not be realised.

Whatever the gastric / alimentary / urinary / defecatory call, in extremis it will not be denied. Many were the bags and small containers utilised in attempts to contain liquid surplus and to project it into the night through the windows. However, this was before the age of plastics, and as paper is of very limited durability, the contents mostly reached the floor, or were liberally distributed over fellow passengers as the bags burst en route to the window. Attempts to direct the unwanted flow directly through open windows met with equal lack of success. These were drunks on a wildly oscillation bus, and this endeavour inevitably resulted in liberal distribution and a widely shared resource as mid flow balance became projected into mid flow flight.

Those who had eaten unwisely of dubious local fare or for whom the temptation to eat to excess had been too great, now suffered with the imperative requirement for evacuation. Our pleas for a halt were met by rebuff. This part of our route was heavily wooded, and road conditions imposed slow progress.

"Too hazardous here, maybe half, maybe three quarters of an hour."

The alimentary systems of some were approaching the point of explosion, and with the only reasonable option out of reach, the means to provide relief must be devised. The direct evacuation approach, as attempted earlier with limited success, would have required the most extraordinary prowess of a highly skilled contortionist, even without the added perils of a bucking bronco bus. A limited supply of newspaper was at hand, but was clearly inadequate to the task, and might be of greater value in the aftermath. The only solution was sacrificed items of clothing. Though there were quite indescribable mishaps, used in tandem with the newspaper, and quickly ejected into the night, some were thus relieved.

The rock 'n' roll journey proceeded, but then came the vomiting. Even for those who were more robust of constitution, or who were not quite drunk to incapacity, the increasingly overwhelming stench in the vehicle became the catalyst to a gastric performance of operatic quality. A kind of ghastly Gregorian chant, as each gurgle, grunt, and horrid ululation projected yet another part digested meal into the central aisle. Those foolish enough to attempt to achieve an upright stance for some misguided reason, were quickly swept from their feet in the treacherous mess as the bus banked to left or right, and until they were able to regain equilibrium slithered inelegantly from end to end of the vehicle.

This apocalyptic scenario continued until the driver finally pulled off the road and on to a gravelly open space. As the bus came to a halt he issued the instruction that we would be permitted leave the vehicle for no more than ten minutes. Alas, by this time, and by one means or another, most of the passenger complement had become empty, and had been drifting in the general direction of insensibility. However, most left the bus to make one final attempt to relieve any remaining burden. Some elected to discard items of clothing that were no longer fit for immediate purpose. The less incapable made some attempt to clean up the interior of the bus, and after a roundup and head count we continued to destination.

It was a pale, ghostly, partly unclad, and hugely subdued group of individuals that dismounted the bus into the chill Cape Gata moonlight, and dispersed to their respective tents. Had our first organised outing since the cessation of hostilities been a success or an embarrassment? There would be more, none quite so spectacularly awful as the conclusion to the first and so this one became relegated to 'an experience'. Its highest and lowest points would be remembered, with much in between that has become lost to memory, or conveniently forgotten.

As 1959 drew toward a close, the freedom to take time out without escort or arms was a relief to everyone, and afforded the facility to experience and to enjoy the many other facets of a very beautiful and historic island. However, for some time yet, there remained the imposition of some measure of curfew, and the requirement to sign out of camp and to be signed back in again on return. Failure to comply with this regulation, or to have failed equally to respect the limited period of grace, placed any miscreant into the 'Absent without Leave' category, serious charge, and subsequent denial of future prospects of liberation.

Blissfully, for those who would aspire to exploit any chink in the armour of officialdom, the later period of 1959 also introduced the prefect contrivance. During the emergency, the families of serving personnel had been repatriated, but in late 1959 and with the acceptable reduction of the considered hazard, families were now returning, and were being housed in 'protected' residential areas. These 'Living Out Personnel' were at liberty to invite anyone to come and stay with them during off duty periods, and by so doing they provided an approved address, and relief from the need to observe the daily / nightly requirement of curfew and return to camp.

The exploitation of this system required no more than the hand of friendship. That hand would sign a form of release that would afford an identified location wherein the dodger would allegedly be living during the stated period. At the termination of that period the LOP friend would sign him back into camp and the system had been satisfied. During the period between signing out and signing in, of course, the truant could be anywhere, and many were the Limassol refuges where an honest skiver might find a place to rest his head.

The first half of 1960, and up to my repatriation and demobilisation in June of that year, was a period of increasing freedom, which permitted even more exploration of the many delights that the island had to offer. The public transport system on the island was sparse to non-existent, and in any case could only be put to purpose after arrival in Limassol. As this was the destination of many of our forays into the sinful wider world, this limited utility served equally limited purpose. Mostly we awaited a passing truck heading for Akrotiri, hung about at the main gate and guardroom pending the same mode of transport heading towards Limassol, and took the lift. It was standard practice, and however unreliable, it was never denied. Nocturnal return journeys, often in various states of disarray, required the use of a taxi.

When venturing beyond the city's decadence, and into the hinterland, hiring a car afforded choice of route, timing, and destination. Away from the summertime heat of the coast, the central and northern mountain ranges provided temperate conditions, splendid scenery, abundant history, and a very welcome ambient change. Tourism had not yet arrived, villages remained unspoiled and natural, and cottage gardens provided harvest of fruit and vegetable from the fertile soil. Trailing vines provided shade for patios where a glass of wine could celebrate the end of the day, and provide harvest to ensure the next bottle. Elegant monasteries, some of which had been earlier implicated in the concealment of arms for EOKA, such as Kykko and Stavorouni added history and culture to journeying. During one such foray, four such mountain wanderers were tempted into an unattended vineyard wherein hung huge, luscious bunches of purple grapes. The temptation was too great, as indeed was the avarice, for not only did we purloin sufficient to satisfy our immediate personal requirements, but we stacked the rear shelf to capacity with sufficient to satisfy the daily fruit intake for half of the camp. What we had intended to do with them all was not so readily apparent.

We continued until mishap struck during our return to Limassol. A brief moment of temporary distraction by the driver, a particularly narrow section of highway, a looming stone bridge across a stream, and an instant of noise and confusion as we struck the parapet. To our good fortune, the impact was not severe, the hired vehicle, a Hillman Minx if memory serves, had already suffered at the hands of others, and the additional damage could be largely fudged or concealed. Of more immediate concern was the content of the rear shelf, which had become airborne on impact, and which now adorned us all, and the interior of the car, in juicy and sticky festoons. While the stream provided some facility to remove the adhering pulp, and a little mud to mask the damage we returned to 280 in the aura of a bar-room floor.

My first ventures into the seamy and seedy nightlife preferences of service personnel, and of Limassol, were shocking. Perhaps I had simply been unprepared for the depth of its brazenness or perhaps my own rural and relatively sheltered background had denied the existence of human behaviour at this level. My boarding school rules and regulations had forbidden any form of contact with 'members of the opposite sex', and those caught indulging in even the most innocent discourse and conversation became subject to a thrashing and to 'gating', the withdrawal of the Saturday morning privilege to venture into the local township. In the tiny community that was home there had simply been no 'members of the opposite sex' with whom to make contact of any kind. The relatively brief period between school and conscription had opened my adolescent eyes a little, but only sufficiently to be aware of the differences, and insufficiently to find any engagement beyond those heady moments of fumbled euphoria.

On those early occasions it was hollow and timorous bravado that accompanied me, and many equally ill-equipped innocents, to face the perils of the Limassol dens of iniquity. Always in the company of others, and generally staying fairly close to the most streetwise, who were serving as unwitting tutors to my inexperience, until my own consumption of alcohol banished my trepidation and threw a little of my caution to the winds. However, shock is a transient emotion, a passing phenomenon that fades with each exposure to its source and as each exposure instils the confidence of experience.

"You wan' jig-a-jig Johnny?"

A glittering lady of huge proportions, most of them on open display, approached with this alarming invitation.

"Er! No thank you!"

"Good, very cheap. I make special for you."

The lady in question had clearly been poured somehow into a lycra costume that was several sizes smaller than her ample frame. The lycra was fighting a losing battle in its futile attempt to prevent substantial proportions of her substantial anatomy from oozing forth under the influence of her diet of gin and chips.

"Another time perhaps."

The bars were almost always crowded to capacity, in semi-darkness, and slippery with booze, food remnants and equally slippery people. Moving at all would inevitably lead to unintended indiscretion, or imposed indiscretion, the intentions of which were very clear.

"Jig-a-jig Johnny?"

Was the ratio of male to female out of balance? How could there be so many of the fair sex passing the jig-a-jig invitation at the same time, and why were not most of them jig-a-jigging as they were proposing. Some of the answers to these questions were become clear as familiarity with the some of the darker recesses of the bar increased.

They were!

Gone was the requirement to retire discreetly to a seductively decorated and perfumed boudoir.

In dark corners, on bench seats, standing in corridors or in recesses, I even encountered one couple thus engaged while sitting on a bar stool at the bar. Though they were entirely oblivious to my presence, I exercised my preference to find service at an alternative section of the bar.

"Jig-a-jig Johnny?"

However limited, the freedom to wander the nocturnal streets of Limassol, and to savour some of its not-too-perfumed delights was not without its inherent hazards, and for some, its inevitable pitfalls. One such slightly remorseful individual, who had conceded that he had indeed succumbed to the invitation, and had lingered among the warm abundance of one of the ladies of the night, had become fearful that he might also have succumbed to one of the delinquent associated disorders so graphically illustrated during those distant early days of his RAF career. To avoid the embarrassment of medical scrutiny, treatment, and probable humiliation, he had decided upon a more home-grown remedy. Perhaps to his good fortune, he had been apprehended in the ablutions while in vigorous application of soap and a nail brush to the offended portion of his offending organ. As the potential damage that he could impose upon his bleeding member could well ensure that he was never again able to indulge in such activity, he was persuaded to desist, to wrap a handkerchief around the already imposed injury and to head quickly to seek the wisdom of the medical department.

Perhaps a change of venue. Happily for the more discerning young gentleman, there were alternative venues, where a modest Keo could be sipped without the attendant risk of an over voluptuous portion of the female anatomy being plunged into his beer or thrust into his face with the familiar and ubiquitous invitation. The Trocadero and Delices Bar both offered entertainment of the more discerning variety, and pleasing venue in which to find ready relaxation.

Some of the more commodious establishments provided floor shows in addition to the customarily abundant drink. Interestingly, drugs were unknown at this time, so we were free from the threat that they and the corrupt industry they support poses today. The quality of each floor show was a direct reflection of the bar in which it was staged. Some were fairly select and respectfully modest in their presentation, while others were graphically vulgar to the point of utter obscenity. The greater proportion of the performers were girls and young women, a few of whom were singers, while the majority seemed to have been employed for the sole purpose of gyrating seductively for, and usually among, the audience. Though these girls were mostly European, their collective backgrounds would have ranged from Shanghai to Lisbon.

Some of the costumes that adorned these lovely ladies were entrancingly elaborate, though none would have imposed a serious material outlay, Scantily clad would have been a generous term for most, while at the lower extreme, complete nakedness left nothing to the imagination and very little to the interest.

The dancing on stage or among the customers was clearly intended to titillate, and to induce the drooling overheated male audience into an ever increasing frenzy of drinking. In this function, it was generally highly successful. However, in those houses that imposed rules, the rule of the house stated that members of the audience must not touch, in spite of the temptation of perilously, provocatively, and closely flaunted anatomical delights. The exception of course, was the pelvic undulation that was the clear invitation to stuff banknotes of any denomination down the front of the performer's knickers. Alas, the excessive drinking and the cardinal rule of the house rarely found agreement. At some late stage it was almost inevitable that some slobbering drunk would lurch to his feet, would make a random attempt to clutch, grab, and grope, and chaos would ensue. Restraint, resistance, flying fists, overturned furniture, broken glass, screaming girls, the threat of intervention by the military police. Time to leave!

At the lowest end of the scale, the kind of performance that was staged was one of desperation, for performer and audience alike. The nature of these depraved shows did not appear on the billboards outside or among the neon lights in the windows, and relatively innocent carousers could be, and were taken by surprise. Naked girls performed and demonstrated their anatomical versatility by making use of sundry pieces of hardware more normally associated with the culinary art, or empty coca-cola bottles for the more seasoned performers.

Many of these girls were working under huge duress. They had been tempted to work in the clubs and bars by unscrupulous entrepreneurs offering free passage and the first steps to stardom and untold riches. They were paid a mere pittance and thus were prevented making an escape. They were provided with appalling living conditions, and many, if not most had become obliged to resort to the oldest profession in order to survive. These were not good time girls on the game, but deeply unhappy young women who were being horribly exploited, and who yearned only to return to Shanghai or to Lisbon. Within their deeply unhappy society, suicide was not uncommon.

Our sympathetic response to this unhappiness led to a measure of more friendly relationship, which they welcomed. They were eager to talk, to learn about life distant from the sordid nature of their places of employment, to share the details of their earlier lives, and perhaps to dream of return. We learned that daily recreation sometimes took us both to opposite ends of Ladies Mile beach. This long curving strand of lazy beach extends from the north eastern corner of Cape Gata to the suburbs, and now to the docks of Limassol. Meeting in the middle afforded us the opportunity to simply enjoy their company, and for them to find a little companionable freedom from the distasteful demands of their miserable employment.

Despite the fact that some of my friends at 280 might have delighted in the civilian facility of fine wines and gourmet dining, while I was rather more familiar with fresh goats milk, pigs trotters, and crusty whole meal bread, we had all suffered, and equally, at the incompetent chefdom of 280 SU Cape Gata. Thus, our freedom to roam afforded us, for the first time, the opportunity to sample and to savour local fare.

The delights of Greek cuisine became pleasurably familiar as we prospected the many cafes and restaurants of downtown Limassol. At least in that sector of downtown Limassol into which we were permitted. Sadly for us, though hostilities against the British had largely been put to bed, Greek continued to growl at Turk, and Turk continued to growl in return. The authorities had taken the view that local enmities could flare up at almost any time, and that they were most likely to find their kindle in the Turkish quarters of the major towns. Thus, these areas were off limits to service personnel.

Well! Off limits? A stalwart and defiant few tended to ignore the restriction and used ignorance as a defence whenever we were apprehended and directed back into the land of approval. So far as I am aware no-one was ever charged for straying into Turkish territory, in spite of bellowed vulgarity from the military police and threats of fearful indignity if ever we were to repeat the offence.

We were old hands by then.

Alas, the Greek-Turk posturing did continue, and did flare up into local skirmish from time to time until 1963 / 64 when violence escalated across the island. At this time, Turkish civilians began to migrate into cities, and in particular into Nicosia, where they occupied shanty accommodations in the Turkish quarters. The unrest continued for a decade until Turkish military forces invaded in 1974, and the Turkish government demanded partition. Later that year, a cease fire was declared, the 'Green Line' was drawn, Turk occupied the northern one third of the island, and Greek the remainder, imposing the horrors and divisions of partition upon the civilian population.

It is not known how many perished during that period of conflict, but the death toll is estimated at 4,500 to 6,000. A huge cemetery in Nicosia bears witness.

Chapter 9. The best laid plans... gang aft a-gley.

... "Have you a lobster I can buy from you?" ...

*

If a more cultural approach to relaxation and leisure is your preference,
regular performances at our theatres of excellence
attract thespians, musicians and artists of the highest quality.

Tragedy or comedy, pathos or slapstick, symphony or syncopation, cantillation or choral,
all are guaranteed to invoke a smile or a tear, joy or enchantment.

Audience participation is encouraged and never fails to add local charisma.

We have provided springboard for some remarkable talent,
some of whom have continued to perform in local bars, in metro stations,
in public parks, on street corners
and in public conveniences throughout the land.

*

Life at 280 was never a plod. Equally, very rarely did it break into a gallop. It was a routine that was repeated day on day in five or six day bursts, depending upon the success of skiving, volunteering, or the validity of excuses to be somewhere else. For we conscripted, non-career men whose future lives did not depend upon a good end of term report, it was relatively carefree, without onerous responsibility, and for some, it was a period from which to derive the maximum life enhancing experience.

Most lives are readily divisible into chapters, periods in time that are dominated by a particular set of circumstances or disciplines. Whether mundane or frenetic, inspiring or dull, difficult or a ride in the park, each chapter will be punctuated by a series of incidents or occasions that deviate from the routine, and which are thus committed to a more secure place in memory. From them may emerge euphoria or despair, satisfaction or disappointment, success or failure, an adventure or an anticlimax, but whatever their nature and whatever their effect, they will leave that almost indelible blip in the recollection of the routine.

280 was one such chapter, and a relatively brief one for most. Though it was most unlikely ever to be repeated, if viewed as part of life's wider embrace, it would surely have been remembered as a very large blip in its own right. Though regular routine was dominant and daily directional, the incidents and occasions that were its punctuation are well remembered for the excitement, the companionship, the amusement, or the distress that were their legacy.

Our first charabanc trip to the world outside had concluded as a seriously messy affair, and fairly shamefully so. In spite of this, or perhaps because of it, the same competitive scramble for available seats quickly followed the announcement of the next one. Distant Kyrenia on the north coast was the intended destination, a location new to the entire passenger complement, and a buzz of anticipation filled the bus as we took to the road.

A few miles short of the outer limits of Nicosia, we pulled in to a cafe to discharge the early morning mugs of tea. A somewhat strange establishment, with some of the seating facility located on a platform among the spreading branches of a nearby tree. Sufficient time and space also to enjoy a coffee, or an early Ouzo for those so minded, but also to sample our first encounter with one curious Cypriot delicacy, the *Ambelopoulia*. Now a strictly illegal practice, and even then of highly dubious morality, small songbirds are captured, cooked and pickled, usually for celebratory consumption on special occasions. They are entire, save for head, legs, and feathers, and are pickled for sufficient time to soften the bones into edibility. Hmmmm! Quite nice, but morally reprehensible.

Through Nicosia, across the arid northern plain of Mesaoria and up into the foothill of the Kyrenia or Pentadactylos Mountains, which take their Greek name from the five-fingered peak visible a few miles to the east. Our first destination, a short distance ahead, and at significantly greater altitude, was the castle of Saint Hilarion. St. Hilarion, it seems, was an oddball cleric who elected to live up here among the limestone caverns, and amused himself by yelling obscenities and waving sticks at passing goats. He eventually constructed for himself a retreat, which in turn, was replaced by a monastery. The castle is no neat and symmetric keep surrounded by walls, but a complex series of battlements among the limestone pinnacles, on three distinct levels of elevation. Quite how waving sticks and yelling obscenities at passing goats qualifies for beatification remains a mystery.

Constructed and fortified during the 11th and 12th centuries, it finally fell to Richard the Lionheart, and presumably the mortal remains of the bold St. Hilarion. Though much improved today, back in 1959, the tortuous and precipitous track leading to the lower entrance provoked sufficient alarm to induce most of the passenger in the bus to alight and walk. The loose surfaced track was narrow and very steep, and demanded much of the driver as he inched around corners, fore and aft, as front bumper scraped the rock and tail end hung over the precipice. We wandered the buttresses and pinnacles of Hilarion's disparate cathedral for a couple of hours before proceeding to Kyrenia.

Then, a sleepy and picturesque fishing village, where fishermen repaired their nets, traditional boats bobbed in the harbour, and local cognac was abundant in the snoozing harbour-side cafes and bars. Now, sadly, the fishing boats have been replaced by floating gin palaces, the fishermen by smartly attired waiters, and the cafes by the glitz and glamour of expensive and excessive gourmandising. The mountain slopes of the hinterland, once the home of abundant flora and fauna, have become transformed into just another city, and one that demonstrated all of the ugliness of rapid development for the satisfaction of the single objective of touristic profiteering. On that first occasion we lingered and imbibed a little on the waterfront. One of the cafe proprietors demonstrated to me the explosive volatility of the stuff that we had been drinking, by setting fire to it and taking two paces to the rear. It was good stuff!

On the more recent occasion we found no motive or reason to do other than look and leave.

We took the short drive to the substantially ruined but still partly serviceable and beautifully preserved Abbey of Bellapais, located in the village of the same name. Then a separate and distinct community, now conjoined with pregnant and expanding Kyrenia. On that quiet occasion, our host and guide was the curator of the site and location, Kostas Kollis. Kostas was a kindly and genial man, who exuded an aura of friendliness, and for just a few of us, this first visit triggered a friendship that prevailed until we left the island.

During the ensuing months, when the duty rota or the skiving permitted sufficient free time, we engineered our passage to Bellapais, making use of public transport or by hitching, and we always found a welcome and a haven of peace in the house that Kostas occupied just across the dusty square from the abbey. Many bottles of fine wine were consumed during many hours of splendid conversation and robust laughter in the house or in the tiny wooded garden that hung perilously over a deep vegetated canyon. Kostas was a great raconteur and a great friend of the author Lawrence Durrell who lived for a time in the village and also spent much time at the house. Kostas features large in Durrell's famous book about the island, 'Bitter Lemons'.

During a later visit to Bellapais, I searched in vain for the house. The day was busy, the abbey and its surrounds thronged with tourists, and every available parking space occupied by a motor vehicle. In 2017, the situation remained unchanged except for the singular lack of tourists, the absence of motor vehicles, and the electrifying revelation that the car park of the earlier occasion was in fact the transformed dusty square across which we walked to the Kostas Kollis house.

It still stands, unoccupied as it happened on that day, perhaps now a holiday house, or maybe a more spectral cloister. The tiny triangular garden, as unkempt as ever, complete with spindly-legged table and an upturned chair, still carried the whispers of our conversations and the echoes of our laughter, over the wall and into the woody canyon below. Equally memorable, and with no less cheerful banter, were the many thus dedicated evenings in Clito's cavernous, wine-soused bar in the company of a hearty local cognac or a glass of the sweet, ruby Commandaria.

Kostas Kollis died around 1965. Though the youthful ticket vendors, gate minders and part-time guides may have scant, if any knowledge of Kostas Kollis, his proud and graceful legacy to Bellapais remains. In 1940, he planted a short avenue of Cypress trees, and to this day they sway elegantly in the breeze, bringing sometimes welcome shade to the cloisters, and to the touristic successors to the earlier men of the cloth.

Our return journey was as uneventful as the previous one had been abominable. We paused along the route on a couple of occasions to take a little libation, and returned, mellow and in good spirits, fully clothed, unsullied and unstained, to the welcoming arms of 280.

***

During my early months at 280, the hierarchy and procedures that related to eating, drinking, and carousing were clear and established. The commissioned ranks ate and drank in the officer's mess, the senior non-commissioned ranks did the same in the sergeant's mess, and everyone else shared the airmen's mess and the NAAFI. For reasons that remain unclear, the corporals felt aggrieved at this failure to recognise and acknowledge their individual rank and status, and they set up a demanding howl for the establishment of a Corporal's Club.

Perchance at this time, The NAAFI had become re-homed in a building constructed for this purpose, and the large marquee that it had succeeded had thus become redundant. With the blessing of the CO, this was re-erected at a location close to the domestic facilities and between the sergeant's mess and the airmen's tent lines. For reasons that were equally misunderstood, the establishment of this simple facility seemed to attract an unreasonable degree of criticism and resentment. Jealousy on the basis of 'why should they have', would seem to have been the only possible source of resentment. This was an illogical sentiment, as now, everyone had their own facilities as defined by rank and station. Among these, perhaps the airmen were best served, as they enjoyed the comfort and facilities of a recently custom-constructed building.

Amid the rumblings, reasonable harmony prevailed for some time, each social and hierarchical group making full use and purpose of the facility provided for the relief of its daily stress. Any lingering complacency about the potential longevity of this cosy arrangement became abruptly and dramatically extinguished in circumstances that remained ever unexplained.

At around 03.00 one dark night, the fire alarm sounded. The tent canvas of those days was not treated with any form of fire retardant, and once ignited, it burned fiercely and rapidly. Safety regulations instructed that everyone must turn out in response to any fire alert, and that roll call would follow. On this occasion, and at that dead hour, the corporal's club had mysteriously caught fire. On-site extinguishers were no match for the escalating inferno, and by the time that the fire services from Akrotiri had arrived, the marquee and the club had become committed to inevitable extinction. As the fire appliances tackled the blaze from one side, moments of abrupt unexplained incandescence erupted at the others. It was later alleged that during the course of the conflagration, individuals had been observed surreptitiously dropping empty coca-cola cans into the inferno. This action remained unclear until it became linked to the incidents of spontaneous incandescence, and the suggestion that the original contents may have been substituted for a modicum of paraffin. It was true that empty cans were discovered among the charred remains, but they were inconclusive, and could well have been the careless remnants of the same evening.

There was no reason why anyone should have been abroad on the domestic site at that time, except perhaps to make a necessary visit to the ablution block. The nightly patrols could have been attending to their duties at any point on the perimeter, or at a more sensitive location on the campus. The Corporals Club was marginally out of direct line of sight from the guard hut. The mystery remained unexplained. However, speculation had frequently offered the suggestion that this had been a deliberate act of retribution in return for the incessant and hideously loud playing of a popular tune of day entitled 'Yaketty Yak' performed by a group called 'The Coasters. If memory serves me correctly, the action was probably justified.

The fire had been brief and fierce, and while it had not been of prolonged duration, it had been totally destructive. Roll call followed, everyone was accounted for, and we all went back to bed. The enquiry lasted far longer than the fire, the blackened and charred remains of the club yielded nothing that would point to cause or implication. The matter was closed as simply recorded as 'unexplained'.

However, some few months later, and in even more mysterious circumstances, the incendiary incident was repeated. The location had been cleared of its charred debris, a replacement marquee had been erected, and the Corporal's Club had found reinstatement. The record does not indicate any repeated abuse of the tranquil evening ambience by the strident tones of 'Yaketty Yak' or perhaps someone harboured an unreasonable grudge against the corporal clan.

***

In the depths of bleak midwinter, when the worthy citizens of Northern Europe languish under leaden skies and rain drenched days, the upper elevations of the Troodos Mountains, and Mount Olympus, are clothed in a glittering blanket of ice and snow that holds every tree, structure and artefact in frigid embrace. The only sound is the deafening resonance of silence, broken only by the wind as it whispers, whistles and wails through the trees.

Vehicular traffic has become stationary, pedestrian progress can be achieved only by making use of skis, snowshoes or with great difficulty. The deep covering of snow invokes an aura of peace and tranquillity. During the months of conflict this was to be either cherished or envied, depending upon which side of the snow line you had elected to find residence. These elevated conditions imposed cease fire. Vehicles could not find passage, or did so only with difficulty, and the deep snow and lack of cover hampered guerrilla activity. Thus the risk of ambush was significantly reduced. During these periods, I made endeavour to enjoy a little of this frigid tranquillity at wintertime Pingo's Sunshine Corner.

On one such occasion, I had contrived a few days of absence, and I boarded a truck bound for Mount Olympus and Pingo's with the forecast confidence that the journey could be completed. This was not to be the case. At about three quarter distance up the steep and torturous road, we encountered the early snow line. Passable at first we struggled on, but a very few miles short of Troodos village, the increasing snow depth brought us to a halt. The driver was without option or alternative, he had to find a turning location and he, and the escorts, must return to Akrotiri. I elected not to do this, and after securing the confidence of the truck crew, I chose to proceed on foot, intending to embrace the short distance to the village, and then on to Pingo's in an hour or so, or if snow depth increased significantly, two at the most.

It was steep, deep and hard going, and there were times when I questioned my decision, but I had deprived myself of choice, so I plodded on. The snow depth did increase, I was without ski or snow shoe, and the company of constant difficulty was becoming distinctly less appealing. However, I knew that the steep incline would abate on reaching the village, and that created tracks would aid my progress through it and on to the road to Pingo's.

As my surroundings had become more familiar, and had afforded the realisation that the village lay less than a half mile distant, I relaxed my pace and my anxiety. Abruptly, I found myself under attack. I had permitted complacency to substitute for earlier urgency, and within twenty minutes or so of refuge, I had plodded directly into an ambush. I paused, for a moment somewhat bemused. The war cry that accompanied the attack did not resonate to the deep guttural tones of a murderous Eoka guerrilla, nor were the missiles whistling dangerously close to my unprotected head bullets that were set to wipe me out at any moment. The vocal challenge that echoed through the trees was much more feminine in character, contained more laughter than war cries, and was clearly the product of a number of more youthful larynxes. The missiles, which were now finding target, as my attackers drew closer and aim improved, were a barrage of snowballs.

I was a solitary warrior against a veritable army of twenty or thirty schoolgirls. An unwitting though not entirely unwilling victim, I stood no chance whatever. However, honour must be defended, and while I retaliated in bold defiance and defence, I was a relatively feeble force and became quickly overwhelmed. During the minutes that followed my defeat, snow flew in every direction, laughter filled the air, and I was finally escorted, as a prisoner of my youthful Amazons, to the village where truce was agreed, and cease fire negotiated.

It was with a renewed spring in my step that I continued my progress through the village, and for the additional mile or so that brought me finally to Pingo's Sunshine Corner.

***

Not all of our notable incidents were so agreeable.

The worthy citizenship of 280 SU Cape Gata were not entirely averse to enjoying the company of other members of the animal kingdom for social or domestic reasons, or with humanitarian motives. In common practice was the custodianship and confinement of chameleons and praying mantids. During the summer months flies emerged from the latrine blocks in plague proportions, and these flycatchers were without equal in helping to reduce the troublesome and inevitable in-house populations. Their reward for incarceration - easy to capture lunch. A fair deal!

A number of cats were present on the 280 campus, and so far as I am aware none of them laid claim to specific ownership of any member of the human menagerie. Where the cats came from was known only to the cats, though their distant lineage may have related to a close association with a reverend lady who was to become Saint Helena.

She it was who made the first attempt to establish and found the monastery of Saint Nicholas of the Cats on the Akrotiri Peninsula in AD 327. During the early construction, legend has it that a great drought resulted in the huge proliferation of venomous snakes that drove out both the builders and the local population. Undeterred, and to engage the reptilian invasion in battle, St. Helena imported 1000 cats from Persia and from Egypt. These felines were carefully trained to respond to the sound of two bells. One chimed to indicate feeding time, and the other to summon the cats to the hunt. During the ensuing battles, many of the cats became mutilated and bruised, but in spite of the opposition, the felines were victorious. Thus, the construction of the monastery could be resumed, was completed, and was appropriately dedicated jointly to St. Nicholas, but equally to his feline allies.

The cats, and their offspring, remained in residence through several periods of reconstruction, but in 1983, when the stewardship of the monastery was passed to an order of nuns, the cats had apparently deserted their duties, and the snakes were once more marauding the peninsula. Replacement cats were hastily obtained and installed, the battle resumed, until once more the snakes were repulsed. A large bevy of cats remain at the monastery to this day, some still bearing the scars of battle, the signs of chronic ill-health, or perhaps genetic mutations inherited from the ecclesiastical crusades of a thousand years ago. The tradition became established that stray cats brought to the monastery would be afforded bed and board, in honour and respect of centuries of service. A bell still rings to summon the cats at feeding time, but the second one has lost its clapper and has become silenced forever.

Similarly perhaps, the 280 moggies were simply feral wanderers that had elected to shake off holy orders, had stumbled across some tasty kitchen waste, and had concluded that decomposing sausages were superior fare to the monastic morsels for which they had to engage in daily conflict with their spitting companions. Whatever their individual origin and background, the 280 cats had simply become fat and friendly. Utter deserters to their original calling, but now enjoying the luxury of abundant food, anyone's bed, and a lifestyle of utter indolence. One favourite was Winston, a haughty tabby, appropriately named, whose daily demeanour was simply one of deserved ownership. Though lacking the bowler hat and cigar, he was imperious master of all that he surveyed.

Winston

Dogs, on the other hand, lacked the ecclesiastical pedigree or the theocratic sanctuary that may have afforded advantage to the felines. Dogs usually arrived on the station by much more secular means. Like many towns and cities across the globe, Limassol could boast its fair share of feral dogs. They survived by scavenging, on handouts, or by their canine wits. Most were reasonably friendly creatures, having learned perhaps that handouts were unlikely to be forthcoming if canine teeth had just been buried in the prospective donor's leg. From time to time, a reveller from 280 might strike up an association with one of the feral pooches, as he and it meandered the bars, conclude that it was just the dog that he had always wanted, and take it home in a taxi. That was probably how all of the 280 pack had made their arrival. All were of mongrel stock, and all were quick to make themselves at home among the handouts, the unaccustomed kindness, and the waste products of the culinary department.

Station Standing Orders carried no hard and fast rules about the keeping of pets, and the most recent arrival would merely join the others to live a far better life than had been the case on the streets of Limassol. The foster parent of the previous night may well deny all knowledge, concede that he had indeed been the canine vector, make the excuse that it was a lovely dog and that his parents had never allowed him to have a pet, or more likely, shrug his shoulders and pat the dog on the head. Alas there would inevitably come a time when the dog population had increased to noticeable or even to occasionally troublesome levels.

This had become the situation late in 1959. At that time 280 Signals Unit was undergoing a metamorphosis that was being directed by the authorities at Akrotiri, and implemented by the military police. Our canine companions had been observed, and authority had concluded that their numbers were too great, and indeed, they issued the edict that dogs would no longer be permitted on the unit. The order concluded with the instruction that all dogs were to be removed from the unit within two days. Any that remained after that deadline would be destroyed.

The record, and for some the memory, revealed that this was not the first incident of its kind. A little over a year earlier, a similar situation, and a similar order had resulted in the deaths by shooting of several dogs. This had been a shocking act, and at the time it had been condemned for its blatant brutality and the manner in which it had been conducted. The dogs had been buried on the peninsula and at least one headstone bore witness to their deaths, recording that Patsy, Chai, and Tango had met a violent death on 23rd June 1958. After the outcry on that occasion, surely they would not do that again?

These dogs were free roaming across the peninsula, they slept in the bundu, they entered camp when they needed food, they probably hunted in the bush, they were out of sight for most of the time. In 1959, though every effort was made to locate the dogs, to round them up, and to take them to a safer place for release, most could not be found. Only one, the gentle, docile, lovable Sandy, was located a short distance from the tent lines, was quickly attracted, lifted, and hidden in Paradise Lost, safe we hoped until an alternative future could be devised. We later discovered that two more had escaped the roundup and execution, had found concealment in the bundu, or had been afforded safe refuge. Dusty and Sally reappeared a few days later.

As the morning deadline passed, instruction from the RAF Police demanded that all personnel not currently on duty would remain within the domestic area until instructed otherwise. The boundary patrols were called in. The RAF Police arrived, and without greeting, acknowledgement or recognition, they fanned out into the bundu. We waited, and the entire camp held its breath, hoping that the dogs had perhaps jumped into the sea, fled across the airfield, found their way to Ladies Mile, or simply kept their heads down among the local archaeology. Not so! Several shots were heard. The truck that had brought the posse, drove off into the bundu, and a short time later was driven back and out of the camp without stopping. The curfew was lifted. The shock waves resounded through the camp for many days.

We never saw any of the other dogs again. Sandy, Dusty, and Sally were later smuggled out of the camp in a taxi, and were returned to Limassol, from which location, and from which perilous feral life they had earlier been rescued.

***

A short time before Christmas of 1959, RAF Akrotiri became host to a squadron of aircraft from the United States Air Force. A mixed bunch of aircraft, and an equally mixed bunch of people to fly and to service them. They were, of course, based at Akrotiri, where they were provided with everything that they would require, and consequently, we had little direct contact with them. However, they were well aware that many of their aerial activities were observed and controlled by a bunch of guys on the cape, and they made the request to spend a day at Cape Gata, to meet, to learn, to mingle, to socialise. They were, of course made very welcome, and especially so as it was clear that meeting and socialising was a principal motive, and that most of the customary protocols that related to rank and status were to be abandoned.

The formal visit and tour of the technical unit, which involved just a few of our officers, and those who were on duty at the time, was followed by lunch in the officer's mess. No post-lunch activities had been organised, and I think that the expectation had been that the Americans would simply return to Akrotiri. They had other ideas. The remainder of the day was at their disposal, and their declared preference and intention was to drop any remaining formality and to linger for the rest of the day among the rank and file. For some, this included a long evening in the NAAFI, and in the company of a not inconsiderable quantity of Keo.

Much of our conversation during those hours revolved around our respective lives and times, and I believe that our American friends were genuinely shocked to learn, and to see for themselves, the conditions in which we lived. In a good humoured fashion, some of their conversation was laced with a generous measure of bombast and bravado, until our recall of a single incident that induced a pale and silent shock reaction to a few.

Shortly after their arrival at Akrotiri, and well before their visit to 280, three or four of their pilots, who been in aerial practice, decided to introduce themselves to us by 'beating up' the unit. They approached the cape at speed and at very low level, and when making their pass, they were close to zero feet, and with accelerating decibels that challenged our future hearing. They gained altitude, wheeled, and returned to the airfield to land.

In later conversation, we made the remark the one of them at least, in the centre of the pack, had been flying a little close to the limit when he had flown between our two tall slender radio masts. There was silence for a moment. We took the group outside and pointed out the masts, which towered above the radar transmitters. The silence continued. They had simply not seen them, and providence had smiled on that day in their favour.

A few days before their final departure, they staged another flypast, this one in farewell, at a more sedate velocity, and at a secure and safe altitude. We waved our responding farewell to the squadron as they passed over the unit, and then watched with slightly puzzled anticipation as another aircraft brought up the rear. Some unknown kind of transport aircraft, it was being flown at a low but safe altitude and at modest speed as it made its approach. As it passed across the unit, a succession of small packages were projected from the aircraft, each landing with a resounding thud on the ground. Fortunately no-one on terra firma fell victim to one of these falling missiles, which were retrieved and opened with some anticipation.

Toilet rolls! Each package contained one of those simple commodities that had been so conspicuous by their absence at 280 for these many months. Our parlous living conditions had clearly created a sympathetic reaction among our American friends.

Epitaphs for those felled by cascading toilet rolls?

After comfortless months in a paperless privy,
Taken out by an errant airborne bog roll!

Genuine manna from heaven!

***

Two or three weeks after the last of the Christmas and New Year shindigs had passed into history and vague recall, 1959 had become 1960, and daily life and times had re-established their customary and familiar routine. As everyday life continued in pursuit of its ritual, the unit sustained a tragedy so dreadful that shocked silence hung over the entire campus for several days. Emotions were, and remain, difficult to describe, just as the event and its aftermath were difficult to embrace or accept. For those most severely affected, counselling was a prescribed necessity; for a small and intimate number, compassionate repatriation; and for most, a period of very subdued and shocked emotion.

It was the middle of a January night when commotion, and the sounding of the fire warning, roused the entire domestic camp. One of the tents was ablaze, ignition of the fabric had been rapid and all-consuming, and there was little that hand-held fire extinguishers could achieve except to damp down the adjacent tents. Perchance, the two adjacent tents had been empty, the normal residents either being on watch or on extended Christmas leave. Occupancy, or not of the affected tent was uncertain.

Those first on the scene had reported that the origin of the blaze appeared to be close to the apex of the roof, though it spread with terrifying rapidity into the entire body of the tent as burning fragments fell into the void. In the ensuing confusion, no-one could provide answer to the question of the likely location of the occupants of tent B2. The unfolding event proceeded with horrifying rapidity until the arrival of the Akrotiri fire crews who were able to quickly suppress and extinguish the blaze.

The full horror became revealed. The body of one of the tent occupants was discovered on the charred remains of his bed. By fearful coincidence, both of his tent mates had been elsewhere as had been the occupants of the adjacent tents. An enquiry and inquest concluded that the victim had probably fallen asleep without switching off a naked light bulb, and that remnants of paper Christmas decorations, which may have been in contact with the bulb, had been the source of the ignition.

***

While Christmas festivities at 280 may have lacked the glitz and the extravagance of the equivalent celebrations in the civilian world, even at the tail end of the sixth decade, they were entered into with no less enthusiasm. No strings of brightly coloured lights festooned post or pillar, the bundu failed to provide a tree of stature adequate to suspend a bauble or two, and the NAAFI was adorned with a picture of Santa Claus clipped from the Daily Mirror, that had been attached to the wall by a dart through the poor man's genitals. In an adjacent image, something unspeakable was happening to Rudolph.

Work and the watch system continued unabated and as normal. No less normalcy was applied to off- duty hours, though the festive season provided excuse for the normal to be pursued with somewhat greater gusto, for longer hours, and in somewhat increased abundance than a routine week in November or February.

For those of us who had been resident on the unit for only three or four months, Christmas of 1958 had marked the end of a period of familiarity. Those of a more enterprising or acquisitive nature had become totally familiar with the when and how and where that would add diversity greater comfort, or alternative occupation. For the initiates, the months to come would witness these attributes being put to best possible use. It had been an initiatory period of survival or submergence. If the former, continued guile would ensure that onward and upward became the daily battle cry. Alas, for those who had failed to survive the initial immersion, life at the bottom of the pond was perhaps their inevitable 280 destiny.

My personal recollections of the Christmas of 1958 are somewhat limited. Up to and until that time, doting and concerned families had been dutifully despatching parcels of food and other craved commodities to their impoverished sons. Some, very sensibly perhaps, had hoarded tinned supplies in preparation for lean cookhouse times ahead. Others had chosen to splurge the lot in one huge gastro-binge, frequently accompanied by unwise quantities of Keo, and often with the aftermath of one huge gastro mess. In Paradise Lost, we stored a little, pooled a lot, enjoyed the occasional tin of peaches to complement yet another plate of cookhouse sausages, and enjoyed just the occasional bean feast. Our in-house, three course Christmas dinner of 1958, cooked and coddled on our twin Aladdin uprights bore ample witness to our culinary dexterity.

On a daily basis we were not much inclined to consume intoxicants in any other form except Keo. Wine was a rare commodity and only available when imported from outside, and though some spirits were available as small measures in the NAAFI, they were of niggardly stature and expensive, and not much favoured. As our staple, Keo reigned unchallenged and supreme. The Christmas festivities however, afforded cause to take a celebratory libation or two of a different nature. Cyprus is famed for its fine wines, and many of these become subject to distillation and the production of equally fine brandies. However, where there is fine there is also ullage, and where there is nectar, there is also gnat's piss.

In the preparation of brandies at both ends of the quality spectrum, Haggipavlu was, and probably still is, a well-known distiller. One of their products, Zivania by name, loosened the teeth, burned the palate, and induced a slow and prolonged explosion in the stomach. If taken in quantity the same process was repeated in reverse. It was early on the eve of Christmas in that year. I was alone in my tent, it was uncannily quiet at my end of the tent lines, and I guess that I was feeling a little dejected, or maybe even homesick. I was uncertain of the location of my nearest neighbours and companions, but I would no doubt catch up with them later. For the moment, I would be content to sample the bottle of Zivania that happened to be in my possession. Well! A snifter became another, and then another, until a surprising quantity of the contents of the bottle had completed its primary attack and was well into major assault mode. Time to move on.

On selected evenings during the Christmas period, an above average selection of films were screened in the cinema. As a further small gratuity these performances were without charge, though hidden costs did filter into the ample purses of the crooks who managed the refreshment kiosk. I decided to desert the Zivania bottle, and head for the cinema to effect a measure of recovery, before making a later visit to the NAAFI. My route seemed unusually torturous, faulty navigation perhaps, or maybe someone had moved the cinema. The body of the house was crowded and noisy, perhaps Quimby had just made his appearance, so I found a seat at the back. The audience settled as the credits for the main feature were appearing, though to my puzzlement, I found them curiously difficult to read. As the film proceeded, I continued to find difficulty in achieving focus and concentration on the action, and must have concluded that my seat was too far distant from the screen.

To rectify this difficulty, I staggered forward a little along the central aisle to achieve a more advantageous position. The problem persisted. Still I continued to move to the fore, until abruptly, I walked into the screen. Alas, this was not a permanent structure, but was suspended for each screening in front of the small stage. As I tripped and fell forward, the entire screen became detached from its suspension gantry, collapsed around me like a parachute, and left me scrabbling ineffectually around in its folds.

I recall a certain degree of indignant anger and protest as I was thrown out of the building and into the dust outside. Somehow, and by whatever means of perambulation and latent auto-pilot I could muster, I found my way back to A12, where I promptly fell asleep.

The next morning, I awoke unusually early, and to my somewhat relief, I found that the worst effects of my Zivania abuse had left me. My tent companions had evidently returned at some stage during the night, and remained firmly in the arms of Morpheus. I made a quiet exit, and headed for the cookhouse to seek a restorative sausage.

On military units, perhaps especially those in areas of conflict, a time-honoured tradition is played out on Christmas Day. The non-commissioned ranks all assemble in the mess, and Christmas lunch is served to them by the officers. Rank and status are not entirely abandoned, but it is a light-hearted occasion, abundantly punctuated by cautious mickey-taking, and more than just a little deliberate ribaldry.

Christmas 1959 enjoyed a very different atmosphere to that of its predecessor. The Cyprus emergency had mostly become consigned to the history books, though much, much more of the same was to follow towards the end of the next decade and beyond. Personnel numbers were slowly being reduced as the increasing use of automatic technology replaced manpower, and many at 280 were anticipating repatriation and a return home.

While Christmas may indeed come but once a year, some things seem not to be so subject to change, and the one-day herald of Christmas once more bore witness to the Zivania scourge. On this occasion, Zivania may not have been the culprit, but I guess that responsibility may rest equally with one of its close cousins.

Christmas Eve 1959 was party time, in tents, in the NAAFI, in the mess, in the cinema, in the dust outside, it really didn't matter where or which party, everyone was welcome at every venue or location. It was indeed a most sociable evening. Most people who were regular tipplers, pursued their chosen purpose in the correct attire, the principal item of which was a drinking hat. These pieces of seriously maligned headgear took on many forms, most of which were battered far beyond original purpose or recognition, and had been signed by many whose company had been enjoyed on many and varied occasions. This Christmas Eve was no exception, and drinking hats were in plentiful evidence, bobbing atop a bellowing head, crumpled and slightly detached from a silent head, lying where it had fallen, or being used for one of a number of unlikely purposes.

At some stage during the evening, Zivania, Five Kings, Three Star, Keo VSOP, Anglias or related beverage began to assert its authority and to dismiss those instincts that might beget or sustain reason. With the aid and abetment of a similarly plastered companion, a discomfiting plot was hatched. The latrines, as earlier described, were of exactly the same pit and pedestal variety for commissioned and non-commissioned alike. However, the commissioned pedestal enjoyed the added privacy of partitions between individual depositories, each of which was covered by a hinged lid, clear privilege in excess of necessity or reason.

The plan was to make a quick and deadly assault on the officer's latrine block, nail down the lids and melt like silent wraiths into the darkness. The entire camp was infused that evening with noise to rival a football stadium at the instant of the winning goal, and provided that we were not apprehended, nails in hand, there was a very reasonable chance that we would complete the dastardly deed unchallenged. It was at the point of departure to our grisly undertaking that all sense of reason left us. Since then, and to the present day, I have been unable to find purpose, motive, or even a hint of sanity in our next decision. We decreed that we would undertake this grisly deed wearing only a drinking hat and a left sock.

Thus attired, or more correctly unattired, we left the tent lines and described a wide arc to avoid any possible visual contact close to the mess. Here were two pale figures, not in the least suspiciously, padding silently through the dust and thorns in the direction of the officer's quarters. The latrine block was located some distance from the officer's living accommodation, but no more than a few moments shuffle from the domestic arena. Each miscreant, armed with a hammer and a handful of nails, accomplished the task of driving a single substantial nail through each lid and firmly into the pedestal in just a few minutes with the minimum of noise and without detection. Job done, we discarded the hammers and surplus nails in the bundu for daylight retrieval.

Then came our next folly. The officers were provided with a separate urinal. This curious construction comprised an overarching roof and a single wall that supported a line of funnels. Each of these galvanised gargoyles was loosely cradled in a metal hoop, and pointed vertically downward into a trough. Perhaps the elaborate design was to avoid splash from the trough, which carried the flowing micturant into a pit. For reasons also totally unclear, and mystifying to this day, I removed one of the funnels.

We began a diplomatic retreat from the scene of our misdemeanour, and as we approached neutral territory, we passed the fire tent wherein was a telephone connected directly to, and only to, the fire station in Akrotiri.

Here, the venue of our next serious error of judgement.

What a jape to call the fire station and to tell the people in the fire station that the fire station was on fire.

That was our final folly.

Our brief, one line call, "The fire station is on fire!" was overheard by the duty officer. We were promptly, solemnly, and formally charged, on the spot. This, despite the inability of the charging officer to suppress his hilarity and to maintain his composure. There can be few more incongruous sights than two almost naked men, each clad only in a battered hat and a left sock, and one still clutching a urinal funnel, being formally charged with making a bogus fire call. As it would have seemed highly probable that the formal reading of such a charge at the properly appointed location, would have reduced the presiding officers to some measure of hysterics, the charge was later dropped. It is likely that this was the only incident of its kind in military history.

In accordance with tradition, Christmas Day bore witness to service once more by our contingent of commissioned waiters. During the meal, one of the officers approached my table.

"Do you know what happened last night?" he asked.
"Not a clue sir! Nothing untoward we hope."
"Some bastard nailed down the bog seats in our latrine. I almost shat myself, and had to go in the bundu."

My immediate reaction to this apparently unsolicited remark, almost projected a roast potato from between my teeth to the opposite side of the room. I suppressed the mirth, feigned surprise, and even commiserated a little. This had been the very same officer of the sock and hat charge of only a few hours earlier. I was most surprised that he had failed to link sock, hat, urinal and bog seat, but perhaps he had been equally plastered at the time.

***

Christmas 1959 provided 280 Signals Unit, Cape Gata with an addition to its customary and traditional Yuletide festivities. A couple of groups of likely lads put their heads together and concluded that there was sufficient talent, or in its total absence, sufficient brass neck, to prepare, choreograph, and present a home grown show. The venue would be the cinema, entrance would be free, and the entire off-duty camp complement would be expected to attend.

In and among any significant assemblage of human kind anywhere, there can be identified a comprehensive cross section of all of human society. 280 was no exception to this generality, and among the plethora of skills and professions there lurked an aspirant thespian or two. Indeed one of our number trod the boards professionally, though at that period in his career, he had, he claimed, been 'resting'. It was he, and his professionalism that masterminded the principle presentation in our Christmas extravaganza.

Preparation for this splendid event commenced in the autumn, as we busied ourselves with ideas, with early scripts, with cast members, even with rehearsals, before severally scrapping it all and starting again. As preparations slowly began to take shape, we turned our thoughts to the indecently naked cinema stage. We were entirely without stage props of any kind, and our manufacturing genius would be limited to whatever material we could obtain in the usual manner. In the event, we did nothing, but simply adorned the stage in the elegantly suspended drapes of some parachutes that we had liberated from the Akrotiri stores.

We practiced, we rehearsed, we even prepared a programme, and come the day, we thought that we were ready. The show would comprise two principle theatrical performances, aided and abetted before, during and after, by a supporting cast drawn from the amazing cornucopia of 280 talent. Among our number there were a few creditable musicians, one or two who believed that they could sing, and just a few comedians who would recite a few risque ditties and jokes to keep the audience tittering.

The auditorium filled to excess, and a peek through the curtain just before the show was due to begin revealed that every corner and crevice had been filled, gratifyingly, to a point somewhat beyond capacity. They were a cheerfully grisly, Keo fuelled crowd, mostly clutching additional bottles to ensure that the jeering larynx remained lubricated throughout. They clearly were in high expectation of great things.

Our minstrels played a jolly tune, to be followed by a singer who may have done his best, though this failed to find the approbation that it may or may not have deserved.

"Rubbish!" "Get 'em off!" "Tickle your arse with a feather!" All encouraging stuff!

The first sketch was delivered by a motley bunch from Scotland. The scene was a crowded tram in Glasgow, a conveyance that came complete with a well-bosomed, blonde conductress who was attempting to collect fares from each of the passengers. None of the passengers was seated, and the tram was evidently swaying perilously. The passengers included a drunk, an individual carrying a huge stack of parcels, one attempting to read a broadsheet newspaper, one with no money, and a belligerent sod who refused to comply in any way with anything. While they were clearly working to a sketchy script, much of the dialogue was gloriously ad lib, and was genuinely funny. The applause it received was well deserved.

A little more music and song, even one or two of those vulgar ditties that normally found voice in the dead of night in the NAAFI or in some ribald tent.

Our second presentation was Shakespearian, or more correctly, it had once been Shakespearian. It took the form of a truly mangled scene from 'A Midsummer Night's Dream', cunningly entitled 'A Midwinter's Nightmare'. The scene, a wood near Athens, the characters, lovers Pyramus and Thisbe, aided and abetted by Moonshine, Wall, and Lion (played by Sandy, one of the resident dogs). I adopted the part of Prologue, and used it to introduce the performance and to support the nonsense as it proceeded. My costume for this part was a bedsheet toga generously adorned with painted symbols of dubious character. Other costumes and props were appropriate to each character and included lantern, bush, staff, and Pyramus' trusty blade fashioned out of a leek. In keeping with the revised title, though the original dialogue had flowed from the quill of the bard, it had been heavily abused and amended, and peppered throughout with constant and irreverent ad lib.

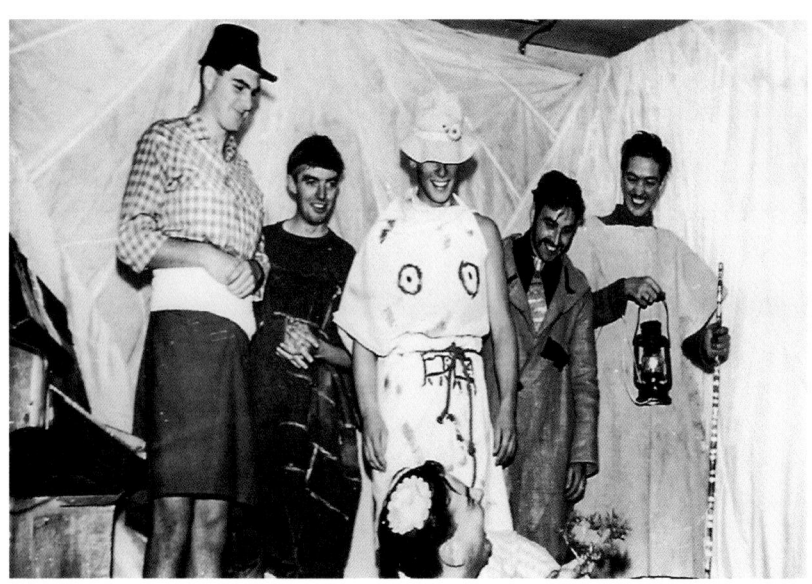

"Wall, that vile Wall, which did these lovers sunder;
And through Wall's chink, poor souls, they are content
To whisper, at which let no man wonder."

Wall's chink? Better not to ask!

It was a ghastly but hilarious parody. Those of us on stage were rolling about as the dialogue became ever more spontaneous and out of order. From the auditorium a veritable torrent of good-natured abuse was projected towards those capering about on the stage, only to be met in kind and in equal by the players. Though descent into chaos could have been the inevitable prediction, good humoured mutual verbal abuse simply added to an atmosphere of good cheer. This was pantomime, pandemonium, farce, slapstick, harlequinade, and utter foolishness all immersed in a tornado of unrestrained audience participation. It was light hearted if a little vulgar. It was different. It was a perfect remedy for any among us who may have been suffering the pangs of some measure of Yuletide gloom. It was simply brilliant, and it is without hesitation, shame or embarrassment that I am proud and content to make that statement.

The festive season would not be permitted to pass without a Hogmanay delivery from our Scottish colleagues. The first day of January would be celebrated with a parade, with a gathering of the clans, with a salute, and with the formal raising of The Saltire. As they possessed not a single kilt among them, many and varied were the skirts, the loincloths, the kirtles, the farthingales, and of course the sporrans that they had manufactured for the occasion. Equally diverse were the tunics, the cassocks, the togas and the boleros; the wigs, the headpieces, the plumes and the tiaras. Badges of rank had been invented, and two columns lined up face to face. A motley array of weaponry, which included spears, swords, manufactured fowling pieces, a bazooka, and half a horse were presented to the order. A solemn inspection was conducted, the Saltire was proudly raised on an elevated stick. 'God save Bonnie Prince Charlie'.

***

One morning, a short time after the elevation of the water tank to its pedestal atop the Pillars of Hercules, the discovery that someone had painted a large, red, Hammer and Sickle motif on one side of the container became abundantly apparent. No-one ever confessed to this offence, and not surprisingly, enquiry failed to identify a culprit. The offence was considered a serious breach of allegiance, and uncharacteristically perhaps, the Commanding Officer was furious. A working party was immediately assembled, and given the order to remove the offending blemish immediately. After all, at that time, the reds were still undeniably under the beds.

***

1959 expired, and we slithered into 1960. For the class of '58, that transition brought with it the sobering realisation that the irresponsible days of our National Service were approaching their terminus. Not too far distant was re-entry into our own personal worlds of reality, of destiny, and of a future that extended far into the bewilderment of unpredictability.

Perhaps some of the words of the American mathematical minstrel Tom Lehrer are apposite, though penned at the time in celebration of the imminent conclusion of studentship.

Soon we'll be out among the toil and strife.
Soon we'll be sliding down the razor blade of life.

Our remaining months, and those of the first half of the year, were months of relative freedom from threatened conflict, freedom to explore the island that was our temporary home, freedom to make the very best use of our allocated or contrived free time. We visited Kostas Kollis, we wasted wanton nights in Limassol, we took time to explore the cultural and ecclesiastical history of Cyprus, we visited Nicosia, Famagusta, Larnaca, Paphos (before it became a city), and picturesque Kyrenia. We wandered parts of its beautiful mountains and coastlines. We explored the fascination of an island hidden from us and denied to us during all of the earlier months of our residence.

We abandoned our weaponry, we stayed out all night in the sin spots of Limassol, or we made our taxi-borne return to Akrotiri deep into the wee small hours, and far beyond any hope of a lift along the night-time road to 280. A temporary billet at Akrotiri could usually be located, though for the most part we preferred to make the trudge up the road to 'Hell on the Hill'.

One such moonlit occasion brought us an unexpected bonus. Shortly after exiting the perimeter of the main Akrotiri camp we encountered a vehicle. A diesel driven road roller of modest proportions had been in use for its intended purpose, and had evidently been parked up for the night. Well! Why not? The answer was self-evident. None of our small party had ever propelled such a vehicle, and we had absolutely no idea how to start it. Quite how we did achieve this is lost to memory, but after some furtive fiddling with switches and controls, and much to our abrupt and collective surprise, the machine roared into life. Well! After that impressive demonstration of nocturnal engineering genius, driving the thing must surely be a doddle.

Walking pace may well have been quicker, but would have lacked the spirit of stupid adventure. As we trundled towards the entrance to 280, domestic guard duty had long been withdrawn, we became bound to ponder the question of what to do with the machine now. A quick decision and rapid disposal became somewhat imperative, as the sound of the engine would soon carry on the breeze and alert the curiosity of some light sleeper. Mischief prevailed. We drove as far as the officer's mess and discovered that the width of the entrance porch exceeded that of the front roller by a margin of several inches. We inched the machine forward until, and without damage, the roller tucked snugly inside the porch. We then cut the engine and fled.

There was of course a brief local enquiry, but so far as we knew, no-one had logged our return to Akrotiri, no-one had seen us trundle past the latrines, the silent domestic facilities, and onward to the officer's mess building. No-one in fact had any idea how an errant road roller had been spirited silently along a couple of miles of road to be abandoned with creditable precision, in the porch. The power of autosuggestion perhaps.

No damage had been sustained. Heads were shaken in tittered denial. The following morning, apparently, the driver had reported the theft of his machine.

"Try 280!!!"

Chapter 10. Nothing if not valiant on the sporting field of valour.

... "Ring the bell verger, ring the bell ring," ...

*

*For many, leisure and relaxation remain incomplete
without the adrenalin-inducing accompaniment of competition.
The 280 resort record is brandished with pride.
The resort and its guests have placed themselves in the constant forefront
of competition, and on occasions too numerous to record,
have returned with prize or trophy.*

*No less supportive of our glorious sportsmen, and their equally proud record,
has been the happy band of followers and cheer leaders
who have made their worthy contribution
to team and to individual success,
and who have made fulsome, vigorous and usually noisy contribution
to subsequent and well-earned celebration.*

*

For 280 Signals Unit, Cape Gata, 1960 heralded the beginning of the end. RAF Akrotiri was expanding, and the distance between 280 and the main camp was reducing, both physically and psychologically. 280, as it had been known and loved, was in decline, and continued thus as ever more of its electronic functions became accommodated by the more up to date technology that had been established on Mount Olympus in the Troodos Mountains.

The decline continued, and in 1962 the domestic function at 280 Signals Unit, Cape Gata was brought to a close. The remaining personnel were moved to new accommodation in a custom built billet block on the main station. By the end of that year, all of the tents had been removed from the domestic site, all of the permanent buildings had been dismantled or demolished, and as radar heads and communications equipment were becoming redundant, these too were gradually being decommissioned and removed.

By the end of 1962, 280 Signals Unit Cape Gata, that once vibrant, celebrated, irreverent, noisy place, oozing with character and bursting with comradeship, had simply ceased to exist. During the ensuing years and to the considerable dismay and chagrin of some of those who had been part of its history, its energy and its dynamism, it gradually became expunged from the record, lost to successive memory and consciousness, and denied even the distinction of an honourable demise. Unlike the other more remote signals unit detachments, Cape Andreas (751A. SU), Cape Greco (751 SU), Cape Kormakiti (7 SU), and Pano Kivedhes (751 SU Detachement); Cape Gata had simply been buried in an unmarked grave.

It is sometimes to our great benefit therefore, to have in our midst, those who are reluctant to discard, those for whom an artefact represents an occasion or an event, those who will store and hoard items of the moment as memorabilia and recall, as the future catches up and becomes the present. A few such people, for whom time at 280 was creative of a worthwhile memory did choose to retain items of the moment that were, to most, mere ephemerals, items in possession for a specific purpose, to be discarded as soon as that purpose has been satisfied. To these people, the archive and its compilers owe a considerable debt of gratitude. Without these nut-gatherers, their sentiment, and their treasury, local and detailed heritage would surely be bankrupt.

While the early 280 years had been preoccupied with ensuring that the present would evolve into a future, the paucity of the written record had indicated that the fact that it would also become a past had been ignored. 1960 had conceived and had given birth to a simple tool that would ensure that the remaining years did not stumble into this same pitfall, provided of course that product was sufficiently attractive to the memory hoarders.

The Gata Gazette enjoyed a brief but informative life, its survival being dictated by the limited span of years that remained to the unit. In those days, well before the advent of the silicon chip, it was laboriously typed and duplicated on cheap paper that was almost soft enough for an alternative purpose, and which, in any case was unsuitable for casual storage. We are thus indebted to those who elected to find shelf space for these irreplaceable portions of the archive, and who, by so doing, have permitted the shared memory of the few surviving copies.

The Gata Gazette was a journal of whimsy, of humorous offerings, jokes, and anecdotes. It contained articles of general interest, personal experience, and occasional factual paragraphs. It carried items of news; of people interest; of updates on current matters; of games, crosswords, and puzzles; of promotion and advertisement; in short, of all of the familiar paraphernalia of a local journal. Its splendid pages allowed for the kind of banter and competition that could transcend protocol and procedure, and allow for the rank and file to occupy the same unprejudiced space as those who carried the Queen's commission.

One entry in the 'Lost and Found' column serves to illustrate:

"<u>WANTED</u>. Two stretcher bearers to carry officers back from rugby training. Recently, two corpses were left behind by twelve fit and strong young men on the road between Akrotiri and 280 Signals Unit."

Much more important, it also kept a record of sporting information, of fixtures and of results, and may indeed be the only surviving record of 280's dazzling sporting history.

Down among the bullshit and the tidy corners of the Akrotiri main campus, the slightly more aboriginal residents of Cape Gata were ever the butt of derisory joke and comment. Perhaps this demonstrated and frequently expressed contempt was the source of, or the inspiration for the determination that was clearly demonstrated on the field of sporting endeavour. The sporting men of 280 were formidable opponents, and a force to be reckoned with when, and where ever, they took to the field of competitive opposition. Never, of course without due and full regard for the 'Queensberry Rules' of every sporting activity. No foul play among the 280 sporting warriors, no red cards expected here.

Though boldness it was that propelled the valiant and determined sportsmen of 280 along the paths of glory, there could be little doubt that boldness alone would be insufficient to ensure that 280 would be etched upon every shield or cup. Insufficient to ensure that the 280 captain would take his place on the top step of the podium. Insufficient to ensure that he would receive the regimental champion laurel from the wife of the CO, or from some big-busted bimbo who was part of the travelling circus here to entertain the troops. No indeed, boldness could only be an accompaniment to training, hard work, and dedication, and just the occasional kick on the shins when the attention of the referee was elsewhere. It was in these areas that the sporting heroes of 280, solo or team, laboured under considerable disadvantage.

A few miles distant, in the huge garrison of Episkopi lay a green, verdant and irrigated place known as Happy Valley. Here were to be found and enjoyed by the few or the fortunate, pitches, courses, greens, tracks, courts, rings, and gymnasia of every kind. Here were played the ultimate events of any tournament, here were championships won, and here the most coveted silverware was distributed. Here, the big boys played, while the big girls watched.

Closer to home, at Akrotiri, facilities were modest in comparison. They may not have been quite so verdant, but they were green, at least seasonally, and a generous range of sports were catered for. They were no less available to the 280 ruffians, but this increased the competition for time and space, for our remote reservation, and for any equipment requirement.

On the home patch, and in comparison with almost any equivalent sporting situation on the globe, the situation at 280 had no parallel. Down at the nether end of the technical site, and adjacent to the motor transport compound, a rough rectangle of unwilling earth had been cleared of bundu. The clearance had not been in any way custom prescribed, but had been incidental to the clearance of the entire station, and this derelict patch had simply not yet been claimed for any other purpose. Any flimsy remaining vestiges of topsoil had been sluiced or blown away by the elements, leaving behind a space of irregular dimension, comprising bare rock, loose gravel, sand and dust, and not a single vestige of any kind of vegetation. A more unprepossessing location upon which to conduct any sporting activity was difficult to envisage.

However, it was the only location that was available for our use, and so we used it. Perimeter and internal pitch markings would have survived no more than one game, one rain storm, or one gust of wind, which ever be the first arrival. Thus, the perimeter of the playing area was marked, with some success, using rope, and secured where possible with tent pegs. Internal pitch markings were generally left to the imagination, and infringements to the referee, so the more competitive meetings were frequently dominated by a barrage of misdirection, misinformation, misunderstanding, and mistaken identity.

In truth, the pitch was simply not fit for purpose. Its loose and broken surface ensured that movement at any speed greater than a dawdle was quite likely to result in a trip, a stumble, a fall, and a series of painful abrasions. Not only was the pitch unyielding, witchcraft would assert that it was also scheming and malevolent, awaiting and entrapping the unwary, protruding yet another stony convolution to interrupt the progress of a passing boot and projecting its occupant into unintended flight.

No sporting venture was immune to its capacity for entrapment, though some fared slightly better than others. Alas, the armed forces league did not support marbles, or tiddlywinks, or quoits, or boules, all of which might have proved practicable on its surface, while its merciless and unforgiving nature ensured that mishap during some of the faster and more vigorous sports would, and did result in abrasive injury of flesh-rending proportions.

The pitch was surrounded on three sides by an additional hazard, in the form of the all-embracing, dense and spiny bundu. For almost all of the sports that made use of this obdurate and bloodstained patch, a ball of one form or another was an essential and critical artefact. The smaller variety, if projected beyond visual contact from cricket bat or tennis racquet, were almost certainly lost forever, and to this day the bundu within the radius of a lusty knock could yet yield a positive treasure trove of lost balls. Even the larger variety, though subject to a much more modest projected radius could equally become lost to view or simply be lodged inaccessibly among the thorns and spikes of a million bundu bushes.

Most sports that make use of balls, make use equally of the term bounce when describing the trajectory of a ball after it makes contact with the ground. Soccer or rugby balls will normally adopt a post-bounce direction that is dictated by spin or the shape of the ball, The 280 pitch dictated its own terms, and many the players whose limbs flailed in futile fashion as the target of their intentions took a random course at the whim of another rocky undulation. For fast moving cricket or tennis balls the term ricochet is the only one appropriate, leaving the intended recipient with little hope of contact let alone positive response.

When occasion permitted possession of the ball, both football and rugby players did at least enjoy the facility to mark up a score. Somewhat makeshift posts had been raised at each end of the field of play, but with a crossbar that was required to satisfy the requirements of both games. The compromise height clearly did neither, but as the posts were loosely permanent, dismantling and reassembling for every change of game was somewhat beyond the call of reason.

In one corner, a temporary cricket net helped to reduce the gross sacrifice of balls to the voracious bundu. However, as relentless ricochet dictated that the ball rarely reached the crease unless delivered like a cannon ball in free aerial trajectory, the net served to reduce the risk of broken legs among the onlookers. The tennis teams had drawn an even shorter straw. Any attempts to play tennis without net or court markings, may induce a tut or a titter among the bystanders, but imposes serious difficulty for the scoreboard. Hockey practice fared little better. Among the pebbles and limestone chunks that littered the field of play, the modest hockey ball could readily lose identity, and the cry of triumph was, on occasion, choked into a gargle with the realisation that a small stone had been projected forcibly between the goalkeeper's legs.

No sporting activity was without the risk of injury, and any fall, however lightweight, would result in the loss of skin and a millimetre or so of the tender flesh beneath. Rugby was the most injury susceptible of our activities, and many who sustained the deeper abrasions, probably carry the scars to this day. Something to show the grandchildren - this one won at the battle of the Cape Gata playing field. A really heavy tackle on any playing surface of this unyielding character could, of course, quite readily result in more serious injury. Many were the hobbled and assisted visits to the medical centre at Akrotiri in the wake of a heavy tussle.

One experience of my own remains clear in memory, though I think that the scars have healed. During a home rugby fixture, a particularly heavy tackle brought me down, leaving most of the external parts of one knee and one elbow smeared across the ground, but also bringing my head into heavy contact with terra very firma. Confused, disoriented, and semi-concussed, I crawled off the pitch on hands and knees and through the line of spectators. There I collapsed in a dusty heap until the increasing pain where the skin of knee and elbow used to be brought yelping awareness, and a return to the fray.

I guess that there were fewer trivial injuries on the field of conflict than there were in training, principally because the playing surfaces at Akrotiri and elsewhere were much less user unfriendly. While some passing injuries were sport related, others seemed to have closer ties to an environmental relationship. A worthy 280 batsman stands proudly at the Akrotiri crease, awaiting with customary aplomb for the next delivery by the star opposition bowler. Alas, he faces not only the deadly bowler, but also the sun directly above and ahead. The delivery is high and fast, and as he raised his head to track the trajectory of the oncoming ball, it becomes entirely lost to view in the celestial glare. With bat poised to do very little, the ball strikes him, with a resounding crack, on the side of the head. To his knees, to his elbows, to the unyielding ground and to the medics to check for signs of concussion.

Rugby fared similarly. The final and winning try of the game was on the point of entry into the record books. Only a few yards from the line, and the only member of the opposing team with any chance of preventing defeat made a wild lunge and a very clumsy tackle. Checked but not arrested, the almost-scorer, lurched, lost his balance, stumbled at speed to the right, and wrapped his face around one of the posts. He slid to the ground and groaned as the blood erupted from his shattered nose. He was also hauled off to the medics to check for signs of concussion.

A football match is in full swing. One swift player was guiding the ball deftly and rapidly in the direction of the opposition goal. Abruptly he stops, puts his hand to his head, the ball rolls ahead until claimed by the opposition. The player remains immobile hand to head, and complaining of a severe pain in one eye. Inspection reveals a grisly truth worthy of the Hammer House of Horror.

A tiny invertebrate larva, akin to a small maggot was inching its way back and forth across his cornea, or maybe even inside, no-one seemed sure. To the medics and an urgent requirement for a knowledgeable entomologist. Not the only time that the Gata Eye Fly had seen fit to make use of a human orbit as a maternity ward.

No-one, to my knowledge ever attempted the victorious knee slide beloved by football players in temperate regions, in celebration of scoring a goal, or indeed the triumphant flying try-scoring belly-flop beloved by rugby players. To have inadvertently attempted such a gesture at 280 would surely have been to sacrifice both knee caps, expose most of both tibias to risk of sunburn, or impose serious re-arrangement to pectorals, nipples and belly fat. The risk at Akrotiri was somewhat reduced, and I suspect that the practice was followed at Episkopi, not in celebration of success, but because there was the awaiting orgasm of real, green, soft, even wet grass upon which to do it.

One most prestigious football match was enacted on Christmas morning of 1958. It had been one of those wild and irresponsible proposals that fell into the category of 'a good idea at the time'. Incubated and hatched during the Keo drenched festivities of Christmas Eve, two scratch teams had entitled themselves 'The Wheels' and 'The Wasters' and had vowed to do battle in a pre-lunchtime clash on 280's unyielding ground. True to promise and pledge, most of the players turned up, all in various conditions of disarray. Some nursing the debilitating effects of events that were painfully recent, other brandishing the euphoria of stimulated recovery. The match was a good-humoured shambles of miss-kicks, stumbles, vomiting, the occasional accidental goal, and refereeing that was of no consequence whatever. The final score has been lost to history, but I guess that it was as inconsequential as the proceedings. An obituary or two may have appeared in the Gata Gazette.

Hockey could never realistically be attempted at 280, and matches were always played at Akrotiri or Episkopi. Hockey was not a particularly popular sport, and the 280 team were very frequently without a full complement. To make up the shortfall, additional players were recruited almost at random, but usually from the football or rugby teams. It was of little consequence that they possessed no knowledge whatever of the rules of the game, what did matter was that they were big, and with a stick in hand, they were dangerous. Thus, new and usually irregular rules of the sport were devised and operated on match days, and while the regular players maintained a respectful distance from the highly irregular and equally hazardous action, the auxiliary force bamboozled the referee and lambasted the opposition. In the process, they generally bestowed considerable enhancement upon the score sheet.

In advance of one prestigious match at Episkopi, the hockey team captain was offered a lift by a playing officer. In preparation for the game, the officer had just washed his shorts, and he made the request of the captain to hold the wet shorts out of the car window to enable them to dry. The 'oops' moment was a great temptation, but as the officer was a key member of the team, diplomacy won the day.

Despite the absence of a home ground training facility, 280 SU were the proud winners of the inter-island hockey championships of 1959, and the equally proud recipients of the cup to prove it.

Perhaps one of the most bruising of our sporting endeavours was Rugby Sevens. This pursuit of competitive glory is always fast, furious, and not for the faint of heart. It involves large men moving at high speed in frequent collision with equally large men moving equally rapidly in the opposite direction. It might be compared with rival pachyderms vying for supremacy on the Amboseli Plains, or Red Deer stags at the rut in Glen Shee.

When played or practiced on the plush and yielding turf of Oxfordshire, or even on the somewhat less cushioned greenswards of Episkopi, contusion, laceration, abrasion and bruise were invariable outcomes. When practice and preparation were required on the bone shattering surface of the 280 pitch it was not beyond the bounds of possibility that body portions if not body parts would be abandoned to the shrivelling mercy of the sun. More regularly, portions of that unruly patch of stony waste became deeply embedded in the unhappy flesh, to be removed wincingly later by use of a surgical device normally used for sowing buttons on a tunic.

The Middle East Sevens was a well supported and hard fought annual tournament. Historically, the bold men from 280 had fielded a side, and while they had never been outright victors, their track record was an honourable one. 1960 was to be no exception, and the team won through the early rounds to earn a place on the field of conflict in Malta. Playing, in reserve, avid supporter, or just a seeker of illicit passage, this was one not to be missed. I don't remember being selected to play, but RAF Luqa was a change, just as Valetta provided distraction and delight. I don't suppose that we won the glittering trophy, but the rewards were certainly worth the effort and the skiving.

More locally however, the 280 seven-a-side rugby squad enjoyed singular success. In match after match, the premier teams from service units across the island fell victim to the heavy-duty determination of the 280 underdogs. Just a few of the victory celebrations fell foul of over exuberance, and at times when emotions still ran a little high, a rescue mission became a requirement. After one successful game in Nicosia, some of the wandering conquerors had taken a little too liberally of the Keo nectar, and had removed a small selection of smart brass identity plaques from the entrances to several offices. This somewhat vandalistic act had outraged a number of locals in a subsequently visited bar, and they threatened a measure of mayhem. Wisely, the miscreants elected to leave, only to find that a local worthy, who had been canvassing for an election, had whipped up a crowd that was lying in wait outside the bar. Just at the point of imminent open conflict, a whirlwind rescue saved the day. Two land rovers, bearing armed military police swept into the square, quickly dispersed the crowd, bundled the intimidated 'victims' into the vehicles and sped off into the night. No further action was taken, and the relieved plaque collectors were instructed to get back to their bus and to leave the city. It might not have been quite such an easy passage had the military police squad been aware of the committed vandalism that had been the original catalyst to the riot.

Six-a-side football enjoyed equal success. In a tournament that embraced a period of several months, teams from all of the Akrotiri units and 280, engaged in furious sporting competition in pursuit of a much coveted trophy. At one game towards the close of the contest, during which the 280 team had played badly but fortunately, and had squandered many chances, the score remained stubbornly at no score for either side at the final whistle. A quirk of the rule that related to corner kicks awarded the 280 team with a nominal victory, and a clear path to the final game. The final victory provided a moment of glory for the warriors from the hill, and a worthy tribute to their determination. Until that moment, the trophy had always proudly graced an Akrotiri cabinet.

One rather odd event took place in Limassol. This was a football game against a local Turkish team, and the service opponents were drawn from various units at Akrotiri, including 280. Once changed into football strip and ready to play, the visiting service team were escorted into a securely fenced compound through a hefty gate, and this was locked behind them, presumably to remain thus until the Turkish side had claimed victory by fair means or foul. There could be little doubt about the allegiance of the crowd, which bayed and howled for British blood throughout every moment of the game and beyond. This was off-putting, so perhaps it was a diplomatic convenience that the Turks did indeed win, by a margin of three goals to nil.

Whilst the training on the 280 pitch, as well as injury during competition, took serious toll of the 280 players, their success on the football field especially during the 1959 – 1960 - 1961 seasons, was remarkable. The tournament for the equally coveted Wing Shield, also embraced an extended period and was open to all of the Akrotiri units. The league tables were something of a progressive conundrum, and periodically the 280 captain would be summoned to a meeting of the football judiciary to be provided with a progress report. As it transpired, progress was good all the way to the two final games.

The hard fought penultimate had 280 trailing by one goal with a mere five minutes on the clock. A misguided pass from a corner kick struck one player on the leg, and became deflected past the bemused defenders. The default afforded victory, the margin of required points, and the critical step along the road to the final game of the tournament. Their opponents were the most successful sporting unit on the station. 103 Maintenance Unit was everyone's arch rival, and they were the proud and jealous guardians of the majority of the sporting silver. Could the hilltop minnows take on their might, and match them skill for skill?

Well! Perhaps not! It was a grimly determined team that descended the hill on match day, complete with their followers, their supporters, and most of those who were off-duty. This was a big, big occasion! Much was at stake, and if the minnows could pull it off, the victory would be sensational. They played hard. They were supported with passion and with maximum decibels from the crowded touchline. They played harder. The touchliners roared until they were hoarse. The crescendo increased with every passing goal, whichever side claimed the score. The minnows kicked and dribbled, thrust and parried, feigned and passed, and shot for goal again and again. As the final whistle blew, the entire arena erupted in stentorian exultation and in celebration of a glorious victory. At the end of play, the score stood at 7 - 3, and 280 'A' team had, at last, vanquished their arch rivals at 103 MU.

During these sporting seasons the victories and the trophies continued to accumulate. Another football cup final and a 4 - 0 victory over a powerful army team. The trophies from five major football and rugby tournaments enjoyed pride of place in the 280 Trophy Cabinet. Football cups, the Hockey League and wing cups, the Tennis wing cup and the men's and mixed doubles trophies, Though 280 also fielded two Cricket teams, they narrowly missed out on the honours.

No less dedicated to their sporting endeavours, athletes ploughed their sometimes solitary training furrow through the year, to maintain their competitive fitness in preparation for the annual Akrotiri Sports Tournament. This major event in the sporting calendar embraced several days, and provided opportunity for competition in a wide range of track and field events. No such tournament could be inaugurated without the ceremonial prelude of a march past by the entire assemblage of hopeful and anticipatory teams, all under the respectful and supportive eye of the station commanding officer. The team from 280 proudly joined this colourful cavalcade, intent upon taking fiercely competitive part, and taking home whatever silver it could earn. It did, but as always on the field of individual athletic endeavour, the inevitable and invariable score sheet reveals the truth of the adage, 'Some you win, some you lose'.

Swimming was the daily pastime pursued by most, but it was strictly a leisure activity, and little interest was shown in the first organised swimming gala. Few attended, and even fewer made the winners rostrum, preferring perhaps the more languid luxury of our own, far superior swimming pool. Here was lazy indulgence, there was breathless thrashing of the water in pursuit of a distant floating flag. In the sun-kissed surroundings of 280 Pool, an over-heated body could be cooled in its depths, and the dreamer could indulge in the vision of the lithe body of Esther Williams emerging from the gentle swell and taking her elegant place among the less elegant bodies on the rocky platform.

280 excelled at the annual Akrotiri Sports Day tug of war contest. The heaving power of the team of apparent minnows simply could not be matched by opponents from any other unit on the island. The secret of their success was inherent in their training methods and the identity of their training opponents. Their rhythmic and musical, 'heave… heave… heave', was pitted against the immobility of a three-ton truck - with the handbrake applied.

Another successful solitary sporting venture was the 280 performance in hurling the javelin. Our spear throwing stalwarts propelled a mean spike, and proved a worthy match for all-comers.

Not all of our later sporting activities were competitive. In the later years, when freedom and facility permitted, cycling became popular, as did go-karting at Episkopi.

Whatever the sport, whatever the occasion, whatever the competition, 280 would be represented. A veritable army of supporters and followers, gave voice and inspiration to those who were striving for glory on the field of honour. To collective delight this extended far beyond a rag-tag bunch of vociferous flag wavers, and included rank as well as file. On the field of sporting conflict, and even in the dressing room, rank was ignored, and a degree of reasonable equality reigned supreme. More important at 280, the commanding officer afforded his personal patronage, and urged the same from every off-duty member of the unit. His allegiance even extended a short distance beyond the hallowed covers of the book of rules. On some of those occasions when honour was at stake, and the competitors on pitch or field required every available voice in support, he would instruct that the radar was to be put on to stand-by and maintenance, to permit maximum audience support and participation.

The regularly participatory supporting army were a fine body of men whose attendance at each sporting event was heralded by the unmistakeable cacophony of discordant acoustics delivered on a miscellany of home produced instruments. Principal among these were percussion devices in the form of a variety of redundant cans and culinary vessels of multiple size, some beaten some rattled, and wind instruments that were the early precursors of the vuvuzela. Dress, on these occasions was optional, sometimes fanciful, sometimes adorned by elaborate rosettes, but always dominated by some of the finest examples of the milliner's art ever encountered. Mostly towering in stature, and always splendid in decoration, these cranial adornments ranged from the more modest fez, tarboosh, or tam o'shanter, to include glittering tiaras and waving plumes, and ultimately top hats of extraordinary elevations.

The banner borne aloft, and carried at the head of each procession proudly proclaimed:

UP THE BONNY 80'S.

This slogan, chanted noisily during our march to each event, and generally continuing throughout the proceedings was calculated to disrupt similar gestures in support of the opposition, and indeed, whenever contrived, to disrupt equally the opposition on the pitch.

The monotony of it all did reap its benefits, as well as earning its sometimes well-deserved criticisms, especially when delivered with sufficient fervour to undo the fine musical efforts of the frustrated maestros in the military orchestra, and its apoplectic director.

"Up the eighties!" "Up the eighties!" "Up the eighties!"

"Up the Eighties!" Strident vocal inspiration for the boys from 'Hell on the Hill', and equally vociferous terror for their opposition of the day. Thus did each of our glorious sporting undertakings commence, and with no less enthusiasm did they conclude.

Chapter 11. That sweet illicit nibble on the other side of the fence.

... "Fiddle diddle dee fiddle dee, said the fiddlers," ...

*

*Let us not ignore the many pleasures interests and delights
that lie beyond the boundaries of our resort.*

*Those who are more upwardly and outwardly mobile
prepare their makeshift machines
and head for the temptations of the hinterland.*

*Others, lacking the good fortune of mobility ownership,
may obtain their means of transportation from other sources,
and follow similar routes.*

*Just a few, upon whom providence shines more generously,
connive passage to more distant places.*

*

There came times, not many, just an occasional smattering, when the opportunity to leave the unit for a more substantial period of time became available. Some were highly attractive, and inevitably became subject to competition among the more practiced of the 'volunteer' force. Others were significantly less so, the 'volunteers' made themselves scarce, and the positions became filled by compulsory postings.

RAF Troodos located on the summit of Mount Olympus in the Troodos Mountains, already mentioned, was a far more comfortable location in which to work, and in which to live. Its relaxed ambience attracted many, and any vacancy in staffing did not usually remain a vacancy for long. For many however, the sporting activities, the superior facilities at Akrotiri, the fleshpots of Limassol, the leisurely delights of 280 pool and the swimming, or perhaps it was simply the unabashed charm of Cape Gata that directed most to be faithful to the location.

RAF Troodos began life as an experimental unit. Technological advances were perhaps beginning to suggest that an all-seeing eye at an elevated location might successfully embrace the surveillance functions currently being carried out by disparate, and vulnerable, units presently operating from coastal promontories. Its establishment as 751 Signals Unit actually preceded the establishment of its titular namesake at Cape Greco. At first it became staffed by personnel seconded from 7SU RAF Kormakiti, as 7A SU, before becoming linked to 280SU. In its more independent role and function, it adopted the title 280A SU, RAF Troodos. With the ultimate close-down of all of the smaller units, RAF Troodos continued to serve as the principal radar unit on the island, a function that continues to the present day.

In spite of the seductive lure and unabashed attraction of daily life on Cape Gata, reasonably regular skiving visits to Troodos and to the accommodation at Pingo's Hotel added welcome diversity, a change of scene, and in the summer, an escape from the heat. The ever ascending route to Troodos afforded rapidly reducing temperatures, a green environment, forest and mountain scenery, gently whispering pine trees at the higher elevations, and vines, grapes and oranges in abundance. Deep snow was a bonus for those who ventured this far during the depths of winter.

The comfort and relaxed atmosphere at Pingo's was simply incomparable. As the name implied, a former hotel, the two storey timber and stone building, with sleeping quarters for the rank and file on the upper floor, bedrooms and bathrooms below for the officers, store rooms to the rear, and a large and well-appointed lounge. A large open log-burning fire assured comfortable living even in the depths of the most severe winter weather, and a tea and snack bar in one corner of the lounge provided most extra-prandial requirements.

Though Keo may not have been on tap, or quite so available as the Cape Gata supply, the villages of Platres and Troodos were not too far distant. One small benefit enjoyed by those at Pingo's, and which certainly did not feature at Cape Gata, was the daily issue of a small ration of rum. No doubt as an aid to keep out the cold, the instigation of this naval tradition on top of a mountain remains unclear.

***

Throughout the year, and at its location in the Eastern Mediterranean, Cyprus becomes the annual recipient of a diverse range of climatic conditions, and especially along its southern coast. While the long summers are unbearably hot, and the winters cool and occasionally very wet, it is the brief interim seasons that impose the greatest climatic diversity. Spring is brief, floristically colourful, and on Cape Gata always brought warm and pleasant relief from the wet and the attendant mud of winter. The lady wearing the cloak of autumn could be something of a harridan who elected to dispel the torrid heat of summer, but to replace it, during her brief transit, with discomfort and inconvenience that was beyond the tolerance of many.

Conflicting and opposing temperature gradients; continental, oceanic, desert, mountain, African, Asian and European, imposed intermittent atmospheric turmoil upon the island land mass isolated in their midst. The close of summer was always heralded by the arrival of the huge North African Sirocco winds, blowing in a northerly direction, and hauling hot air from the wide open wastes of the Sahara Desert. In the company of the hot air, there also came a substantial quantity of the Sahara in the form of cloying, irritating, choking, all-enveloping dust. It clogged, penetrated, blanketed, infiltrated and infused every moment of every day and night. During its mercifully brief transit of a three or four weeks or so, we ate it, drank it, inhaled it, dressed in it, slept in it, and lived life in its shroud in a choking permanence.

Its grisly dominance usually met with a dramatic demise. Storm clouds would gather, and in a huge show of electrical pyrotechnics, and Thor's fury, the celestial regions emptied a million tons of water on to the blotting paper landscape. At first the heavy water droplets lifted little spurts of dust at each landing, much as a pebble being thrown into soft sand. The dust dominance was now in its death throes, and was soon being swept into rivulets and erosion channels to become lost in the bundu. At first a cheer echoed around the camp, and then figures emerged to stand naked between the tent lines and revel in this free cleansing shower. But not for long. The deluge increased alarmingly, and equally so did the volume of liquid mud that began to swirl around the tents. Ditch clearance became a pressing matter, and naked or otherwise, hands, shovels, beer cans, pieces of timber, all were brought into employment to ensure that the flow of water was directed around the tent, and not as a gloopy flood into it. Regular curfew was an urgent discipline during the rains to ensure the continued integrity of house and home.

The wet and stormy weather would persist for a few weeks, and though this imposed permanently saturated and very uncomfortable conditions, it was far less serious than the genuine threat of house moving. On more than one occasion, slumbering inmates were awakened to the fearful rending of canvas and breaking of ropes to find themselves gazing helplessly into the stormy night with the remnants of their tent being carried across the bundu, or flapping furiously in the gale. Perhaps even more morale sapping was the return from a period on watch to find tent and possessions slowly being absorbed by the environment.

It was usually during the interface between sand and flood, at the time when the climate was at its most confused and eruptive that we encountered an odd climatic phenomenon. Waterspouts were a fairly frequent feature of the autumnal climate, and seemed to find their genesis around the cape, or more especially in Limassol Bay. Just a few of these adopted huge proportions and all of the characteristics of hurricane vigour and potential. Mostly they were relatively short lived and collapsed back into the sea where they belonged. However, a small proportion of them were driven ashore by the wind, the direction of which was apparently influenced by the Cape Gata cliffs, and they invariably collapsed at the southern end of the main Akrotiri runway, depositing thereon their discharged cargo of fish, seaweed, stones, timber, sundry flotsam, and a significant proportion of the local sea bed.

It was during this period in 1959, that the towering grandfather of all of these sodden cyclones raised its head in the familiar location just off the end of the cape. Far larger than any of us had ever seen, this angry cyclonic leviathan lifted its marine cargo ever higher, reaching the very cloud base that was the heart of the storm. It began to move, and for a brief time it appeared that Akrotiri was destined to become the recipient of unusually abundant manna from oceanic heaven. Then a change became imposed upon the integrity of the maelstrom, a change of wind direction perhaps, some strange magnetic force, or the mysterious hand of destiny. Whatever the influence, the monstrous column began to move towards the end of the cape, a feature that quickly disappeared it its embrace. It continued its progress, crossing the cape and for just a few moments became suspended above the 280 technical site. Apparently usurped by its contact with the lumpy outlines of terra firma, it promptly collapsed, cascading its enormous weight and volume directly on to our radar transmitters and receivers.

When the storm had passed the extent of the damage caused became revealed. Fish flopped and squirmed, seaweed festooned, and broken debris lay everywhere, but most important was the severity of the damage to the exposed equipment. Those few brief moments of marine blitzkrieg had clearly rendered the station impotent. Some of the revolving or nodding heads had become twisted into complete non-functionality, metal spars and rails had become twisted, some of the smaller items had been toppled, and less durable parts had been smashed beyond purpose or recognition. Clearly, the station could no longer function, and was out of commission.

The ensuing few days became a whirlwind of emergency measures. Here had been created a serious breach in the defence of sovereignty and of continued peace in a troubled world. It quickly became clear that the task of repair, replacement, and restored function would require weeks and not simply the generous application of electronic sticking plaster. An understudy station would be required to fill the gap pending the successful conclusion of the Cape Gata recovery period.

Some distance to the north and east, and to the south of the second city of Famagusta, the promontory of Cape Greco protrudes southward into the ocean. Here, an existing signals unit was being closed down and removed, its useful purpose having become inherited by 280 Signals Unit, and the expanding station at Mount Olympus. Some of the equipment had already been decommissioned and taken elsewhere, and the remainder had been mothballed in preparation for the same destiny. Most of the personnel had been transferred to other locations, leaving a skeleton staff of electricians, technicians, and dismantlers. Hasty restoration and re-commission would permit Cape Greco to deputise for Cape Gata during the period of transition and refurbishment.

Displaced equipment was quickly recovered, the red button was pressed on the equipment that remained on site, and all that was required to restore functionality was a team of operators to enhance the skeleton crew that remained during the decommissioning period. This team could only be recruited from Cape Gata, and the call for volunteers once more appeared on the notice board. Though the obvious choice for this task were the members of a small group of operators who had recently arrived from redundant Cape Greco. The tentative suggestion that they should undertake this mission, unhappily met with a vociferous demonstration of reluctance to return that bordered on mutiny, and thus, the notice and its call for volunteers remained in place.

No obligation was enforced, and the sluggishness with which the list of volunteers increased revealed that some of the dark and dubious delights of Cape Greco, had been shared over a Keo or two in the NAAFI.

"Well! Why not? It will only be for a few days, and it will provide a change of scene."

So a couple of three-ton trucks containing a contingent of thirty or so anticipatory volunteers, and disgruntled conscripts in fairly equal proportions, appropriately and necessarily armed, left 280 for their holiday camp at Cape Greco.

On arrival, it required little time and no imagination whatever, to appreciate why the recently departed squad had been so resolute in their determination not to return. Almost an island, the Cape Greco peninsula is connected to the mainland by a narrow, rocky, naked isthmus. Had this neck of land been well vegetated, it might have been an ideal place for an ambush but then, as now, the dusty road snaked the quarter mile or so across its length. Known as 'Hell Hole' by the recent former residents, and now immigrants to Cape Gata, for whom 'Hell on the Hill' had provided a very welcome refuge and alternative.

Desolation is an evocative and expressive word, and one that was used, in unrestrained and abundant tandem, accompanied by a string of additional and descriptive expletives, by the small group of recent immigrants that were enjoying their first view of their temporary home. The road that exits the isthmus enters the peninsula at a slightly elevated location beneath the rocky hillock known unimaginatively as 'High Point', and from this position of advantage, the entire peninsula and its trappings were contained within the same sweeping vista. Desolation applied very appropriately to the dusty, rocky. parched, finger-like promontory that jutted indelicately into the ocean, but no less so to the confusion of part dismantled tents, semi-derelict temporary buildings, cabins, electronic equipment, sundry vehicles, radar and radio antennae, and domestic disarray that occupied the closest quarter. Home from home! A nightmarish reincarnation of the cosy and familiar Cape Gata that we had so recently deserted.

It was clear that some of the habitation tents were in process of re-erection to accommodate the incoming team, and after the allocation of shared home and bed space, familiarity and sustenance rapidly became the top priorities. A cookhouse and mess, a corrugated iron construction with a field cooking range to the rear, served up fare that was in every way of the same abysmal standard as that at 280, so little familiarisation was required. Adjacent to the cookhouse, and of vital social importance, a similarly constructed and equally scruffy building served to provide the welcome facilities of the NAAFI, and in spite of the considerable hazards involved in delivery, an abundant supply of Keo was always readily available within. A large marquee with rows of frame seats had served as the camp cinema, but had become redundant at intended close down, had not been re-commissioned, and was thus was no longer functional.

Our first working day revealed familiarity of equipment and of practice. Radar heads revolved and nodded, cabins were equipped with screens and strobes, plotting tables and chinagraph, with the result that the substitution, Greco for Gata, evolved seamlessly and with a break of no more than a couple of days. The equally familiar working routine of watches to ensure function, security, and protection, quickly became established, and while the damaged station at 280 became restored and repaired under a cloak of great secrecy, its function in the defence of the realm was handled adequately by its small dusty cousin.

The familiarity of daily routine quickly established the equally familiar emotion of overwhelming boredom. Here, on Cape Greco there were even fewer locations on the list entitled 'Nowhere to Go'. Almost entirely surrounded by the sea, we worked, we swam, we worked again, all in an endless cycle of repetition. We enjoyed the considerable benefit of generated electricity, and when not in the sea or the NAAFI, playing cards, reading or listening to the music of the day on slowly revolving vinyl discs, provided most of our entertainment.

Waste disposal of every kind presented a considerable challenge. A substantial quantity was simply dumped into the ocean, but in the absence of any regular tidal flush, most of it remained where it was dumped. Combustible material was incinerated in pits excavated for that purpose, but this process was rarely complete, and the well-toasted remains provided an easy and attractive source of food for rats, and for multitudinous infestations of breeding flies. The limestone peninsula presented a unique challenge to latrine designers. The rocky substrate prevented any hope of excavating deep pit facilities, so relatively shallow, and singularly grisly grottos had to suffice. These, of course, filled very rapidly, and the team of Armenian unfortunates whose unwholesome function was to dig and fill, seemed to be present on the station at almost all times.

In functional terms, there were differences, Greco to Gata. To sustain a basic but reasonable standard of cleanliness and tidiness around and within the camp, everyone was allocated a duty of cleansing care. As a part of every period of daytime duty, a rota to involve all personnel, ensured the collection of litter, the disposal of general rubbish, an element of cleaning, and even sweeping, though this latter was inclined to induce and not reduce, in the dusty world of Cape Greco. All of the other additional duties related to security, to guarding, and to protection, and during any period of twenty-four hours, airmen were deployed in equivalent numbers in the operation of the radar and electronic equipment, and in the security of the station and its occupants.

Cape Greco lacked the defensive buffering of an RAF Akrotiri that was enjoyed at Cape Gata. Thus, the potential for attack was of paramount consideration. In addition, every item or commodity that arrived at the station, had to be transported there by three-ton truck or equivalent. This included every drop of water for any purpose, and this provision required a daily water bowser collection and delivery from Ayios Nikolaios. With almost the same regularity, all consumables were transported from the same location or from Famagusta. Any journey to or from Cape Greco, required passage through the large and narrow village of Paralimni. This location was revered as the considered birthplace of Archbishop Makarios, the Greek Cypriot leader, and first elected President of Cyprus. This is contentious, as history records his birth name as Michael Christodoulou Mouskos, and his birth place as Panayia in the District of Paphos. Whatever the historic validation of his arrival on the planet, to the worthy villagers of Paralimni he was a deity. It was his oft-broadcast vilification of colonial British rule that directed these same villagers to so many extreme acts of hate and violence against the alleged British oppressors, mostly at that time in the form of youthful and politically innocent National Servicemen.

Cape Greco was vulnerable. Its flat promontory would permit ready and concealed landing from the sea at almost any point along its coastline. The narrow isthmus led first to Cape Greco village, and then to Paralimni, and in both of these villages welcome would more likely take the form of a bullet or a well-aimed stone, than tea and cakes. The unit did not enjoy the defensive expertise of professionally trained troops. No military police were stationed here, nor were members of the RAF Regiment or equivalent army platoon. We were on our own, and if defence against an oppressor were to become a requirement, we would remain on our own.

Consequently, every individual on the unit, regardless of rank status, or persuasion, was required to become skilled and proficient in the use of every available weapon. Of these, there was a modest miscellany, and one which included side arms, .303 calibre rifles, Sten guns, and the heavier and more purposeful Bren gun. Of necessity, the station boasted an armoury. This was not an impregnable steel and concrete monolith, but a large tent that contained a number of secured lockers, crates and boxes. Its principle defence was the cocoon of tangled barbed and early razor wire in which it was entombed. This impenetrable entanglement was supported by a miscellany of steel and wooden poles, and the entire tangled and convoluted reticulation would have proved perplexing to a weasel. To one side of the similarly fortified single entrance, and with just a hint of whimsy, a sign bore the title and message:

751 SIGNALS UNIT

ARMOURY

OUT OF BOUNDS TO
EOKA.

In whatever guise, security figured large in our daily lives, and on site, on every watch period, every member of the watch was detailed to undertake guard duty. The issue of arms and ammunition was scrupulous, and as at 280, if twenty rounds of ammunition had been issued, twenty rounds were expected in return. Failure to make this return, required the evidence of a body, (wandering goats and donkeys were not in evidence as substitutes), a witness to the discharge of the weapon, or a bomb proof excuse.

From the earliest days of square-bashing, indoctrination insisted that the rifle was our personal best friend, it should never leave our possession, never be out of reach, and never, ever be out of sight. Such pieces of weaponry and the matching ammunition were much sought after by EOKA, and clearly, any successful violation of the armoury at Cape Greco would provide a bonanza beyond terrorist imagination. Consequently, this prickly location was guarded, padlocked, illuminated and alarmed at all times. Elsewhere, guards were posted, in pairs, in strategic places, and allocated the task of patrolling specific sections of the perimeter wire that enclosed both technical and domestic locations. The most sensitive areas were those that provided natural concealment among the rocks of the elevated ground to the rear of the camp.

The most prominent guard post location was on the summit of High Point. Here, an open-sided wooden hut provided shelter from unremitting day time sun, and some protection from the chill of the dark hours. The High Point lookout was equipped with a permanently mounted Bren gun, a powerful searchlight, and radio communication. The elevated location provided panoramic views of the entire peninsula, but more important, of large areas of open ocean and adjacent coastlines. Always manned by two guards, it was a reasonably agreeable job by day! Nothing to do. Play cards, read a book, keep your eyes open and occasionally scan the horizon. By contrast night watch was deadly dull in the extreme, and as boring as hell. Security forbade the use of lights and in the dreary dead hours, remaining awake demanded a supreme effort. Nothing happened at High Point. It was never attacked, no vigilante pirates ever launched a sea-borne invasion, no submarines flying the Eoka flag were ever sighted in the bay, and no dark and silent parachutes ever fluttered down from the night sky.

Boredom ruled! To ease its miserable burden, we occasionally resorted to a momentary illumination of the searchlight. This was strictly against standing orders, but could readily be dismissed by an alleged suspicious splash or something moving across the moonlit water. A penance beyond endurance demanded that an entry be made in the log book every fifteen minutes. At the point of every fifteen minutes precisely nothing had happened since the last fifteen minutes, or since every other fifteen minutes since nightfall. What the hell did you enter into a fifteen minute log book during the deadly mausoleum of the night? Fantasy fashioned one such set of fifteen minute entries.

"Moderate swells on ocean surface. Could conceal small craft."
"Unidentified object sighted at distance."
"Unidentified object moving rapidly towards cape. Distance too great to challenge or identify."
"Crew of unidentified object making use of powerful searchlight and flares."
"Unidentified object moving rapidly towards coast. Now suspect fire on board."
"Unidentified object has become stationary."
"Object now identified as rising sun."

Making false entry in an official log was a chargeable offence, or one at least that would attract a severe bollocking. None happened.

While a considerable degree of flippancy did pervade guard duties on camp just as they did at 280, perhaps in both situations as a reaction to boredom or possibly apprehension, no such levity ever accompanied outside escort duties. As an escorted delivery service was required for everything from beer to bog paper, some on a daily basis, the escort duty requirement came around fairly frequently. Stores of any kind were transported on three ton trucks based on the unit, were driven by in-house MT drivers, and were accompanied by duty guards recruited from the watch of the day. Two of the guards occupied the rear of each truck, while the third stuck his head above the parapet in the cab turret.

Preparations were always carefully measured and meticulous. The issue of appropriate weapons followed a briefing and procedural check. At the armoury, each issued weapon was carefully checked for purpose and condition, and a counted number of rounds of ammunition followed. Each of the guards then checked his weapon personally to ensure, to his own satisfaction that he would be comfortable if called upon to make use of it. Lives, including his own, could well depend upon these simple but vital checks.

As lone vehicles would have been extremely vulnerable, whenever possible, trucks travelled in convoy, with heavily armed escorts fore and aft. These comprised land rovers with permanently mounted Bren guns or armoured cars with heavier weaponry as escort for larger convoys. These were driven and protected by airmen and non-commissioned officers of the RAF Regiment, who were based at Ayios Nikolaios, and who were on daily deployment to Cape Greco for the purpose.

A serious potential threat accompanied each and every journey. From the cape, and once through the tiny village of the same name to seaward, the route afforded two choices. A coastal route through Protaras enjoyed a reasonably intact surface and could afford higher speed if necessary, while the slower traversed Ayia Napa before turning north. Alas both routes required the slow and torturous traverse of Paralimni, its narrow streets, its hostile population, and the likelihood of barricades. On approach to the village, the 'weapons ready' instruction was always given, magazines were checked for locking, and each weapon held at readiness. A traverse of Paralimni was always terrifyingly slow, was almost always accompanied by thrown projectiles, was sometimes shocked by anonymous shots, and just occasionally was subject to the destructive power of a land mine.

Even if adequately armed, there is little real defence against an unseen assailant, and especially one who is defended by the anonymity of a throng. Though vehicles were afforded some protection, they remained highly vulnerable in a situation where speedy escape was precluded. As a protection against missiles or thrown grenades, some of the vehicles were fitted with high sides fabricated from rigid, heavy duty wire mesh. They deflected some of the missiles, but not those that were rolled down sections of drainage gutter from the flat rooftops, or lobbed like hoop-la rings at a fairground. Whatever the disturbance, and provided that vehicles remained on their wheels, the menacing, metallic rattle of a Bren gun from the front or the rear of the convoy, usually signalled a shuffled dispersal of the menace and the crowd.

During earlier times of greater unrest and hazard, and when Cape Greco had been significantly more populous, the extreme vulnerability of the turret man had long been recognised. With head, shoulders, and most of his torso projecting prominently from the roof of the truck, he was invariably first in line as recipient of any projected missile, be it a rotten apple or a lethal projectile. To afford a slightly enhanced degree of protection, bizarre contraptions, akin to upturned and bottomless dustbins, were secured to the roof of the cab. This provision did afford a shield to turret man's body, as only his head now protruded above the contrived parapet. However, the time and difficulty involved in the raising and deployment of a weapon while occupying this restrictive cylinder, rather diluted turret man's potential capability as a force majeure. (The Dustbin Bandits. Terry O'Reilly 2014.)

In reality, by mid-1959 disturbances were few, and perpetrated by the remaining hard liners, who seemed uncertain about their allegiance or their adversary. Turk continued to snarl at Greek. Greek rumbled on about Enosis. In due course, the British would remove their influence, leaving Greek and Turk to their own disagreeable devices. Occupation would fade into the pages of the volumes that record the history of this troubled island, and yet another war would be unleashed that would claim infinitely more lives than before, until it finally degenerating into the obscene and unhappy spectacle and practice of partition.

In due course, Cape Gata became restored to fully operational capacity, and the story resumed. The 'borrowed' operators and technicians were returned to their customary location, those remaining continued to dismantle the Cape Greco hardware, the entire encampment was bundled up and removed, and 751 Signals Unit, Cape Greco was despatched into history.

So what now of unhappy, abandoned, derelict, windswept, parched and ever dusty Cape Greco? Unloved, and apparently unwanted, a security barrier across the isthmus precludes entry by the curious, the casual or the nostalgic. A single unworthy installation, imposed by the Cypriot armed forces, suggests that some authority may have tendered an earlier interest, but of the lines of tents, the flapping marquees, the Keo induced jollity, the noisy panoply of confined life, the vibrancy and the purpose of 751 Signals Unit, only the ghosts remain.

"Cannons to the right of them, cannons to the left of them, cannons behind then volleyed and thundered."

The silence of today's Cape Greco is disrupted by armaments of a different calibre. Gone the rattle and ping of the Sten gun, the concussion of the .303, or the dull and ominous thud of explosion. A new army of occupation has conquered the adjacent coastline, and probably generates rather more noise than the occupants of yesterday. To the east, the formerly somnolent village of Ayia Napa has become transmogrified into a vast hollow chamber of touristic Babel. Oozing in a westerly direction, it has spawned dive centres, beach resorts and clamorous holiday villages, now nudging the sea caves and the landward stem of the isthmus.

Northward along the eastern coast at Protaras and Fig Tree Bay, similar, if slightly more sophisticated development, has given birth to another tourist conurbation, while the former menace of Paralimni has dissolved among its urban byways and alleys. Asphyxiated among it all, Cape Greco remains silent and unattended, harbouring only memories of distant days, and denying access to the brash and vulgar world of the seekers of leisure and pleasure.

***

To a life (however brief) on the ocean wave.

Some of those in possession of larger ears, those who were quick to interpret the messages of the jungle drums, or those whose position in the scheme of things permitted early access and interpretation of incoming messages, had become aware that a visitation was being planned. The word on a very restricted grape vine suggested that a ship of the line would shortly be dropping anchor in Limassol Bay, and maybe, just maybe, some of the crew would be coming to tea.

HMS Broadsword (D31) had been a Weapons Class Destroyer, but had recently undergone a major refit designed to carry and utilise an advanced (965) radar capability. Currently in deployment in the Mediterranean, the ship was heading for Cyprus, and whispers bore the message that a training exercise may be under consideration. Sure enough, the authorities, marine, aerial, and terrestrial had considered that it would be of benefit to the crew to learn a little of the function and operation of land based radar, and in particular of its operational relationship with its sister equipment aboard ship.

A reciprocal arrangement? No-one knew, but here, me bonny boys, was a possible opportunity with potential far beyond the dreams of avarice. If it came to pass, it would be extremely limited, and those best prepared would surely enjoy a foot on the gangplank while those dragging their heels through the mire of unpreparedness would remain gasping in the slow lane. To the more experienced of the 'volunteers', time spent awaiting an announcement that the Royal Navy had graciously extended an invitation, was time wasted indeed.

Lists were prepared, and were replaced by counter-lists. Names were dropped names were added, names were erased, names were abused. Honour among thieves there was none, and it quickly became clear that the plethora of accumulated lists of aspirants, would simply compete each other to an early death. None but the bold would find success, and pre-release knowledge would afford clear advantage. No source of potential information was left untapped and at first whisper, a list, anonymous of course, was spirited on to the desk of the station adjutant while his attention was diverted elsewhere. The invitation was announced the following day.

While an unseemly scramble ensued, the 'first come, first served' rule was admirably enacted. A couple of days later it was a somewhat self-satisfied, and unbearably smug group of jolly 'sailors' who climbed aboard HMS Broadsword to commence their brief, contrived, and completely undeserved periods of loyal service in the Royal Navy.

As we were being directed to our quarters, someone lit the blue touch paper, we pointed our stern toward Limassol Bay, and slowly headed into the blue. Our superficial attempts not to look too smug as we looked forward to our brief experience on the briny, were demonstrably futile, as we began our familiarisation of the ship and its facilities.

The captain, officers and crew were hospitable in the extreme. Though we were service persons of a lower order, mostly of the national service category, we were treated as guests by the entire crew, and afforded equal, if not privileged status as comrades and as friends.

Shortly after being welcomed on board, lunch provided our first revelation, and an indication of life's daily pattern while we were aboard. In those days, the splendid tradition of a daily rum ration remained a time-honoured pursuit, perhaps it still does. Served at lunchtime to all who wished to participate, it was available to take or to leave as preferred. Guests, of course, were equally participant, but in addition, it was no less traditional for crew members to offer any unwanted daily ration to honoured guests. Thus, smug expressions fairly quickly morphed into silly grins as tot followed tot followed tot.

On this first day, lunch preceded a detailed briefing. Though we were to enjoy the relative freedom of the ship, there were certain areas that were off limits for reasons of hazard, security, or personal integrity, and others where we should first engage the direction and guidance of a member of the crew. Our subsequent tour of the ship clarified all of these protocols. We were, of course, still in uniform, this was not, strictly speaking, a cruising holiday, and it followed therefore that all of the customary protocols that related to courtesy, seniority, rank, and authority, would be followed and respected.

For our briefing tour, and to avoid unnecessary operational congestion on the days to follow, our party was divided into pairs or groups of three. We were introduced to the bridge and the means by which every aspect of the ship's operation was directed. We gazed in awe at the immense power house deep in the bowels of the vessel that drove it ahead at 25 knots, astern at something rather less, and which could accommodate the versatility of its every manoeuvre. We made inspection of the galley and remarked ruefully that victuals aboard were far, far superior to those that hit the platter at 280. The defence and attack capacities of the ship were explained as we examined its armoury and its fire power. Most important, particularly in respect of the principle purpose of our visit, we considered the communications systems aboard the ship, its radar, its radio, and the part that it could play in early warning and defence, in tandem with land based units such as 280 Signals Unit and Mount Olympus.

In the few days to follow we were invited to become more practically involved with most of the operational functions of the ship. Our first demonstration afforded us some morning excitement. The captain elected to undertake some sea trials, and while we arranged ourselves on the deck, the ship was put through its paces. Impressive indeed were its top speeds, its manoeuvrability, its turning, and the degree of heeling as the rudder was thrown successively to port and to starboard at high speed. Later we were each invited to take the wheel, and to follow the instructions relayed to us from the bridge. The helmsman's visibility is limited to a compass reading, and his task is to achieve and sustain the instructed direction. To the untrained hand and the inexperienced eye, this is no simple task as the directed bearing is achieved and exceeded, achieved and exceeded, time after wobbly time. To the merriment of more familiar and dextrous mariners, our wavy lines across the ocean were well evident in the ship's wake, and relayed for the benefit and entertainment of all on to a monitoring screen.

We didn't get to fire the guns, nor did we seize power piratically from the captain, but we did temporarily deputize for officers on the bridge and relayed instructions to functional areas of the ship. Principally these were to the bemused and struggling 280 helmsman, as his endeavours to maintain a steady course, or to synchronise smoothly to an adjusted one, imposed an ultimate test upon his somewhat embryonic skills of helmsmanship.

Of course, the principle purpose of our voyage was the reciprocal of that enjoyed by the nautical visitors to 280, and should be considered more correctly under the all-embracing category of 'training'. In its pursuit, we each undertook practical exercise in operating, transmitting, receiving and recording, all of the elements of the daily work with which we were familiar. However, while most aspects of the task enjoyed considerable similarity, practice was required to furnish the necessary adjustments to accommodate a moving vessel, the motion of the sea, and elemental differences between our two locations. It afforded some satisfaction to enjoy the facility to communicate directly with our colleagues at 280, without gloating of course.

The afternoon provided the highlight of each day. For an hour or so after lunch, the captain ordered that the ship should heave-to, and that the engines should be silenced. After a hearty lunch and a rum ration made the more generous by donation, the on-board guests were ready to indulge in their daily dip. The swimming pool was abundant by any standards. When the ship had finally become stationary in the water, and the crew had become distributed around the deck to maintain vigil for sharks, salacious mermaids, or any other sea creature that might choose to take advantage of a small group of plashy innocents, the bonny lads from 280 simply and literally jumped ship and took flight into the ocean below. A simple but enduring memory of mine is the vision of the side of the ship, complete with barnacles and a sparse coif of weed, passing vertically through my vision as I headed for the depths. We wallowed the while, until summoned back to the rope ladder, the deck, and the steady rumble as the engines were brought back to life.

For a couple of days, life was good, enjoyable, and extremely interesting for a bunch of semi-itinerant and conniving refugees from Cape Gata, though the dusty cape finally waved an insistent beckoning finger. We waved back as we nosed into Limassol Bay, but there was no bosun's pipe, no colourful bunting, no garlands and grass-skirted maidens, and no welcoming committee, only the trudge down the tent lines to 'Paradise Lost'.

***

During the period of emergency, six satellite radar stations operated from strategic locations around the island. In addition to Cape Gata, Cape Greco and Mount Olympus, RAF Kividhes was located to the south of the Troodos Mountains, RAF Kormakiti occupied the tip a peninsula on the north coast, and RAF Cape Andreas occupied a location at the extremity of the long north-easterly pointing finger of land, formally the Karpas Peninsula, though more commonly and affectionately known as the Panhandle. At the extreme fingernail of the Panhandle, Galounopetra Point and Cape Apostolos Andreas provided a rocky platform for the base of RAF Cape Andreas.

Though it was never my pleasure to find reason or excuse to visit this station, some of the Air Defence Operators with whom I served at Cape Gata, had found temporary station at this location, and it is their service at Cape Andreas that has inspired this inclusion. I was never knowingly in the company of anyone who had served at Kividhes or Kormakiti.

In the closing months of 1958, new arrivals, whose destination tickets bore the name Cape Andreas, were transported initially from their arrival point at RAF Nicosia, to the garrison at Ayios Nikolaios for final kitting out and briefing, before being taken to long-term transit at Cape Greco. Here they endured a couple of weeks of immersion in the complexities of daily duties, the unfamiliar use of equipment and its operation, and familiarity with living conditions that bore not the slightest resemblance to anything that life had hitherto presented.

Dress codes at Cape Greco mirrored those at Cape Gata, and uniform abuse was even more extreme. Here, it was not exclusively self-administered but enjoyed the tender caresses of an occasionally imported civilian tailor. His abilities in the snip and stitch department transformed the standard tropical uniform to a somewhat risqué hybrid between Christian Dior and the Afrika Korps. The standard issue of shorts, if left unmolested, drooped unappealingly and somewhat baggily to the knees and beyond, not a situation that could be tolerated by the athletically flamboyant Grecoese airman. Tassos the Tailor required a mere hour or two to reduce these voluminous culottes to a point alarmingly close to the suspensory and supportive capacity of the issued undergarments. The finished product could have readily posed an encasement challenge to a modest loin cloth.

At the termination of their two-week transit holiday, the innocents abroad piled all of their worldly possessions into the back of a truck to begin the long and hazardous journey to Andreas. Through hostile Famagusta and ever north-eastwards along the panhandle, through villages and small townships that bore no love for the occupying British military. Cape Andreas was truly remote, and though afforded some supportive protection from Royal Artillery units located elsewhere on the panhandle, none were within ready proximity, and any defensive approach could have been readily arrested by a carefully located ambush along the only approach road. Though EOKA terrorists were not particularly active on this part of the island, the nearest township of Rizokarpaso enjoyed the same actively resentful reputation as did Paralimni, close to Cape Greco.

The approach to Galounopetra Point snaked through a series of steeply sloping convolutions as the road descended to sea level. RAF Cape Andreas was a small unit. A huddle of tents, a couple of adjacent buildings that housed the cookhouse and a NAAFI, two radar heads, one operations cabin, a couple of Nissen huts that had formerly been occupied by men of the Royal Artillery, and two diesel generators that operated noisily around the clock.

Small in size, and equally limited in personnel. The total unit population of a little more than fifty included only one commissioned officer, who commanded the unit, and a sergeant who served as his second in command. The remaining hoi-polloi of other ranks, included two lost souls from the Royal Artillery, and a single ship-less naval rating. In the apportionment of responsibility, the two Royal Artillery squaddies would probably be expected to provide the first line of defence in the event of attack, and the naval rating had become inexplicably responsible for the management of the NAAFI. A somewhat obscure arrangement, though in reality, the Royal Navy maintained offshore surveillance to seek and apprehend any illicit arms smuggling or gun running in enshrouded fishing vessels or other sea-going small craft. Its solitary on-shore representative, who maintained ship to shore communication, doubled up as the station NAAFI manager.

In tandem with all of the other satellite radar stations, the daily working principle dictated that everyone made equal contribution to every aspect of the operation of the station. As ever, security was of paramount importance, though its application at Andreas could have been considered a little more casual than the imposed and adopted procedures at Cape Gata. As elsewhere, coils of barbed wire were the first line of defence and completely enclosed the encampment from two clifftop points. The only entrance was defended by a boom barrier and a guardroom, though the latter rarely if ever enjoyed the defensive attention of a sentry. Alternative provision took the form of a guard tower and gun pit. These facilities were located a little closer to the centre of the camp and were equipped with searchlight and Bren light machine gun, in addition to individually carried rifle and small arms. This defensive unit was manned at all times, and provided viewing facility for clear surveillance across the entrance and approach road, and the surrounding coastline and ocean.

The domestic provisions were no less crude and basic than those at Cape Greco, and here, as there, the necessary maintenance was carried out by domestic work parties allocated to these tasks. Frequently unpleasant, always essential, and though these tasks were a penance and never a skive, they were undertaken in a spirit of communal necessity. Pit latrines, camp tidiness, an orderly home and workplace, and not a rubbish dump or building site, it was a sense of personal and communal pride that directed the domestic obligation. Though scruffiness remained endemic, it was invariably worn with a sense of bravado and male pride, and not as a slovenly gesture of youthful angst.

The toilet facilities at Cape Andreas had clearly been designed by the same architect who had earned his blue plaque at Cape Gata. A raised pedestal had been equipped with holes of the appropriate shape and size, doors had been considered unnecessary, but a thoughtful addition had been low dividing screens of height sufficient to support an elbow. Support perhaps for those of narrow rump dimensions or an easy arm rest for the studious or the more leisurely squatters.

Alas the single facility was restricted to four standing (six, with the risk of a potentially damp squeeze), and four sitting. The requirement to form an orderly queue was as regular as daily rhythms dictated, but as the only such facility, it was shared, without priority or discrimination, by rank, file, and officers alike. Unless under alimentary attack, the first come, first served rule dictated queue etiquette, and the morning assembly was ever an occasion of cheerfully and willingly imposed equality.

The building that combined the essential function of the cookhouse, and the equally essential social function of the NAAFI, was situated on the periphery of the little-used parade ground. It lacked the space and essential facilities required for eating, and meals were received through a serving hatch in the external wall. The positively orgasmic delight of eating the daily fare was enjoyed in a suitably equipped Nissen hut at the other side of the parade ground. It can be reliably observed that any windswept, rain lashed, or dust enshrouded coastal peninsula is probably a fairly unsuitable place to consider alfresco dining. Equally, any endeavour to transport the roast beef and Yorkshire pudding or sausage and reconstituted spud to a more sheltered location, and to expect it to arrive at the table in the same condition as it left the serving ladle, enjoys the same degree of futility. In the most amenable conditions it may make the short journey intact, if a little cool, but in conditions dominated by no more than a modest tempest, the self-waiting service invariably dictated that it arrived stone cold at the table, had become saturated or imbued with the gritty airborne surface of the parade ground, or simply have left the plate altogether.

The supply of every required commodity was undertaken in the same manner as that at Cape Greco. Every item of daily use and purpose was delivered by three-ton truck from Ayios Nikolaios. In addition to serving numerous villages and small townships, the long road between these two locations was also an ecclesiastical highway that was used by pilgrims making their way to the Apostolos Andreas Monastery. As a result, it was maintained in a reasonably passable condition, at least as far as the monastery entrance. The final, steep and convoluted section of track to the camp entrance deviated from the principal highway at a point around a half mile from the monastery before making its descent. The surface of this final half mile or so left rather more to be desired.

With exception of the regular supply convoys, visitors to the unit were unknown. Anyone making passage along the dusty highway would face the requirement of a gauntlet of hostile villagers and townships, the risk of ambush, or deadly hazard in the form of pressure mines. Notwithstanding all of this, those on security detail found surprise one day at the approach of a small motor car as it made its way down the convolutions toward the camp entrance. From it there stepped a middle aged, uniformed lady of diminutive stature who requested entry. Though this was refused on grounds that remained unclear, she remained steadfast, collected her accompanying cargo from the boot of her car, and returned to the gate.

She was an emissary from the Church of Scotland, and had driven from Ayios Nikolaios to deliver leaflets and magazines for the spiritual well-being of the lost souls of Andreas. Regardless of the religious persuasion of the inmates, her risky gesture was appreciated, and her collecting box jingled healthily as she began her return journey, though it seemed a shame that she had not been permitted to make entry and to enjoy a cup of tea. Perhaps authority had viewed her as a security risk, or perhaps refusal had been considered in her own best interest. These young guys had been isolated for many months, and perhaps security had been fearful that reaction to the unexpected company of a representative of the opposite gender might have emulated that of more permissive surroundings. It was hoped that the same guiding hand of providence provided her with an equally safe return journey.

The single vital commodity that imposed exception to the supply and delivery routine was water. To satisfy the essential nature of demand, daily or seasonally more frequent deliveries, were an imperative prerequisite to life on the unit. Clearly, it would have been a totally impracticable proposition to haul daily water from distant Ayios Nikolaios. To satisfy the daily requirement, long standing concord had been reached with the monastic authority at Apostolos Andreas Monastery, about one mile distant. As and when required, water from the deep well at this location was pumped into a one-ton tanker to be transported the short distance to the camp.

It was a simple logistical difficulty that was to prove fatal. From the camp, the approach to the junction with the main road demanded a slow ascent of the rough and twisting exit track. At the junction, the track joined the highway at an angle that was too narrow, and too acute to accommodate the wheelbase and the turning circle of the truck. The devised and utilised alternative was to turn in the opposite direction, direct the truck for a short distance down the opposite side of the hill, make use of an abandoned field to describe a turning circle, and return to the junction to proceed in a more direct line to the monastery. It was a simple procedure and it worked well.

On every occasion, the collection and delivery was made by a driver and an armed guard. It was just a few days before Christmas, the tanker had been driven to the turning point and was in process of describing its circle when it struck a buried pressure mine. The resulting powerful explosion blew the truck to pieces, and inflicted fatal injuries upon the two occupants. The explosion had been clearly heard and recognised at the camp, and personnel were at the scene in minutes. Among the scattered remains of the shattered truck, a solitary boot, complete with sock, stood forlornly in the middle of the field. These boys had been a national serviceman aged nineteen, and a serving airman aged twenty-seven. Neither had harboured the slightest enmity against Greek or Turk.

A comprehensive search was conducted in the immediate vicinity and more widely, but no evidence was discovered of perpetrators. As a provisional truce in the area had already been established as an aspired forerunner to more lasting settlement and peace, it was considered that the mine may have been planted on a much earlier occasion, and had lain under the ground for an indeterminate period. Given the regularity of this short journey, it could only be considered remarkable that the device had fortuitously been avoided on the many subsequent occasions when the truck was being manoeuvred through its turning circle.

Less than four months were to elapse before RAF Cape Andreas was finally decommissioned, disbanded and closed down. The serving personnel were returned first to transit at Cape Greco and then to 280 Signals Unit, Cape Gata.

A Yuletide Blessing!

***

My experience during these years had evolved a belief and practice, that opportunity should never, ever be dismissed out of hand. Cometh the more enlightened hour, it can always be rejected if circumstances or more specific details reveal it to be less attractive than earlier considered. Thus, in June 1959, opportunity raised its bejewelled head once more, and demanded urgent consideration.

The prospect, apparently up for the highest bidder, or perhaps the early bird, was a short term posting to RAF El Adem. RAF Where??? RAF El Adem, it turned out, was in Libya, and was located about thirty Saharan miles south of Tobruk. The posting would be of an unspecified few weeks duration, and required the services of a team of radar operators and fitters. A few who had visited this location described it in very disparaging tones. Hot! Desolate! Remote! Featureless! Totally unappealing! There can be little doubt that these detractions imposed a deterrent upon some, and thus may have reduced the competition. Others would be loathe to desert the blue waters of 280 pool, to find poor substitute in an ocean of blazing sand and dust. Then there was the question of Libyan beer. This was a Muslim state, perhaps there was none. A substantial team was the operational requirement, and the list of willing and volunteered participants fell somewhat short of the target number, thus imposing conscription upon a small additional number in order to make up the shortfall.

Thus it was that a rattling and draughty Douglas DC3 Dakota lifted equipment and innocents from RAF Akrotiri, and headed in a south westerly direction across the blue

Mediterranean and into the grey and yellow Libyan Sahara. It had been cold in the flatulent aircraft, but the desiccating heat as we disembarked into the glare of the North African sun, seared and evaporated with every laboured breath.

In comparison to other signals units of our acquaintance, RAF El Adem was spacious. Distributed generously across a wide swath of dead flat desert terrain, its layout comprised a combination of permanent structures, semi-permanent buildings and the inevitable tents. We were to find billet in the latter, and were afforded a few days to acclimatise, to obtain the confidence of familiarity, and to become acquainted with the equipment and facilities that we would be using during the few weeks that lay ahead.

Our purpose, at 425 Signals Unit, was to make our contribution to a large-scale military exercise, which would embrace a period of around one week, and which would involve members of all three military services. As well as making the provision of new and different surroundings, it promised to be an interesting diversion from the routine and the familiar of daily Cape Gata life and work. Though our first few days were dedicated to training, the equipment and its use at El Adem introduced no procedures or practices with which we were totally unfamiliar, and we were quickly able to slip into a routine. However this training period did prepare us for the much more urgent and high speed activities of the exercise that lay ahead.

During that first week, army divisions arrived from their base near Benghazi, and we were to understand that naval vessels had assembled offshore, close to Tobruk. Our very own familiar HMS Broadsword would no doubt be among them. The aircraft to be involved would fly daily from bases at various locations in the Mediterranean basin. The exercise was indeed, fast and furious. Our experience was tested as never before to ensure that our contribution to navigation and to the activities of the aircraft above, the armoured vehicles charging around the nearby desert, and the rather more distant offshore vessels was accurately interpreted, accurately reported, accurately recorded, and accurately plotted. The exercise continued day and night through the course of its allocated week, and so far as we ever became aware, it was completed without loss or mishap.

Making use of familiar equipment and working procedures in a capacity that enjoyed the excitement of a 'live' exercise, and one where errors would impose extreme hazard or possible fatality, added the stimulation of drama, and banished the soporific qualities of our more familiar function. It had been an invigorating exercise, perhaps leaving us all a little breathless in the wake of the successful team management of simulated combat in the air, on land and at sea.

We lingered at El Adem for a further week or so, and bore witness to another event of note. In 1959 Libya had not yet been overwhelmed by militarist rule and remained a nominal monarchy. Still tenuously aboard his golden throne and still ruling at that time, though somewhat shakily, was King Idris 1, or to afford him his full and proper title, El Sayyid Prince Muhammad Idris bin Muhammad al-Mahdi as Senussi. He was Emir of Cyrenaica and King of the Libya that he had unified. His reign extended until 1969 when he was ousted by a military coup led by Colonel Muammar Ghaddafi. He died in exile in 1983.

At the conclusion of our exercise, no fixed date had been announced for our return to Cyprus, an in truth, we were content to remain a while longer and to use the opportunity to visit Tobruk and its environs. As there was nowhere else to go, and as the road from Tobruk to El Adem enjoyed no other destination, traffic was fairly regular and lifts equally abundant. The port of Tobruk, and the area of Cyrenaica had been the scene of extraordinarily fierce and prolonged battle during the desert campaigns of the Second World War. In particular, the town and port had been bombed and shelled repeatedly, action that had reduced most of it to rubble and ruin. By 1959, some had been reconstructed, new buildings had appeared, the township was beginning to recover character and purpose, and the port and harbour were functioning. However, recovery from such total devastation is a slow process, and the destructive evidence of those dark days was still very much in evidence.

Around the periphery of the town and port, a number of extremely poignant locations remember those who sacrificed their lives during these battles. British, Canadian, Australian, Polish, German, French and other cemeteries bring home to the visitor the magnitude of this sacrifice. Between them, thousands of names and personal details remind us that these had been young men like ourselves, many like us, conscripts or volunteers, and all, like us, had been looking forward to a life of which they and their families had been so brutally deprived.

The huge, pristine, gleaming white cemetery, the resting place of allied servicemen who fell during these battles is a serene place. Immaculately cared for by the British War Graves Commission, the simple, uniform, undeviating lines of white headstones extend from any point in unbroken lines to the perimeter walls. Interrupted only by the collective memorials, by strips and patches of carefully tended green lawn, and by shrubs and trees to invoke the atmosphere and the tranquillity of a garden among the relative desolation of the rocky desert landscape. It is a peaceful place, and while it is inevitably a place of lament for those lost to conflict, it is no less a celebration of life and a memorial to the sacrifice of life in pursuit of the future of mankind.

Some distance closer to the coast, an enormous fortress-like structure stands atop a low hill, and dominates the local landscape. This is the memorial to those members of the axis military who perished in this locality. Square in ground plan, with huge circular towers at each corner, its four massive walls offer a somewhat forbidding facade. Impregnable to the casual visitor, its single entrance requires a key of impressive proportions with which to unlock the equally huge wooden door. The custodian of the key was a member of a Senussi tribal family whose community encampment was nearby. On request, an elderly gentleman surrendered the key, and despatched two more youthful family members to unlock the portal to permit entry. The somewhat unkempt interior comprised a single courtyard with a central memorial depicting a bowl that was supported on the shoulders of four stooped figures. The construction of the interior walls had included twenty or so tall arched alcoves. In each of these, an ornate mosaic spelled out the names of the dead. This was a slightly eerie place, a somewhat forbidding chamber of ghosts. A place to view, to pay respect, but not to linger.

The city of Tobruk, with its natural deep water anchorage had been a port and harbour for centuries. Amid changing fortunes, the years of the Second World War were no exception. By 1959 it had reverted to its peacetime purpose, and had become a thriving port, with all of the facilities demanded by an itinerant seagoing population. Thus the waterside bars, the fleshpots and the sin spots flourished. Any alcohol reservations that may have been harboured by the orthodox Muslim world were swept away on a tide of cheap booze, illegal hooch, and ready profits. Downtown Tobruk was not a pretty place, and after a couple of tentative visits, most rejected its sleaze, its vulgarity, and its blatant and overt promiscuity. The sexual acrobatics of the ladies of the night and bar room performers rapidly lost their appeal. Cheered on by howling bands of inebriates they pursued their nightly routines with an astonishing array of equipment, and even, it was alleged, with the aid of a donkey, surely a spectacle to be avoided.

While there were few places for quiet contemplation, or even where a modest sundowner could be enjoyed without raucous intrusion, compensation came in the form of some splendid and generally deserted beaches close to the town, and it was to these havens of peace that we were inclined to direct our steps during the idle days before our return to Cyprus. Though we were free to come and go without hindrance, we had earlier been advised not to wander from the camp and into the desert, and certainly not to venture beyond the visible distance of camp or road, and never without water. We were afforded graphic illustration of the disorienting and dehydrating effect of dust storms.

One foolish and ill-advised venture was to reveal to me the wisdom of this advice. It was yet another blazing day with breathlessly elevated temperatures, clear skies and not a zephyr on the breeze. In an idle moment, I decided to take a walk. I would not venture far, but far enough to immerse myself in the desert environment. Desert topography is creative of sensory mayhem. The heat, the haze, the constantly transforming illusion, all combine to militate against routine and familiar visual navigation. What may appear as a gently undulating desert landscape may, in reality, be a series of elevated dune ridges and deep valleys and hollows.

The air was suffocatingly still, and though I had not ventured far, the camp had abruptly disappeared from view. Equally abruptly, the still air swirled into motion, obscuring vision and regular aspiration with choking clouds of dust. As the wind, the dust and the raised sand increased in velocity, I was left with no choice but to crouch, to cover my face with a handkerchief, and to remain on my knees until the blinding, asphyxiating maelstrom abated. A few minutes had elapsed, and while the gale continued its noisy abuse of the atmosphere, my little pocket had become reduced to an overheated, lung-violating reduction in pressure. I raised my head to view the whirling tempest around me, to realise that I was the sole occupant of the cyclonic vortex, and that my entire visible world was now locked into a huge turmoil of dust filled gyration. Within a few seconds the tempest returned, concussed, and in a few further minutes had departed, leaving me without conscious location or direction. I had no idea where I was, nor the direction of the camp. While the sun was overhead, just where I had last seen it, the terrain around me seemed to have been adjusted beyond ready recognition, I trudged on, through the loose sand and the dune valley, until I finally achieved elevation and enhanced visibility. The camp was behind me, a mere half a mile or so distant, but in the diametrically opposite direction to my confused trajectory. Suddenly, the wisdom of the standing order was revealed in abundant clarity.

A few days before our departure, notice was posted that representatives of each service and every section would be required to be involved with a ceremony of homage, respect, and welcome. King Idris, who had been seeking medical treatment in Turkey, would be making his return home to Libya, and pausing in brief transit at El Adem. A guard of honour would provide a welcome return, and dress uniform would be the minimum required turnout. In this heat? The announcement was greeted with an audible groan.

The appointed guard of honour was to be mixed bunch of mortals conscripted from El Adem residents, the entire 280 contingent, and the army platoon not yet returned to their base near Benghazi. These groups had not been involved with any form of drill or parade exercise for months, and had never done so together, so muster was dictated for mid-morning to permit time for a period of rehearsal. Our performance would have won few accolades at a military tattoo, but it had to suffice, and we were drawn into two ranks at either side of the taxi runway to await the arrival of the royal chariot, expected at 13.00. The heat under the mid-day sky was searing, the aircraft was late, and the ranks began to wilt.

One by one, individuals and their rifles clattered to the ground. In the period before the incoming aircraft was making its final approach, medics were permitted to scoop up the fallen and take them to recovery. However, once the drone of the incoming aircraft indicated the imminent royal arrival, protocol dictated that the fallen should remain where they fell. They continued to do so as the royal chariot landed and proceeded towards the taxi runway and the somewhat depleted twin ranks of almost upright servicemen. To the observer, and perhaps to the royal personage, the scene bore greater resemblance to a skittle alley than a guard of honour. The no longer contiguous twin ranks had become two lines of wilting, now widely spaced militia, struggling to maintain the required 'attention' posture, while between them, an equivalent number of apparent corpses greeted the incoming and homecoming monarch.

For all of the preparations, the rehearsal, the discomfort, and the heat induced disarray, the entire event concluded in moments. Perhaps Idris was also averse to the mid-day sun, but he stepped from the aircraft, acknowledged the waiting senior officers, and was transported quickly into the reception building, thus permitting dismissal, the near-dead to walk, and those beyond repair to be gathered up and treated for dehydration.

Almost thirty years later, this event was to find an unlikely sequel. The scene was a remote corner of Malawi. I was in the company of four travelling companions, and in the light of our camp fire we were sharing the events of the day, and of life and times in general. One of the company, a pharmacist from Swansea, was to become a lifelong friend and world-wide travelling companion for more than twenty years, until his untimely death in 2002. We had both been required to undertake National Service, he as a medic in the army, me in the Royal Air Force. As our conversation shared our respective experiences of those times, it became clear that he and I both had taken our places, and had presented arms to the arriving Idris on the blazing tarmac at El Adem on that June day in 1959. He had been a member of the army group that had been despatched to El Adem for the exercise, and he had returned to his base at Benghazi on the day after the royal return. We did not meet on that occasion, and indeed had no knowledge of each other until the coincidence of our journey together in Malawi. Small world!!!

Chapter 12. The winds of change were blowing, and the world was closing in.

... "Oh, the seagulls like the lighthouse" ...

*

*After an energetic and exciting day out and about,
and having enjoyed the many and varied facilities of the 280 resort,
a quiet evening 'at home' may be the preference.*

A quiet drink. A good book. A little light music. A game of Ludo or Scrabble.

Charades, musical chairs, hunt the thimble, pass the Moonie.

*Drinking four pints of Keo, while standing on one leg on a chair
always brings a smile.*

*The simple sing-song is always popular, and helps to foster a communal spirit
as guests join new friends for an evening of harmony.*

*Many and varied are the routes to relaxation,
or perhaps to plan and plot for the undercover mayhem of the following day.*

*

During the period between my arrival in the late summer of 1958 to the closing months of 1959, daily life at 280 enjoyed a measure of relaxed discipline that did not feature on the majority of RAF stations. Isolated geographically and socially, the quality of daily life depended heavily upon individual initiative and opportunism, with just a modest helping of bloody mindedness. Hazard and excitement came in small and irregular doses, usually associated with extra-curricular duties. For many, the regular duties of the Air Defence Operator did not associate in any way with personal interests or professional direction, and were thus conducive only to boredom. Relaxation was easy to conjure provided that sunshine and the sea were heavily involved, or that personal creativity could be combined with initiative and opportunism.

However, the relaxed atmosphere at 280 was dependent upon two other factors, the generosity and understanding of the Commanding Officer, and the almost total absence of Snowdrops and their associated bullshit. Of course, in their familiar botanical morphology, these nodding white harbingers of the coming spring in Northern Europe are unknown on dusty Cape Gata, Here, as elsewhere, the somewhat derogatory term was, and probably still is used as title for the nodding white cap cowl that identified the wearer as a member of the RAF police.

Snowdrops shone, Snowdrops glistered, Snowdrops strutted, Snowdrops dictated order among the disorderly, but for so long as this variety of Snowdrop was absent from Cape Gata, imposed dress and personal appearance codes were without manifestation. However, while disciplinarian Snowdrops were the instigators, the perpetrators and the prefects of bullshit, their absence from 280 ensured that this unwelcome, despised and unnecessary discipline was not evident at Cape Gata. At no time did the punitive variety of Snowdrop become resident at 280, and in the earlier days were not known to call in for afternoon tea or a quiet game of Monopoly. Snowdrops preferred to dwell where order was the familiar, and where any hint of disorder could be rectified by a threatening wave of a baton or a barked instruction. 280 was no such place, was considered a place of ruffians, and a place not worthy of the rule of order.

However, towards the end of 1959, the winds of change were beginning to blow. Station standing orders began to carry general camp instructions that were menacingly similar to those posted regularly at Akrotiri. They exuded the imposition of more regular camp inspections, of dress codes, of disciplinary measures, of imposed camp maintenance working parties, and of regular Snowdrop visitations. These appalling prospects struck at the very heart of the 280 doctrine of freedom. There would surely be unrest. They made clear comparisons with the relatively pristine conditions that dictated daily life at Akrotiri. Neatly pressed uniforms, clean and tidy vehicles, swept roads and footpaths, tidy shops, neat living quarters, and even a full-length mirror in the guardroom to ensure that all who passed its portals did so under critical scrutiny.

The Snowdrops did come, irregularly at first, and evidently somewhat timorously in the beginning. They came in twos and threes, and ventured first to the more open and more publicly populated parts of the camp. At first their arrival was always signalled by the on-duty guard at the gate, and this signal permitted sufficient time for concealment, for evasion, or for the removal of questionable artefact. It was all very cat-and-mouse, and ultimately fairly futile, as Snowdrop visitations became more frequent. The more public parts of the camp were their early targets, the mess, the ablutions, the cinema, the NAAFI, and the more open spaces. It took a little more time, and perhaps an injection of courage and self-determination before they directed their critical gaze at the more personal living quarters and the tent lines.

In truth, they were largely ignored, and their influence upon daily life was marginal. Instructions and orders occasionally echoed across the camp.

"Airman, pick up that empty beer can and dispose of it in the proper manner."

"Airman, pull up your bloody socks."

"Where are your bloody laces?"

It was generally far easier to comply than to oppose, especially as regulation was ever in their favour, and whatever the depth of resentment, the opposition could never prevail.

"Uniform will be worn at all times when on duty of any kind". The rule was clear and unequivocal, but it afforded slightly less guidance on how the uniform would be worn, and in what combination. Of course we all knew exactly what was required, but the relaxed attitude to most aspects of life, had reduced all but the few who boasted elegance and etiquette among their idiosyncrasies, to a fairly scruffy bunch. Badges, buttons and boots were the most frequently neglected items of our daily wear, and most readily seized upon by a passing Snowdrop as a cause for bellowed reprimand. They were very rarely exposed to polish of any kind, and the closest they ever came to a buffering was an occasional dusting. Perhaps the classic reprimand referred to the condition of a miscreant cap badge.

"Airman, your cap badge is disgusting, and while we have little hope that you might polish it from time to time, you might give it an occasional weeding."

While the more a la mode among us continued to make their own fashion statements, and the resident versus Snowdrop battle lines continue to hurl brickbats, something much more sinister was rearing its ugly head among the on-camp whispers. Only rumour at first, but with the certain knowledge of Snowdrop opposition to the 280 casual approach to daily life, suspicion focussed strongly that this most recent initiative had been Snowdrop influenced. The intention, it appeared, was to bring 280 into line with every other more 'normal' RAF station, and to impose a regular and routine programme of watch parades.

To date, these events had been irregular, badly attended, and no more than a token gesture toward the 'normal'. Usually conducted at around 07.00, called by the sergeant of the watch, the usually incomplete and ill-clad members of the morning watch were marched to one end of the dusty patch of earth that substituted for a square, marched to the opposite end, about turn, and return to the centre where they were dismissed. No formal salute, the minimum requirement had been satisfied, and the reluctant participants headed for their daily duties.

The word on the jungle telegraph now suggested that the 'square' was to be enhanced and improved, that facilities for greater formality were to be installed, and that respectful parades would become a regular feature in our daily lives. The underlying message, and the Snowdrop implication, were clear, bullshit was set to increase. As the indications of the first practical steps towards implementation of these proposals were awaited, the genesis of a clear determination to mount practical opposition began to evolve.

The first manifestations of intended purpose were the several deliveries of quantities of stones that were dumped centrally and to one side of the intended square. Initial puzzlement was quickly succeeded by the revelation that these were to be used to construct a raised platform or dais that could only become the rostrum from which the officer of the day would make his address and take the salute. Nothing more was to happen or to be delivered for several weeks, which afforded abundant time for the first disruptive plan to become enacted.

The security lights around the square were all directed toward the cabins that were the administration offices, leaving the opposite perimeter of the square, and its pile of stones, in relative shadow. The plan was simple. Each passing night patrol would lift a stone or two from the pile, carry their cargo to a random point on the technical site perimeter, and project it as far as they were able into the bundu. Little by little, the pile of stones was reduced, and it was satisfyingly remarkable that it had become significantly diminished before anyone noticed.

It was of course, replenished, and though the programme of reduction continued, its progress was necessarily much more opportunistic and cautious, until finally the risks outweighed the gains. The prank was finally laid to rest when a team arrived from Akrotiri, armed with all of the materials and equipment necessary for construction. By the end of the day, a small decapitated pyramid had replaced the ungainly pile, and continued sabotage required an element of revision.

Nothing more transpired for some time, and although just a few of the lower stones became mysteriously free from the construction, we blamed a careless driver, no attempt at wholesale destruction was considered. Once the structure had set, consolidated, and concreted, the next delivery was a substantial load of constructional timber. Examination of the timber suggested that the most probable intention was the fabrication of a platform to crown the pyramid, a short flight of steps to make the ascent, and perhaps a single section of railing.

The erosion and evaporation of this kind of material presented very different practical difficulties. Most of the pieces of timber were relatively large, and could not be pocketed or otherwise concealed about the person. Discarded timber would be readily rediscovered if jettisoned into the bundu, and in any case, timber was a commodity far too valuable in the domestic arena to be squandered. In any event, after the success of our sleight of hand with the stones, the authorities were likely to exercise a far greater degree of vigilance. Some of the shorter pieces, those that we suspected were to become step treads did disappear, allegedly spirited away from the site in trouser legs. This cannot have been achieved without significant discomfort and impediment to the trouser wearer, not to mention hazard, in no small measure, to the tender parts in the event of an unfortunate stumble.

Anxious perhaps to avoid repeat of the stones debacle, the authorities did not leave the timber unattended and vulnerable for long. A team of carpenters and nail knockers were despatched from Akrotiri, and in less than a day of sawing and hammering, a proud dais stood atop the pyramid, complete with a flight of four steps and a frontal rail upon which the officer taking the salute would find a modicum of support.

For the residents, the writing was now clearly writ upon the wall, and capitulation had adopted the mantle of inevitability. However, the structure remained incomplete, and could not be properly utilised without a flag. Hitherto, a makeshift structure had served this purpose, but this now would be clearly and shoddily inadequate. The next team of skilled technicians arrived to rectify this final omission. First they excavated a pit directly to the rear of the dais, and this they filled with mixed concrete. The base of the splendid new flagpole had been tightly secured into a metal sleeve, and this they inserted into the concrete, steadying the entire structure in place with ropes and timber until the concrete had set. Any attempt to sabotage this while the concrete remained unstable would have earned a ticket to the guard house and to the cells at Akrotiri, so there it remained, a proud herald of impending and inevitable change. A declaration of authority? A seriously retrograde step?

Points of view would remain at very considerable variance

An order was issued. A flag raising ceremony was to be initiated every morning at 07.00, to coincide with the changing of the night to morning watch. Members of both watches were ordered to attend, while ensuring that the changeover permitted essential operational continuity.

The flagpole stood proud, its struts and anchors were removed, and some little time was to pass before its intended inaugural parade. In the interim, the flag was raised and lowered daily, and it was during this brief intermission that the final two acts of defiance and protest brought closure to this brief chapter in 280 history. Both were somewhat extreme, and both were shrouded in mystery that could never be exposed. One dark night, someone entered the tech site to commit the darkest of deeds, and made his exit, unseen when the deed was done. With care, precision, patience, and silence, he had contrived to saw through the flagpole at its base and had left it lying on the ground beside the dais. His capacity for stealth, both audible and visual had been remarkable. Through his criminal location was shielded from immediate view in the shadow of the dais pyramid, he contrived to saw through the pole so slowly and meticulously that the guilty rasp of the saw remained undetected. To have attempted to remove the pole would have been futile and could not have been achieved without detection. Equally, concealment of such a large item would have posed insurmountable difficulties, and would have been readily discovered, however well concealed. The inevitable noise of sawing precluded any thoughts of cutting it into sections. So with great skill, and in silence in the shadow of the pyramid, the pole was detached from its metal tube, was carefully lowered to the ground, and was abandoned.

The reaction was predictably furious. An enquiry was conducted by an investigation team from the SIB amid threats of serious punishment should any culprit be identified. All of the personnel who were on watch that night could readily be accounted for, but those whose duties for the night had included patrols endured a particularly severe grilling. Among the remainder of the camp complement, some were selected, apparently at random, for questioning, others were questioned in groups, and the SIB delivered one or two pep talks in the cinema to impress upon everyone the serious nature of this wanton act of vandalism. Of course, no culprit was ever identified, no-one was even accused and brought to assize, the flagpole was restored to place in the concrete block, and life returned to its customary daily routine.

At around this time, one disgraceful act of vandalism shocked the entire 280 community. The wheeled cabins that provided office accommodation for some officers and for the station administration function, were situated in a single row at the opposite side of the square to the newly inaugurated dais. They were enclosed structures mainly without window on to the outside world, and only slit windows located at relatively high elevation, for ventilation. One night, a misguided individual, possibly one harbouring a personal grudge, smashed one of the windows of the adjutant's office and directed the contents of a foam fire extinguisher through the small broken pane. The mess that was thus imposed was appalling and destructive, and when revealed, induced universal regret and revulsion. It had been an act of mindless vindictiveness, one driven by an unknown motive, and one for which a culprit was never exposed or revealed.

One further gesture was to bring this episode to a close. Audacious in the extreme, and risky to the point of foolishness, this act of protest required a high degree of self-assurance, effrontery, and brass balls. The plot could be likened to that of John Catesby and his gunpowder cronies, to the Ides of March, or possibly to Macbeth's witches. It was divined by a small group of individuals, who planned and prepared the details, agreed the timing, designated the action, and allocated the task to one most bold. In broad daylight on a normal working day, the elected or coerced man of action walked up to the flag, lowered it, removed it from its halyard, folded it, and left the site. He was not challenged, apparently not even noticed, and he walked away from the flagpole and the technical site carrying with him the most symbolic item on the entire station. The outrage went unnoticed until sundown, when a duty corporal went to satisfy the evening task of lowering the flag. Curious! The flag had been lowered and removed as normal, and the halyard had been secured. Had there been a confusion of duty? No-one else it seemed had performed the daily ritual. He became obliged to report the mystery of a missing flag.

Too late this day to commence a thorough search or investigation. This became the urgent demand the following morning when the matter had been reported to the Commanding Officer. Without its morning flag, the station had been stripped to a vulgar and ugly nakedness. This was the morning after a major amputation, and functionality had become seriously impaired. The SIB were summoned once more, and on this occasion they were especially thorough. With the insistence that one tent occupant be present at every search, the investigation team set about the task of conducting a search of every residence. To avoid any chance that the item could be relocated during the night, the team completed their initial search during the twelve hours or so of daylight. Nothing was found, and the flagpole remained shamefully naked.

The search continued through a second day and endeavoured to embrace every other nook and cranny in every other building and structure. Still no sign of the missing flag. A third day was dedicated to a more general search of peripheral areas, locations yet to be examined, and even areas of bundu for any evidence of recent flag interment. Still they came up with nothing, and perhaps in conclusion that the flag may have been destroyed, they reduced their activities to random questioning. The unclothed flagpole remained an embarrassment and a sustained gesture of silent protest, and as a temporary measure, an urgent request was relayed to all other RAF units on the island.

"Do you have a spare flag that we may borrow?"

Alas, no spare flag was forthcoming.

A few more days passed, and droll observers began to suggest that the abandoned flagpole was beginning to wilt. An increasingly desperate situation required equally desperate action, and a further bulletin was posted on to the station notice board.

TO WHOM IT MAY CONCERN
IF THE MISSING FLAG REMAINS IN YOUR POSSESSION
WE REQUEST THAT IT BE RETURNED FORTHWITH
NO FURTHER ACTION WILL BE TAKEN.

The flag, undamaged and neatly folded, was discovered on the step of the Commanding Officer's office at daybreak on the following morning. The perpetrator of this jape, who remains nameless to this day, had been wearing the flag, like an oversized cummerbund, under his uniform throughout the entire period of the search.

The matter became closed without further comment or sanction.

One further act of fairly passive protest in this war of attrition, made final contribution to trucial conditions and a reduction in the unacceptable escalation of campus bullshit. After all of these years, I feel constrained to confess sole responsibility for this small piece of mischief.

The flag was now restored to purpose and was making its daily ascent and descent of its pole. Internecine conflict had subsided, and routine and regularity had become restored. One morning a party of able-bodied men arrived from Akrotiri, and set about the imposition of yet another assignment of bullshit. They parked their truck on the parade ground and unloaded a large number of small wooden stakes. They drove these into the ground at precisely regular intervals, encompassing three sides of the parade ground rectangle. This done they adorned each one with a coat of white paint. Next, they took a rope, which had already received a gleaming coat of white paint, and they stapled this to the top of each post, ensuring that lowest point of each loop between the posts, was equidistant from the ground. They touched up any bruises or blemishes on the rope, and headed back whence they had come.

The parade ground was now proudly adorned with a low rope fence suspended on posts that measured fifteen inches or so in height. It extended across each end of the arena, and along its entire length behind the dais, perhaps in total length some forty or fifty yards. This was utter bullshit, and its nature strongly suggested a Snowdrop initiative. It could serve no practical or useful purpose, except to trip the unwary. It was bullshit of the most obnoxious and least acceptable kind. It surely would not survive.

The camp was awash with muttering and criticism about this pointless intrusion, and some of this must have reached the ears of those in authority. Consequently this sinuous carbuncle survived for a few weeks and until the initial surrounding furore had subsided. Opportunity to commit my small act of sabotage became apparent during a night shift, when my watch had reported for duty.

It was customary, at the end of each working day, for vehicle drivers to park their three-ton trucks in a neat line at their base in the MT Section. The exception to this rule were occasions when the requirement for a vehicle was expected during the night, or very early in the morning, and on these occasions, a required vehicle would be parked for greater convenience. On this occasion as usual, my allocation of duty included a period of perimeter and site patrol with a companion. While checking security around the offices and the parade ground, I noted that a truck had been parked in the shadows close to the offices, and only a few feet from one end of the offending fence. We checked the vehicle, which was unattended, nor was there a driver in the vicinity or in the canteen. My next move was heavily dependent upon the hope that the truck would not be required for duty until after the change of watch at 07.00.

I asked my companion to maintain a watching brief for ten minutes or so while I quickly deviated to the MT Section where I knew that I would find the item I required, and I duly returned a few minutes later carrying a length of small diameter rope. It was a simple task, and the work of no more than a few minutes to attach one end of the rope to the base of the end stake, and the other to part of the understructure of the truck. With equal ease the exposed length of rope could readily be concealed in a groove in the dust.

The dastardly deed done, we continued dutifully until change of watch when the night watchers went home to bed. For me, temptation was too great. The truck had not been moved at the time of change over, so I lingered in and out of the canteen, doing my best to appear busy or unobtrusive, or out of view. My patience was rewarded. Little more than a half hour had elapsed when a driver jumped into the cab of the truck and started the engine. I muttered a small supplicatory mantra in the direction of no particular deity, but in the sincere hope that my rope proved sufficiently sturdy to tolerate the impact of engagement with the fence. A moment of buttock clenching apprehension when the driver dismounted once more, though happily to attend to something at the front of the vehicle, and well out of view of my guilty hawser, before regaining his seat, revving his engine, and moving off in a cloud of his own dust.

Behind him, as he sped out of my range of vision, fifty yards or so of trailing rattling fence, lost to his visible range in the cloud of dust spewing from his wheels and his exhaust. I felt it diplomatic not to wait to see how far he dragged his unintended cargo. I made haste to leave the tech site, to take refuge in Paradise Lost, and to practice my most innocent countenance in preparation for the breaking storm.

Oddly enough, it never did. There followed no enquiry, no investigation, no intense questioning. The fence was never replaced. Perhaps authority finally came to realise that snowdrop fuelled bullshit enjoys only limited boundaries of tolerance.

...but this was 1960, the fuse was burning down and time was inexorably nudging us towards the unknown quantity of the next phase in life's rich pattern, and the daunting prospect of the return to reality.

Chapter 13. Time gentlemen please!

... "and the sphinx's inscrutable smile." ...

*

*Ultimately, it will become your unhappy task
to make your preparations to leave our resort.*

*Dear to your memory will be your friendships and associations
with the native people of the locality, their sense of humour
and their practical jokes.*

*Faded now, the memory of tricky devices,
placed in original and unusual places to ensure maximum effect
and hearty amusement all round.*

*Attractive or valuable objects, all designed like firecrackers
to ensure maximum noise and confusion,
and to remove treasured parts of your anatomy as they did so.*

*Laughter is such a good remedy, and a worthy accompaniment
for your homeward journey.*

*

A significant proportion of those serving at Cape Gata had been drawn from the ranks of National Servicemen, or those who had accepted the Queen's Shilling and had signed on for an extra year. For some, the years beyond National Service were already prescribed, the return to profession, an awaiting job, the pursuit of tertiary education, or perhaps returning to resume a position in a family business. For others it was not so clear-cut. Some had been obliged to resign a position to respond to the call to arms. The farewell message to others had suggested that 'if the job is vacant when you get back, you can have it'. Frequently it was not. Many who were without profession, craft or training faced the prospect of seeking a living in the small ads, and some, for whom the weekly unemployment benefit had provided their only income, faced the prospect of returning to continued dependency upon the state.

Thus for the intending repatriates, it was a mixed bag of emotions that faced the termination of their collective uniformed years. For some those years had been a period of unwelcome and undesirable servitude, for others it had been a welcome break, and for most it had been an experience, never to be repeated and never to be forgotten, an opportunity to indulge in an experience like no other, and a welcome deviation from the inevitable routine that would follow. Whatever the emotion, for some it had always been customary and the normal practice to complain about the drudgery, to moan about the waste of two years, to express disgruntlement about living and working conditions, to mutter discontentment about almost everything, and to be so consumed by self-induced melancholy, that the experience and its attendant opportunities passed unseen or were ignored. Not so for me. I cherished every chance that came my way, indulged in as many as possible, enjoyed my two years of service and, I choose to believe, emerged much better prepared to face the rigours and challenges of a competitive outside world.

Perhaps as a practical indication, or just an elaborate display of actual or alleged discontent, almost everyone in pursuit of his short-term servitude maintained a kind of chronological record. This was not a diary chronicling events of the day or week just passed, but a forward look at the day or week ahead. Frequently manufactured as a chart, a table, a graph, or a map, it recorded 'days to do'. Mine took the form of a map of Europe and the Mediterranean basin, carefully painted on to a large rectangular piece of softboard. Superimposed on to my map I had pecked three lines of black dots, each of which represented a homeward route, and all three beginning at Cape Gata and ending in Whitby. The three lines represented the three possible modes of transport that I might employ, air, sea and land, and each dot represented a single day. Progress along the 'days to do' dots was marked by a tiny cut out aircraft, a ship, and a motor vehicle, each mounted on a pin, and each progressing dot by dot, day by day, inexorably towards the same destination.

Through the winter and spring of months of early 1960, the familiar routine at Cape Gata continued. Snowdrop autocracy waned to a mutually acceptable level, there were no more protests or demonstrations, and we slithered gently towards demobilisation. We determined to take every possible advantage of our new found freedom to travel, and to enjoy the ambience and the many pleasures and interests that the island had to offer. Skiving had become an art form, and with the gradual onset of 'demob happy' mode, bellowing sergeants no longer struck fear into trembling hearts. Those months remained tense in some locations. We were to receive somewhat frosty receptions in some of those monasteries where arms had been cached. The residents of those villages that had remained loyal to Eoka made it clear that we were not particularly welcome; and in some of the towns, some streets or districts remained out of bounds. However, we did get around, and the privilege of increasing familiarity with the beauty and interest of this historic island promoted an agreeable and appropriate swansong to our more turbulent months of residence.

April and into early May witnessed the passage of the brief Cypriot spring, and the somewhat unpredictable anticipation of transition. The date of my demobilisation would be the second day of June, the second anniversary of my arrival at Cardington, and those distant, hesitant, deeply apprehensive first steps toward the life enhancing enlightenment of the two year period now passing into personal history. At some stage information received would indicate the date of our transportation to Blighty, and to RAF Innsworth for discharge back into the civilian world. We hoped that the chronological juxtaposition of travel and ultimate discharge would be close, and that the tedious limbo of transit at RAF Innsworth would be mercifully brief. In the event were afforded no more than a few days' notice in which to make our personal preparations, and undertake the all-important psychological adjustment.

This was a period of bustling preparation. It seemed inconceivable that confinement of twenty months in one third of a tent, and the limited storage capacity of one upright and one bedside locker would permit any more than minimum accumulation of personal artefacts. This indeed had been the case, and imposed limitations had induced the maxim, so valuable in later travelling and backpacking days, that the personal wardrobe was 'one on, one off, and one in the wash'. Somewhere, suspended in the tall locker, was the little used 'best blue' uniform. As this would be required during the entire transition period from departure to homecoming. The task of removal from the hidden depths of the locker was approached with care, and in the hope that decomposition had not become too far advanced. An onerous task now awaited each intending returnee. The dusty garment would require a process close to purging. Beating it with a stick like a carpet would surely sound its death knell, so the only alternative was the somewhat more gentle attentions of the cleaning service at Akrotiri.

Equally demanding would be the cleansing, polishing and buffering of buttons, buckles, and badges. Gleaming in their heyday, now closer to lime green in their months of long neglect, restoration of that long-forgotten condition would be a requirement. Boots too! The lustre of toecaps, the outcome of the labour of daily hours of spit, polish, and gentle buffering in those distant Bridgnorth days, would require recall and re-establishment.

Permitted transported baggage on our homeward journey would be restricted to the kitbag issued to us at even more distant Cardington, and one standard small pack. However, we were to be permitted the additional facility of a ditty box, into which we could pack any items not required in transit or for some period hence. Though there were no declared restrictions on contents, a brief inventory was required, and the container must not exceed a required maximum dimension. This package would make the journey by sea, and would arrive at its intended destination at some indeterminate future date. It was the responsibility of each individual to obtain a suitable container.

An early search of the unit revealed nothing among the accumulated junk that seemed appropriate and that was not already in use, which directed the quest to more abundant Akrotiri. Here among the hangars and storage sheds were containers in abundance, all designated for some intending purpose, though perhaps just one could be misappropriated without notice. How? This posed a passing dilemma, to which brass neck seemed the most likely promising remedy. I selected one which complied with the stipulated dimensions, simply liberated it from its stored location, and wandered unchallenged from the campus. I was pleased with my illicit acquisition. It was a wooden crate that had been designed for the transportation of equipment that had been susceptible to impact damage, and was thus robustly constructed and internally padded. I removed the padding and some of the internal strengthening in order to maximise capacity, and my ditty box was ready to receive its cargo. It remains in use to the present day, which affords some credit to its durability.

Its intended contents required a little cautious consideration and planning. Surplus clothing and some souvenir items could be used for wrapping and packing, as could the original padding earlier removed. Central to this endeavour, and the box, were three bottles of the finest Cyprus brandy. I considered that these were sufficiently well packed to survive unless dropped from a considerable height. For the next intended items, concealment took centre stage. Over the months, I had amassed a considerable collection of small hand tools, and useful though they had been during this period, it would be embarrassingly difficult to return them to the careless mechanics in the MT Section. More than that, they would be of considerable use to me when stripped of their military livery. Each was meticulously wrapped in swaddling clothing and packed carefully around the bottles. Any remaining space was filled with souvenir items, and the entire box was packed so tightly as to be all but bomb proof. For despatch and further security while in transit, it was tightly roped, wrapped in hessian, and carefully labelled. When I presented the package for shipment, and handed in the stipulated inventory, no-one questioned the latter, nor did they make any enquiry about the contents, or instructed that the box should be opened for scrutiny. Farewell ditty box. Hopefully see you in a few weeks.

During the closing few weeks of our residence at Cape Gata, the confusion of emotions became ever more evident. Some were overflowing with noisy euphoria at the prospect of leaving, while others were clearly struggling with overwhelming melancholy. I was chatting one day to one such, a big lad, an enthusiastic party goer, a significant contributor to 'A Midwinter's Nightmare', and a most gregarious individual. He was struggling to explain his somewhat confused emotions about his impending repatriation, when he abruptly burst into uncontrollable sobs. As the floods of tears began to flow, I led him to one side to ease his embarrassment. He guided me through some of his personal life. Family and home life had been unhappy and difficult. He had no social life and no friends at his home location. National Service had provided the best moments of his life. He didn't want to leave and lose all of his mates. He was without job or evident prospect. National Service, it seemed, had provided him with the only sense of security that he had ever known. I put my arm around his shoulder as he wept uncontrollably, and spluttered his life's history through the falling tears. As he began to recover, I could do more than wish him well and better fortune than had been his destiny so far in life.

We were finally instructed to prepare for departure on a date in late May. However mixed the feelings as we awaited the arrival of the truck to take us to Nicosia, bravado dominated the ambience outside the NAAFI. For me, a few moments earlier, a moment of extreme sadness, a sudden overwhelming sense of dejection as I closed the door of 'Paradise Lost' for the last time. I had taken my last look at the insignificant corner of the world that had become a surrogate home for most of the last two years. However incomplete its surrogacy, that little corner of tent A12 had become an indelible part of my life. The Whitby coat of arms and insignia rather crudely painted on my tall locker door; my 'days to do' chart still the wall, the pins now perilously close to the homeland; the bed legs still standing in the beer cans of paraffin; and the bedbugs smiling at me from every crack and cranny. I closed the door finally and joined the noisy crowd of migrants lest I too would become overtaken by misplaced remorse.

GOODBYE AKROTIRI
FAREWELL 'TOO AYE TEE'
YOU CAN STICK YOUR CHUFFING RADAR UP YOUR JACKSON
'COS I'VE GOT MY CHIT.

A wild frenzy of handshaking preceded our en-trucking, but no sign of officers of air rank to bid us farewell and thank us for our selfless duty. The truck trundled us to Nicosia and dumped us in the unlovely transit camp. Perchance, there were a large number of transiteers in similar limbo, and all of the available Cawood buildings were occupied. Humph! Still in tents. We became obliged to linger here for a couple of dreary days before being allocated a flight. I guess that we were a fairly subdued cargo of passenger that emerged at RAF Lyneham, and who were quickly ushered aboard a bus to take us back whence we had commenced our journey of personal enlightenment. Our residence at RAF Innsworth was as brief as administrative processing would permit, and a couple of days later, on the second day of June in 1960, we were driven through the camp gates for the last time, as freshly fledged civilians.

Clutching our rail passes, we were dumped at Gloucester railway station. Here I fell into final temptation, and embarked upon my final attempted deception. After all of my earlier, meticulously planned schemes, this was the only one that was to fail. My rail pass indicated that I was destined to travel from Gloucester to Whitby via the most direct route, a tedious voyage involving a series of station changes through the midlands. All of my pals were heading towards London, and the temptation to join them for a final few hours, and a final few beers, proved too great. My rail pass afforded the facility to deviate from the allocated route, and in the small box labelled 'via', I wrote London. It was a clumsy attempt, in handwriting nothing like the original and even in ink of a different shade of blue.

The man in the ticket office looked at me sternly and silently before he spoke.

"You have two choices," he said. "You can pay the difference or I will telephone the camp administration."

I paid the difference.

Many hours later, the early morning 'milk' train pulled into Whitby station. It was 06.00 hours, I was half asleep, no-one was there to meet the returning prodigal son, and I was obliged to await the first bus that would take me to my final destination. As I was sitting on the bus station bench, inevitably pondering everything that had happened to my life during these two years past, I was approached by a familiar. This was a sometimes acquaintance, someone with whom I would share a pint and a chat if we met in a pub. Not a close friend. I was still in uniform, and after a brief greeting he posed a simple question.

"Haven't seen you for a while," he said. "Have you been away?"

A comprehensive response would have required several hours, but the arrival of the bus saved me that penance. Nothing had changed - except me!

Home to the unfamiliar familiar. A couple of days later, I stood in the middle of the home property, in the green home hamlet of thirty souls, and I pondered the road just trod and the road ahead. It was a strange, somewhat alien feeling, and the reflection that it had induced was to remain with me for many weeks until the increasing familiarity of the present relegated it to recent memory. A few weeks later, my ditty box arrived. It had lost its hessian jacket, the ropes were awry, and it had clearly been opened, probably by HM. Customs and Excise. So far as I was able to recall, the contents remained intact, and indeed some of them remain in my tool box to this day.

Welcome to the rest of your life!

Epilogue.

... "There were none so fair" ...

Where did they all go? A few kept in touch with a few others, a pattern no doubt duplicated throughout the length and breadth of the land, but these familiars would mostly become estranged through the passage of time, and the in the wake of the many preoccupations of life, and death. Two years previously, we had all been dumped into one place like a handful of ants. Now someone had trodden on the nest and scattered the occupants far and wide.

For me, friendship was sustained over the years with just a very small number. Occasional meetings to share life and times, past and present, served to foster these relationships as life progressed. A large proportion of the temporary close-knit band of warriors that had been 'the boys of too aye tee', had dispersed. They had all pursued life's many and inevitable quests of profession, vocation, family, interests, leisure activities, social endeavours, the entire panoply of the ever changing and evolving pattern of life's enterprise and opportunity. They had all disappeared along the highway entitled 'Destiny'.

Perhaps it is a feature of later life. Perhaps when each individual has reached the apogee of his personal aspirations, and further struggle and competition against a better informed and ambitious younger generation becomes a pursuit without purpose. Perhaps then, the still active and vibrant psyche will find satisfying reflection in memory. Memory inevitably promotes a simple question and an imperative demand. It becomes an obligation, perhaps even something of an obsession.

"I wonder what happened to?"

The answer is frustratingly evasive and elusive, and so frequently the moment of enlightenment becomes dominated by one that will equally frequently induce sadness and remorse. The sinking revelation that all of your many efforts had been in vain, and you had returned to the scene just a little too late.

"I wonder what happened to?"

I guess that question had been in the back of my mind for years, but when and where I began to take a more positive stance on finding an answer, I cannot recall. Nor can I remember how and with whom the first contact outside of my immediate small circle of two or three regular correspondents was established. It is of little consequence. Of far greater significance was the first meeting of a small group of those veterans who had bade each other a final farewell at Cape Gata almost fifty years earlier.

In 2008, we met in a pub in Warwickshire, and once the slight unfamiliarity of feature and form, which had undeniably matured since that farewell day, had recovered its fellowship, the camaraderie continued in denial of the interruption. That meeting embraced a weekend, time aplenty to reminisce, to share life and times, and importantly, to share known contact locations.

Contacts swiftly began to beget contacts, and the number of corresponding members of the veteran group increased. Sadly, all too many of the enquiries revealed the earlier, and often premature deaths of former close pals, and the oft heard lament, 'I do wish that I had made the enquiry earlier'. Perchance, a small number of the group were resident in the Manchester area, and in Leeds, some of whom were no longer able to accommodate long distance travelling. Thus Manchester became an occasional meeting place, sometimes for up to a dozen, as the residents were joined by others willing to make the journey from other parts of the country. Our base for these meetings has been Trafford, where the Premier Inn or Travelodge has provided ready accommodation, and a Wetherspoon establishment has supplied an ample supply of beer, of fish and chips, and of eggs Benedict for breakfast.

In 2007, during a holiday visit to Cyprus, the first such return since 1960, I made the request of the RAF to undertake a visit to Akrotiri and to the long abandoned ruins of 280 SU. My request was granted and on arrival at the station I was greeted by a former serving officer, who had retired to the locality, and who now served as an official guide. I enjoyed my nostalgic tour of those parts of much changed Akrotiri that I could remember, but I expressed a particular desire to visit Cape Gata.

"Why do you want to go up there? There is nothing to see except the radar and radio installations."

"But there was once! There was an entire and self-sufficient encampment that provided home for three hundred or so worthy souls, and in which I lived for almost two years."

"No! You must be mistaken, I have served three tours of duty here, and there has never been anything else on the cape."

"Not so," I responded. "Let's go and see."

A substantial proportion of the familiar route had become absorbed by extensive development in pursuit of the provision of accommodation for the main station, but it was still heading in the appropriate direction. We travelled as far as a large open storage compound.

"Sorry! Security will not permit me to venture any closer. The unit is currently being managed and run by the American military, and if we proceed from here, there is a fair chance that we may be shot."

I was very disappointed. We were still a long way short of the remnants of 280 SU. I described our playground pool, the caves, the cliffs, of fishing, of home-made sea-going craft, of Keo by the sea. He remained in denial.

"Are you sure that you don't mean Ladies Mile?"

"No, no, no! I know Ladies Mile, it's on the other side of the entire peninsula."

An abrupt enlightenment followed. "I know where you mean!" he said. "People still swim there. Great pool. I can quickly take you there."

We drove back to Akrotiri, then once more out towards the coast, terminating our brief journey at a point overlooking a fine sweep gently curving beach, almost adjacent to the sister Cape Zevgari. From this location I had a clear view to the east, to the installations on Cape Gata, and even beyond that to the lighthouse. All of that was two miles and more from our present location.

"No," I said, "I remember this place also. Our pool was directly below the camp at the foot of the cliff. It was a simple steep scramble to make it to the water, not a walk along the beach."

We failed to locate the last remnants of 280 Signals Unit. He remained mystified and in continued denial. I was profoundly disappointed to have failed the principle purpose of my quest and visit, but that was where it remained on this occasion.

Part of our tour had included a visit to the small museum and heritage centre. Here I found exhibits, illustrations, photographs and texts that described the history of Akrotiri since its establishment. I also noted that other units, some extant, some long gone, that had played their part in the defence of this part of the world over the years, had been included in exhibition. Not a single word did I find that afforded mention of 280 Signals Unit, Cape Gata. The curator seemed to share the view of my guide. To his knowledge no such place had ever existed. 280 Signals Unit, Cape Gata, had apparently been wiped from the face of the earth, had been expunged from the record, had been buried in an unmarked grave, and had been lost to the collective memory.

My guide had invited me to check the Cape and its environs on Google Earth, but warned me that the requirement for security will have demanded that much of the area be blanked out. Indeed, this could apply to the entire cape. On return, I made haste to make this check, and to my delight and somewhat smug satisfaction, I was able to bring into the clear focus, and into equally clear recall, the concrete base of every tent and building, the outline of every domestic installation, indeed I found an image so clear that it provided vivid sensual restoration of the vibrancy and the of life of that place and of those distant times.

I was incensed, and determined to rectify the omission, to restore the record, and to afford 280 SU some of the credit it most assuredly deserved, and perhaps even a decent burial. The task would require veteran assistance and advice. I was aware that one of our number had been very busy collecting and collating information about the radar outstations in Cyprus. He had been the author of some highly creditable accounts about the installations, the camps, and the people like him and me, who had manned the PPI tubes the plotting tables and the guns. His accounts would provide an excellent platform, and the basis of our subsequent contribution to heritage, to history and to posterity.

Our veteran numbers had been increasing. Indeed, some forty former veterans, residents of 280 and some of the other stations, have joined our exchanges of correspondence during these years. Sadly, during this period, eight have cashed in their chips and left this mortal coil. Equally sadly, we found the facility to restore our fellowship with only one of these, our more recently late colleagues.

Subsequent contact and communication revealed a sense of outraged enthusiasm, and a willingness to probe the shady corners of memory, and the dusty ditty boxes lying forgotten in the loft. The outcome was a wealth of contributory material, on paper, on electronic disc, or even in the form of original documents of the day. Wonderful stuff, and a worthy, if somewhat bulky contribution to the historic record and to the Akrotiri Heritage Centre. If getting it there imposed any kind of logistical problem, it did not do so for long. The solution became manifest in our first Cyprus reunion, when personal delivery and receipt ensured that 280 Signals Unit, Cape Gata would no longer be forgotten, and would take its well-deserved, and so far neglected place on the roll of honour.

Though the first reunion had enjoyed the limited attendance of only eight in number, it had proved such a huge, and later well publicised success, that several who had rejected that first opportunity, made it clear that their enthusiasm had been rekindled. Accordingly, they pledged their attendance at a second occasion, if it were to be convened. Thus in 2014, a second meeting did indeed convene, and once more made use of the convenience of Paphos as its base. Bearing gifts of history once more to the curator of the day, also the station padre, who pledged the preparation an exhibit dedicated exclusively to 280.

The reunion of 2014 had attracted fifteen veteran warriors whose service careers had, at some stage, dumped them into the welcoming clutches of 280 SU. It is perhaps a measure of the longevity of comradeship that these two meetings had attracted a few who had pursued expatriate lives, and who had travelled from Canada, the USA, Australia, and France. (Appendix).

In 2017 we met again. Once more we made our pilgrimage to the once hallowed, now hollowed ground of dusty Cape Gata. Nothing much had changed. Perhaps the bundu had become a little more dense and deep, perhaps the concrete had cracked and broken just a little more, perhaps it had become just a little more difficult to relate memory to the crumbling dereliction that remains,

Perhaps, just perhaps, the ghostly whispers on the wind are beginning to fade.

One day, there will be a last man standing. Until then…

> *"THERE'S NONE SO FAIR*
> *AS CAN COMPARE*
> *WITH THE BOYS OF TWO AYE TEE."*

This account has been dragged from my dwindling memory, aided and abetted by just a hint of imagination, inspired by those with whom I shared my time at 'Hell on the Hill', ably assisted by the few with whom it has been my pleasure and my privilege to retrieve and restore that relationship, and sustained by the indignation of omission.

It was perhaps initiated by my reading of 'The Dustbin Bandits' by Terry O'Reilly, his account of life at 751 SU Cape Greco.

… anything he can do…

I am pleased and delighted to acknowledge and express my sincere thanks to each and every one of my sources of inspiration, information, and imagination.

Appendix.

... not fade away! ...

REUNION 2014 - A RESUMÉ.

'Paradise Lost'

During the years 1957 - 1961, a large group of young men were afforded repatriation from an interlude in their lives that would bear no direct relationship to earlier youth or later maturity and adulthood. They were among the last to have been called to take up arms and to serve their country as National Servicemen. Most returned to pursue chosen profession, to resume study and education, to raise families, to follow their chosen direction of life's rich pattern, to wax strong and purposeful, and to wane slowly and into graceful seniority. For most, later life would bear no relation to the two or three year interlude of service for Queen and Country.

One curious feature of interlude is its finite characteristic. It has a clear beginning and an equally precise conclusion. It is a moment in time that is without direct association to its neighbours or its successors. It is a mere blip in that passage of time that is life. It is not, however, without influence, and for most who were called upon to assume the khaki or the blue, that interlude was to become one of the most profound that life would impose. Timorous and apprehensive youth was plucked from the complacency of family life, was thrust unwillingly into a world of brutally imposed authority, and later returned to civilian life weaned of youthful illusion and endowed with a maturity that would provide each with enhanced direction into later life.

Our group were blue. We served with the Royal Air Force, training and working principally with signals, and from unit bases that were situated mainly in remote and isolated locations in Cyprus. Cape Gata, Mount Olympus, Cape Greco, Cape Andreas, Cape Kormakiti, Kividhes, Ayios Nikolaos. These places became the hazardous substitutes for everything that we had ever known, and their imposed regime quickly banished remnant adolescence and endowed callow or rebellious individuals alike with a fresh and totally revised set of values.

Upon conclusion of the interlude, we closed the door and walked away. Just a few close friendships were to survive, but in confrontation with the new challenges that work, family, and early professional life imposed, these became neglected and slipped slowly into yesterday. At what point in life yesterday resumes a more dominant place in the emerging world of tomorrow is dictated by individual circumstances, but the arrival of the influence of nostalgia is frequently accompanied by the insistent and compulsive investigative question, 'I wonder what happened to?'.

The question is irresistible and leads inevitably to a frustrated search of unclear and confused distant memory, and a return to dusty, long forgotten personal memorabilia. Photographs, address books, remembered names, and a return to acquaintance more recently lost, directs nostalgic enquiry slowly but inexorably in the direction of more of those who had also closed the door some fifty years earlier and who had each vanished into his own brave new world. Almost forty of these old acquaintances have now found recall through correspondence, and more than half of these have enjoyed the facility for more intimate reminiscence over a beer and in restored company with each other. We would have been closer to our numerical half century, but sadly four of our earlier number have become obliged to enter into that last goodnight during this process of recall. A solemn reminder that comparatively little time remains for the rest of us to initiate the additional recall of others, so important during those interlude years.

The first, rather tentative reunion meeting was convened in Solihull. Here the six attending veterans, strangers after more than fifty years, changed in feature and form though not in temperament, quickly proved that the mere passage of time cannot, and will not erase a comradeship forged in some extremis. Though most of life had passed for us all, as we had metamorphosed somewhat into the wrinkledom of seniority, the interlude that had bundled us together in remote and difficult circumstances and the comradeship that it had initiated, remained collectively clear. A reminder of mortality, and thus of the value of that comradeship, came to us shortly afterwards at the funeral of one of the attending group.

Several meetings were to follow in Manchester. Not perhaps the most romantic venue, and while Wetherspoons and Travelodge may have lacked the charisma of a more tropic location, it provided a convenient venue for two or three unable now to undertake more distant travel.

These meetings had heralded the potential for a return to the place where interlude had initiated our association. Disbanded only a few short years after our repatriation, and like its former occupants now in ruinous progression towards extinction, its former substance remained recognisable. Eight veterans made the pilgrimage. We were welcomed to an unfamiliar RAF Akrotiri. We toured the base and we enjoyed our first hand familiarity with its present function and operation. We relished a lunch that was a far cry from the questionable fare that had been our daily endurance at Cape Gata. We pressed on to the ruins of that once vibrant encampment.

Here, familiarity was all too evident. Though his tent and mine remained only as a broken concrete base, they were as fresh in memory as they had been on the day that the interlude had terminated. The cookhouse where the most unpalatable sausages known to mankind had been served, and which had been later closed by the direct order of John Profumo, the Minister of War; the cinema of sometimes somewhat risqué screenings; the pestilential toilet blocks; the Corporals Club that had mysteriously burst into flames; the ablution block where water only rarely happened; the dust in the summer and the mud in the winter. Memories in the mind, ghosts on the wind, and the bond of distant comradeship a very ready presence for us all.

Our little gathering had enjoyed huge social and reminiscent success. A brief report of the visit to the other members of the corresponding group quickly induced comments of regret. "I wish that I had made the effort", "Sorry that I was unable to make it", "Been to Cyprus many times on holiday", "Count me in for the next one".

Four years had elapsed. No additional members of our stalwart group had fallen from their perches. Continued correspondence had revealed that increasing infirmity would continue to be restrictive though not prohibitive. Interest and willingness prevailed among a greater proportion, and although a few of the first visit regretted that they would be unable to join the party on this occasion, their omission would be adequately compensated by the additional indicated interest. Preparatory and organisational logistics on this occasion would be somewhat complicated by the hugely welcome attendance by expatriate veterans from Australia, Canada and the USA.

Though planning and preparation were as complicated as these occasions always are, the logistical burden enjoyed the huge benefit of unstinting cooperation from the Royal Air Force, for which I remain enormously grateful. In response to popular request, this reunion was to include, if possible, a visit to the only other remaining signals station on the island. Many of our party had been stationed high in the mountains at RAF Troodos, and at the radar and signals unit at Mount Olympus, and this location featured high upon their list of priorities as a visit destination.

Thus it was that the reunion of 2014 found its genesis, its formulation, and its implementation. As on the earlier occasion our base was to be in Paphos. This late 1950s isolated fishing village had become a touristic metropolis of considerable proportions. What it now lacked in charm it could provide in the abundant convenience of accommodation and an international airport. It was here, then, that fifteen veterans, some accompanied by partners, convened on a warm spring day in May of 2014.

Our first day became dedicated to greeting and familiarisation. Only half of the assembled veterans had met any of the others since those distant service days, and just a few who had by chance been out of time and place, were complete strangers. No less welcome for that. The influence of the much earlier interlude quickly became evident. Though face and form of yesteryear had endured the metamorphosis of maturity, the comradeship remained as youthful as ever. We toasted yesterday and bade a Keo welcome to today, and retired in eager anticipation of the two days that were to follow.

Our cavalcade of hired motors made rendezvous as planned at the main gate to RAF Akrotiri promptly-ish at 10.00 hours on the following morning. We were welcomed by Corporal Chantelle Goodall who had been invaluable during the months of preparation and planning, and whose hand I was finally delighted and privileged to shake. Our exchanges of correspondence had been many, and had been a most agreeable and vital component of the preparatory process.

Our first port of call was the SNCO's mess for coffee, and for our meeting with and briefing by the Station Commander Group Captain Paul Kennett. He made us welcome and outlined the function and operation of RAF. Akrotiri today. It was a friendly and informative meeting, and served to introduce us all to an unfamiliar Akrotiri that now serves a function so different to that of fifty years ago. We were grateful for time poached from his busy day and schedule.

After coffee we headed for St. Paul's Church, which now serves as the RAF Akrotiri Museum and Heritage Centre. We were welcomed to this important venue by the Station Padre and Curator, Padre Adrian Dyer. For reasons of history, the museum represented an important pause in our itinerary and to our visit to the station. During a private visit some years earlier, I had discovered, to my considerable dismay, that no trace remained of the domestic camp at 280 SU Cape Gata. It seemed that upon closure in the middle 1960s it had been expunged from the face of the planet, and that no records had been retained of its existence (though surely some must have survived the passage of time in a dusty and forgotten ministry archive). During our first reunion visit to the station, we had attempted to rectify this imbalance through the donation of photographic and documentary material. Equally, Martin Greig, who had compiled a huge amount of information about the unit, and more generally about the history of convoy radar in Cyprus, had supplied similar material electronically and by post.

During subsequent evolutionary developments, changes of personnel, relocation of exhibit venue, the confusion of storage and administration, the location of this material had once again become unclear. In anticipation, I had taken a full dossier, partly recorded electronically, and partly as original documents, for the archive and for display as required. This has represented a huge collection of donated photographs of life during those years, on and off the station, and is a record of life as it was lived at that time. By drawing from the memories of those who shared this interlude, I have aspired to prepare a more anecdotal account of this period. Alas memories become a little faded, and as this is a task of considerable magnitude, perhaps it will simply never find completion.

We were, of course delighted to discuss these matters, and this history with Padre Dyer, and to view the splendidly presented history of the station. Padre Dyer has pledged to redress the historic omission. 280 SU Cape Gata had never been viewed as an integral part of the station, more a wild and undisciplined outpost. It was home to an unruly bunch of odd characters, who made up the rules as they went along. They were highly adept at the art of skiving but however untidy the execution of their daily tasks, however inventive their abilities to create a little creature comfort and self contained recreation, however insistent their demand for improved conditions at 'Hell on the Hill', their approach to duty and to the sports arena were the same. Always with pride and always with determination. It showed! I hope that I shall be able to sustain a corresponding relationship with Adrian Dyer, and enjoy the facility to monitor the development of a corner of the Heritage Centre dedicated to Cape Gata. We, its former inmates, believe that it is well deserved.

Only the hallowed ground remained, and after expressing our thanks to Padre Dyer, this was our next destination. What do you do among ruins that enjoy no place in history, that have not been monumentally listed, that contribute nothing to heritage or culture, that have done little in the furtherance of the history of mankind, that are no more than remnant broken lumps of concrete that have largely been reclaimed by the bundu? I guess that the answer is nothing. Unless, of course those ruins still harbour nostalgia and the remnants of memories of a period that can never be ignored. It's that interlude again. It is that shared period that afforded nothing of practical significance to later life, but which was creative of the comradeship that can never be erased. It is that period which, fifty years later, stirs every fading memory and whispers nostalgia out of every concrete fissure. Broken though it may be, it is that place in which we lived, we walked, we slept, we dreamed of demob. It is the place of rows of tents and the occasional unpopular garden. It is the place of Sandy and of Winston. It is the place where the most inedible food on the planet was consumed and where its remnants were deposited in a pit of equal awfulness. It is a place of joy, frustration, fear, horror, and delight in fairly equal measure. It is a place that dominated two or three of our most formative years and where all of that part of youthful lives became enacted. Even in its ruined condition, it too cannot be ignored. In no less ruined condition, we had returned to pay due homage to that place and to its years.

So what did we do? If nostalgia was a verb I would use it. We simply remembered. We relocated the locations. I made positive identification of the tent I shared with John Murphy, 'Paradise Lost', and for one more final time we shared our respective bed spaces. We located every installation that had been such an intimate part of every day that we spent in the embrace of 'Hell on the Hill'. As we peered over the cliff, we could swim once more in the limpid blue waters of 280 pool. And we remembered comrades of those days, some there present, some unable to have made the pilgrimage, some simply lost to memory, and some lost to the permanence of the inevitable.

However deep our reverie, however profound our nostalgic deliberations, they were about to receive a most dramatic awakening. The aerial wizards of the Red Arrows display team undertake their training at RAF Akrotiri, and by happenstance were present for this purpose at the time of our visit. At the kind invitation of the Station Commander we were afforded the unique opportunity to observe one of their training sessions. From a cliff top viewpoint of truly amazing advantage, we were to observe these intrepid young men in their flying machines as they trained to aerobatic perfection. Adequate superlatives are difficult to find, and we could only observe with muted gasps of astonishment at their demonstration of aerial dexterity as they painted their colourful pictures in the sky. It was a spellbinding hour, for which considerable privilege we were all enormously grateful.

When we had done all of this, we had thought our thoughts, we had listened to the ghosts on the breeze, we had remembered people and moments and events. We had walked the broken paths between the tent lines, we had sought an ancient souvenir but found only the unidentifiable. We had gazed across a more recent boundary to a tech site that no longer existed. We had watched in awe one amazingly skilled section of today's Royal Air Force. When we had done all of this we moved on. Lunch awaited in the SNCO Mess, and they would cease serving at 14.30.

For the majority of the veterans and all of the ladies, a splendid lunch brought this memorable visit to conclusion, and they made their return to Paphos. For just a small group of veterans however, nostalgia had not yet quite been satisfied. Thus we made the request to return to Cape Gata, and we did this in the company of Warrant Officer Alex Balmer, who shoulders the arduous and insuperable responsibility of station security. His was excellent and most informative company, and much of the remainder of the afternoon was spent among his experiences and our thus prompted memories of equivalent situations. We had aspired to walk sections of the cliff that had been familiar in earlier years but security could not allow this degree of freedom at this time. Content to accept imposed limitation, we walked the site perimeter, made partial and secure descent of the upper cliff. We remembered home-made kayaks of doubtful seagoing capacity and diving foolishly and perhaps irresponsibly (surely not!) from the roof of the great cave. We remembered gurgling our way through submarine tunnels, and launching a rescue mission to retrieve an individual who had determined to swim to Egypt.

We had also been pleased to be able to bring correction to a case of mistaken identity. The perimeter fence to the current technical site is absolute and not to be violated. Within its wire enclosure some of the installation is situated atop a structure described throughout our visit as 'the old lighthouse'. Memory suggested that this was in error, and was later confirmed when a more advantageous viewpoint revealed the old lighthouse where it had always been. We returned to the imposter, and in a moment of some delayed revelation realised its true identity. It was the base structure for the huge, revolving Type 254 radar head, much feared in its day as a testicle shrinker and shriveler, and the thief of virility. The memory and the correction raised another smile.

The Royal Air Force had provided and allowed a very special day for us all, and one that had restored moments of yesterday that had been displaced by the delete button of time and tide. We are most grateful for the generosity and cooperation of Paul Kennett and his colleagues.

Our visit to RAF Troodos was to take place on the following day. Once again easy and cooperative planning correspondence with the Station Commander Wing Commander Ken Pudney had ensured that preparations had been without difficulty or unwelcome complication. Rendezvous had been arranged, and all that was required was our arrival at the appointed hour. To afford the occasion an enhanced flavour of a 'day out' and to ensure that everyone could benefit from the freedom from driving or the need to remain Keo-free, I had made reservation for a bus to collect from morning hotel locations and to return at a later hour, hopefully full of the joys of Keo if so desired.

The driver collected and delivered promptly, but on approach to our destination accepted misguided, memory-induced directions from his eager charges. At our request, he drove the bus to a terminal point on the summit of Mount Olympus where we were confronted by large locked gates complete with armed guard, and a second set, equally secured, though without armoury, and both of which led into puzzlingly separate sections of a technical location. An approach to the guard, who appeared to be about fourteen years old, yielded nothing, as he spoke no English. We fared little better with one of his superiors who seemed to know nothing of Wing Commander Ken Pudney or an RAF facility. Thus, a confused group of elderly veterans stood around in the sunshine, pondering any subsequent move that might find purpose. This was the only remaining RAF location known to us, as we were aware that earlier domestic accommodation had either met with demolition or was now out of bounds.

We reasoned that today's personnel must live somewhere, and as we pondered this question it was our driver who brought light into the darkness of our dilemma. Though his command of English was limited, his comprehension of our requirement initiated the response that he knew exactly where it was and promptly drove us there. We too quickly recognised the old leave camp to which overheated personnel from the lowland locations could come to take a few days of the refreshing mountain air. It had become transformed into a far, and almost unrecognisable departure from the wooden huts of yesteryear, the physical location had changed but little, only the smart new buildings had transformed the landscape.

Ken met us at the gate, and we transferred quickly to the smart mess, recreation, and conference building. Here, after coffee, and as part of a briefing for the day, Ken provided a most interesting history of the station and its location, including many fascinating facts of which none of us had been aware. He also allowed that we were welcome to take pictures of almost anything, but strictly not of the Cyprus National Guard installations or encampment. Relationships, we understood, were not as cordial as might be considered desirable. Indeed, Ken had done his best to secure access on our behalf to the Cypriot Guard encampment to allow visitation to Pingo's Hotel, the former RAF principal domestic residence. To our disappointment, this had been denied. However, two of the long term residents of those distant Pingo's days responded to his briefing with their unique and incomparable rendition of 'Pingo's Sunshine Corner is the place for you'. (A stamped addressed envelope and a postal order for 2/6d will secure the rest of the words).

Ken then escorted us to the present technical location. While the entire site has been transmogrified almost beyond our recognition, it was not entirely unrecognisable. However, as the only portion that bore any familiarity was now firmly under the management of the Cyprus National Guard we were unlikely to find any closer access than the bars of the gate, and even there we were met only by the belligerent gaze of the teenage Rambo at the other side. Ken unlocked the barrier to the home patch and we entered a world that bore little relation or resemblance to that of yesteryear. All of the surveillance equipment is now contained within huge plastic covered geodesic domes, which serve to maintain an automated watchful eye over a vast area. No blips, no beeps, no strobes, no PPI tubes, and next door, only a belligerent youth with an elderly rifle.

We lingered to enjoy the view, and to remember the same view of fifty years ago, before returning briefly to the leave camp, to a little reminiscence of some of the artefacts of yesterday, and the present location of those that had been displaced but saved for posterity. From Troodos, Ken guided our descent of the mountain to Makris Restaurant for a mid-afternoon lunch. The Makris came to us with Ken's very positive recommendation, and he had kindly made the necessary reservation on our behalf. He had promised that the manager, Meletios Synnos and his family, would do us proud, and this had been no idle boast. We enjoyed a memorable meal of typical Cypriot fare, and the clear advantage of freedom from the need or obligation to drive quickly became evident.

Renditions of a distinctly dubious nature accompanied the later stages of afternoon. The Boys of Two Eighteee were well remembered as were the words of advice in the event of a recalcitrant truck or a reluctant azicator. City locations were celebrated to include Jerusalem and a large township in Alabama. Little Angeline was afforded fond recall, as I believe was a Lady to the Manor born, a gentleman by the name of Banglestein, and for some reason on a Saturday afternoon, a verger. It was a late afternoon of some choral quality, not much, but some, and it pursued our charabanc of revellers back to Paphos.

As we would be bidding farewell to four of our number on Monday, we reconvened on Sunday for a further spot of indulgence, and enjoyed a prolonged Sunday lunch together, at a harbour side restaurant. The occasion afforded time for reflection on our two splendid days with the Royal Air Force. We were absolutely unanimous in our expression of gratitude for the welcome that we had received at both stations, and for the generous provision of access to locations that allowed the rejuvenation of fading memory; the facility to donate some of the more practical manifestations of that fading memory into a more permanent archive; and the privilege to enjoy unparalleled observation of one truly special and supreme aspect of the Royal Air Force of today.

During our remaining days we each made pursuit of our own preferred activity, but reconvened each evening in continued social endeavour. Our convention had enjoyed a most convivial week, some of the participants meeting for the first time in 55 years, some who had been strangers until this occasion. Whatever doubts there may have been about the wisdom or folly of returning a bunch of retirees back to a location in which they had misspent a portion of their youthful years, in retrospect I do not believe that a single dissenting thought will have accompanied them back to the more sedate security of their retirement. Indeed, I have found huge gratification in a small but significant change of collective view. During the long planning process, all of the speculation had referred to this meeting as the inevitable last of its kind. In a renewed and positive shift towards the future, the anticipation now makes reference only to the next one.

The meeting has owed its success, in equal measure, to all who have been involved.

Per Ardua ad Astra - though you may find the stretch a little more difficult these days!

On behalf of the entire visiting group, my most sincere thanks to:

Group Captain Paul Kennett for his generous hospitality and that of his station.

Wing Commander Ken Pudney for his welcome to Troodos and our visit to his station.

Corporal Chantelle Goodall for her enormous help in setting up, and her company on the day.

Group Captain James Linter for his help and advice in early planning.

Padre Adrian Dyer for granting our access to the museum and for his stewardship of the collected and presented information relating to 280 SU Cape Gata.

Warrant Officer Alex Balmer for our most informative afternoon visit to Cape Gata.

To the assembled group, and not forgetting those who were unable to make it. Thank you for your company, and for your continued communication. It has been very special.

Five and twenty ADOs
Work on their consoles
Brandy for officers
and Keo for the proles!

With apologies to Kipling.

Acknowledgements.

This modest volume found its direction, rather than an inspiration, in the 2007 revelation that 280 Signals Unit, Cape Gata had not been closed down in the middle 1960s, had not been committed to history, had not been afforded a ceremonial final lowering of the flag, but had been erased, expunged from the record, omitted from the chronicles, and entombed without memorial. The rectification of this intolerable situation required urgent contemplation and the creation of an avenue that would find a phoenix at its terminus.

The solitary interrogation of the grey cells of a memory of almost sixty years into antiquity would be obliged to provide the majority of the necessary elucidation. However, somewhere out there, there must be others of those distant days who could add purposefully to the cerebral lexicon and who could add substantiality to my ponderings and to the slowly evolving fabric of my retrospective scaffolding.

There were, and prominent among these was Martin Greig. Martin had served at Cape Gata, and much later when seeking answers to questions not dissimilar to my own, he had collected and collated a vast amount of information that related to life and times in the mobile convoy radar stations in Cyprus, to his own period of National Service, and of the many and diverse individuals who had made up the fighting force. From this huge dossier of information he had compiled several authoritative documents which stand collectively as the only comprehensive history of those closing days of national service in the RAF in Cyprus. I remain enormously grateful to him for his cooperation and assistance in my endeavours, and for the facility to draw freely upon the fruits of his labours.

Equally, I owe a debt of gratitude to many of those who feature namelessly on these pages, and especially to those in whose more recent company I have enjoyed the intense pleasure of reminiscence, and who have continued to echo their support of this retrospective challenge during the months of its preparation. Truly, we were 'the long and the short and the tall', though sadly, the 'time and tide that waiteth for no man' is imposing ever increasing curtailment upon our numbers.

If some subliminal foresight had permitted even a modest appreciation of the magnitude of the task of editing, correcting, adjusting, refining, re-drafting, setting out, and the many and varied pitfalls that lie between the final full stop at the end of the first draft and publication, I might have been tempted to have abandoned the entire project. But not so! In this complex endeavour I have enjoyed the huge benefit of the knowledge and experience of Paul Reed, to whom I am enormously indebted for his transformation of the early narrative into readability.

When reflecting upon life's abundant pattern, I am bound to express a profound sense of enduring gratitude to the beckoning finger for the imposed obligation to undertake my military service. Equally, to the Royal Air Force for the provision of a platform from which to undertake one of the most memorable episodes of my life. At no point in this narrative is criticism intended or applied, only gratitude for the opportunity, and pride in my brief and limited contribution.

PER ARDUA AD ASTRA

The Author.

Ian Tillotson pursued and embraced his period of National Service in the Royal Air Force between June 1958 and June 1960. He made the most of it.

This account is a ramble through those two years, and an attempt to restore to life and memory some of the moments, the occasions, the situations and the events that contributed much to the awakening of a timid youth from rural Yorkshire.

It follows no chronological sequence, but each chapter describes an individual aspect of life in that distant place and time. It tells of the early terrors of initiation and introduction, and of their gradual metamorphosis into the more subtle aptitudes of avoidance. It describes the all-weather delights of life on a large and unruly campsite, and of the many and diverse contrivances that could be employed by the more resourceful to make daily life a little less uncomfortable.

It chronicles work, function, purpose, and our essential contribution to peace in our time, to the defence of the realm, and to the greater good of mankind. It also removes the glossy wrapping paper to reveal underhand contrivances that might permit avoidance for the more ruthless. To the hard working resident populace, time for leisure and relaxation are essential factors in the restoration of body and spirit. To those of somewhat more careless dedication, a little honest chicanery could manufacture adjustment to the balance of effort, and somewhat extended periods in pursuit of those moments of leisure and pleasure......and just a few that we would prefer to forget.

It highlights the many incidents and occasions that punctuated daily life. Though each incident and event inevitably imposed its legacy of benefit, pathos, terror, delight, disgust, amazement, triumph, and collectively they made vital contribution to the individual evolution of maturity, throughout, I have endeavoured to sustain a descriptively lighter mode. Just a few of these occasions, those considered to awful to return to focus, or those which could perhaps run the risk of reawakening painful memories for some, and thus re-impose distress, have been omitted.

Throughout the narrative, the preferred endeavour has been the presentation of facts and details in a manner that owes rather more to burlesque than to tragedy. They remain facts and details.

On demobilisation, he resumed his studies in Forestry, and on graduation, he embarked upon a short-lived career in that industry. He later transferred his allegiance to the world of applied biology, and pursued a life-long career in environmental management and wildlife conservation. In that pursuit he worked for eight years as a wildlife warden on Dartmoor, and for the remaining twenty-five years of his working life as a Chief Warden in Wales. In addition to his home-based responsibilities, he also served as a member of an occasionally itinerant team preparing management plans for conservation in a number of diverse overseas locations. His passion for wildlife, for the environment, for biological conservation in the face of fearful decline, and for broad beans, remains steadfast.

On just one more occasion in his subsequent life did he find the need to recall the memory of those distant disciplines on the parade ground. On 21st August 2016, he joined ranks with a squadron of ageing veterans at the National Arboretum at Alrewas in Staffordshire. This was the occasion of the first service of remembrance at the recently unveiled Cyprus Rock Memorial.

Hewn from the Troodos Mountains, this irregular four-ton granite monolith was transported from Cyprus by the Royal Air Force, and set upon a plinth of polished granite in the Mediterranean Area of the Memorial Garden. The stone is adorned with an inscribed plaque in the shape of the island, also in polished black granite, and bears the insignia of each of the military and police forces in service and sacrifice during the years of the emergency.

Brought smartly to attention by a parade marshal, and preceded by three pipers, the squadron marched, perhaps with a little less elegance and perhaps with a little less precision than might have been the case sixty years earlier, though with no less pride, the few hundred yards to the memorial stone. Though the ravages of time, the North Yorkshire climate and decomposing Copydex had reduced the once proud 'best blue' to a somewhat unceremonial condition, once more, with civilian pride, we remembered those who did not return from the conflict.

He is a proud member of the Welsh Association of Churchill Fellows.

He continues to live in Wales and to travel to the more remote and still relatively unblemished regions of the world in pursuit of his passion.

Printed in Poland
by Amazon Fulfillment
Poland Sp. z o.o., Wrocław